POSTCARD HISTORY SERIES

Clark County

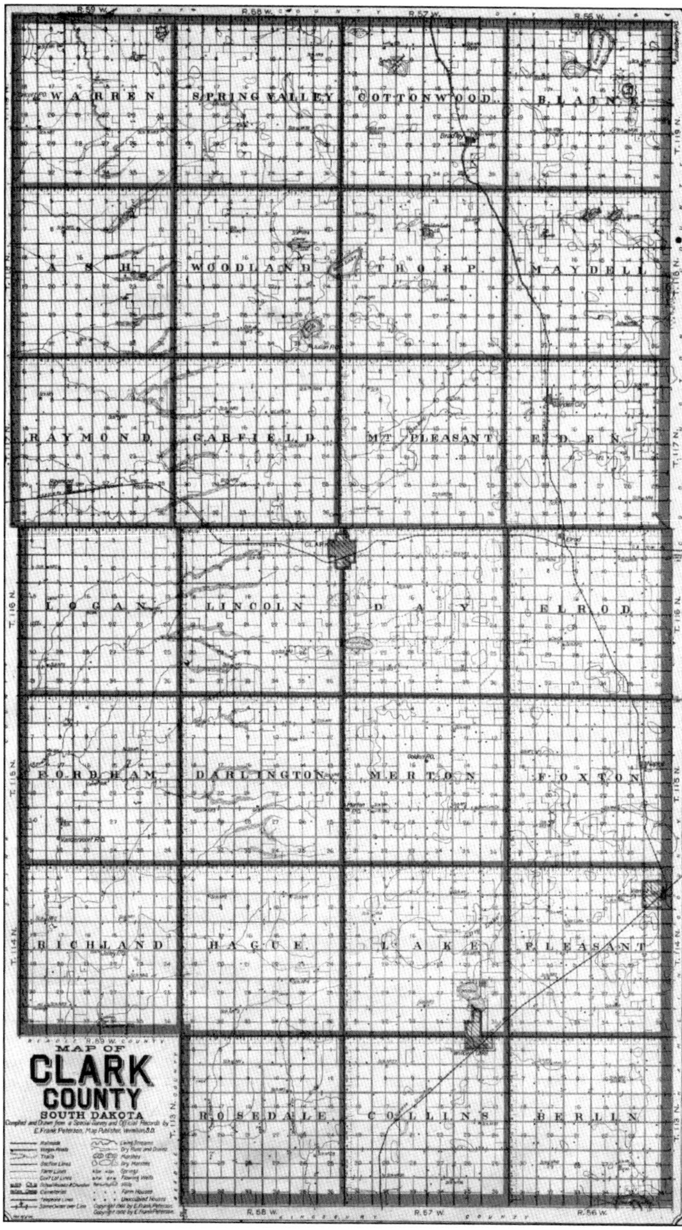

Clark County was created in 1873 by an act of Dakota territorial legislature. It was named for Newton Clark, a territorial legislator. On June 27, 1878, the first white settlers invaded Clark County, which had remained unbroken by civilized occupation. They were John Bailey and his wife and Joseph Woodland and his wife and family, who located in the northern part of the county near a lake, later named Bailey's Lake. Settlers continued to migrate to Clark County and by 1880, there were enough settlers to petition for organization. On May 23, 1881, Clark County became an official county. This map of Clark County is from 1902.

On the front cover: Please see the top of page 40. (Author's collection.)

On the back cover: Please see the top of page 97. (Author's collection.)

POSTCARD HISTORY SERIES

Clark County

Greg Furness

ARCADIA PUBLISHING

Copyright © 2006 by Greg Furness
ISBN 978-0-7385-4026-9

Published by Arcadia Publishing
Charleston, South Carolina

Printed in the United States of America

Library of Congress Catalog Card Number: 2005937811

For all general information contact Arcadia Publishing at:
Telephone 843-853-2070
Fax 843-853-0044
E-mail sales@arcadiapublishing.com
For customer service and orders:
Toll-Free 1-888-313-2665

Visit us on the Internet at www.arcadiapublishing.com

This book is dedicated in memory of Noel Fischer,
a good friend of mine and a friend of Clark County history.

Contents

Acknowledgments 6

Introduction 7

1. Bradley and Crocker 9
2. Garden City and Elrod 17
3. Clark 33
4. Naples and Vienna 87
5. Willow Lake, Melham, and Carpenter 101
6. Raymond 119

Acknowledgments

Postcards to most folks are a way of keeping in touch with family and friends while on vacation, at least in modern times. At the beginning of the 20th century, many postcards were made and sent for all types of greetings: to show off a particular view of a town, depict a school, or depict a residence. Most of "those days" were a way of life then and are now gone forever, but they are not forgotten.

The views in this book, selected from a very large private collection of postcards from Clark County businessman Greg Furness, do in fact present a brief history of Clark County via postcards. Whether you are a current resident of Clark County or a former resident, it is my hope that as you page through this book it will spark memories; the "I remember when," or "I did not know that," and other fond memories from the past. To all of you who have purchased the book—thank you.

I wish to acknowledge the writers and contributors of the Clark County and Southern Clark County history books. Without that information, my job of finding and writing history of some of the postcards would have taken countless hours of research. That information was of utmost value. To Ailene Luckhurst, president of the Clark County Historical Society—your vast knowledge of people, places, buildings, and events could not go unmentioned, you are the best. A percentage of proceeds of this book will be given to the Clark County Historical Society so they can further preserve some of the history of this area. To David Moritz and the late Bert Moritz, former editors and publishers of the *Clark County Courier*, I thank you for your contributions of postcards and stories, they were of much value. I also want to acknowledge Margaret Hallberg, your memory is remarkable at your young age of 95. Your information and ability to identify people and places, especially in the Vienna section, was very valuable, and thank you for your contribution of information on Chauncey Long.

Special thanks also goes to many of my exchange sons, Martin, Hauke, Maik, Lars, and Manuel; my brother Brad and his wife, Marsha; and David Musser, thanks to each of you for helping search for postcards while we were at shows and antique shops. I know you helped, even though you would rather have been doing something else some of the time! In addition to them, thanks also to my parents for supporting me in this endeavor.

I would also like to thank the family of Noel Fischer. Noel was a pharmacist and along with a business partner, Bob Schlueter, owned and operated Bockoven Drug since the late 1950s. One day, Noel stopped by my office to discuss some of my Clark County memorabilia and to leave a couple of items for my collection. As we sat and discussed some items of Clark County, I began to talk to Noel about my postcard collection and my hopes that one day those cards could be shared with others in the version of a book on the history of Clark County via postcards. I can still hear his words, "Why not, a marvelous idea." It was less than six months later when Noel again stopped by and shared some pictures and postcards. He also shared with me at that time a health problem he was dealing with. A short time later, I was invited to his home to further discuss his imminent demise. After his death and settlement of his wishes, I received a note in the mail from his son John along with a monetary gift. The note was an instruction from Noel that upon his death, this gift be given to me to help me in publishing a book on Clark County history via postcards. I sat in disbelief and awe. So it is with that generous gift the book idea could become a reality. Thank you Noel and the Fischer family for believing in my dream.

INTRODUCTION

Several years ago, a book was published on the history of Clark County and the history of Southern Clark County. It is not my intention to replace these books, but to simply show a history of Clark County through postcards. These cards will show nameless people and events that will certainly lead to memories of people, events, and places throughout Clark County. Most of the cards are from 1900 to 1930, with a few from later days of the 1940s. They all provide invaluable accounts of early history.

The early days of Clark County begin where days of the Native American, the old-time trapper, and the hunter ended in 1878. It is interesting to imagine who had roamed this county before that time, and through the centuries. It is understood that this is part of the territory where the buffalo, deer, elk, and antelope roamed in great herds, and wild fowl lived by the millions, all followed by the Native American, trapper, and hunter for food and profit. The bones still on the ground in the early days were evidence that the above situation existed, and it sounds like the days of real sport and adventure.

By 1881, the Northwestern Railway had reached Clark, first called Clark Center, and then reached Raymond in 1882. In 1888, the first courthouse was built in Clark. Of two prominent Clark attorneys, S. H. Elrod became governor of the state from 1905 to 1907, and Carl G. Sherwood served as chief justice of the supreme court.

Besides Clark, the following towns were soon to be formed: Bradley, Carpenter, Crocker, Elrod, Garden City, Melham, Naples, Raymond, Vienna, and Willow Lake(s). There actually have been some 34 post offices in Clark County since the first one opened on April 28, 1879, however, only five full-time postal facilities are still open. Clark County, located in the Glacial Lakes and Prairie Region in northeast South Dakota, is home to some 4,500 residents, but as rural America is, it is "home" to hundreds more.

Clark, being the largest of the communities in the county, seems to have the most postcards. However, all the other communities, including Bradley, Carpenter, Crocker, Elrod, Garden City, Melham, Naples, Raymond, Vienna, and Willow Lake also have another portion of great county history. My collection has grown to over 400 postcards; I am not able to use all of them in this book, but I have included the ones that I think provide a valuable and fun history of early Clark County.

I hope that you will enjoy this book. The captions on each postcard are by all means not always correct, but to the best of my knowledge, and from the history books, and the recollection of some of the "old timers" of Clark County. So sit back, enjoy, and reminisce.

One

Bradley and Crocker

Bradley had its beginning in a small settlement two miles north of the town's present location. In 1885, when the Chicago, Milwaukee and St. Paul Railroad Company was building its line north and south, a water tank and post office was established; this was called Prairie Hill. When the train started operating some two years later, businesses were set up two miles south and this became the town site. Bradley has the peculiar distinction of having been named as the result of an early day fight between a railway official and a group of excited laborers. E. R. Bradley, who was visiting the town, was credited with saving the life, in the fight, of the chief engineer in charge of construction project and was honored by having the town named after him in 1887.

Crocker was named by the Minneapolis and St. Louis Railroad Company when the town was founded in 1906. The post office was established in 1907 in the Hans Rasmusson General Merchandise Store. On February 16, 1947, Floyd Flatten became the postmaster, and the post office was moved from the Spratt store to Flatten's Grocery. Flatten retired in 1980, and his wife, Martha, then served as postmaster. The post office closed in 1993.

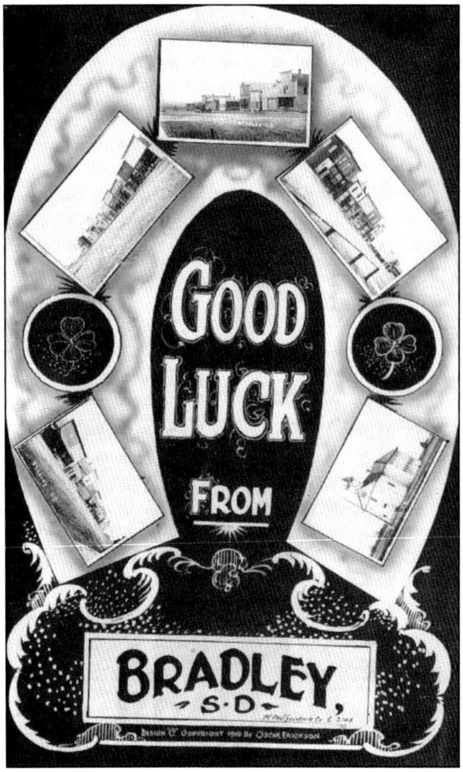

This Good Luck multi-view card was copyrighted in 1910. This card depicts five great Bradley views: four different downtown scenes and one of the wooden Bradley school. This card was not used through the postal system, but was written to an Irene Cutting, compliments of Auntie Bartlett.

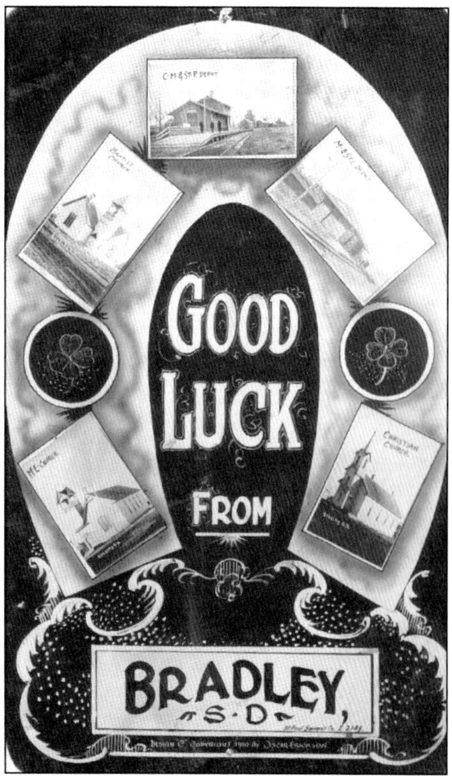

Shown here is another Good Luck multi-view card also copyrighted in 1910, showing three churches—M. E. Church, the Baptist church, and the Christian church—and the Chicago, Milwaukee and St. Paul Depot and the Minneapolis and St. Louis Depot. The text on this card is written by Jennie Kinyon, wife of Frank D. Kinyon, a local undertaker. She writes about him having many funerals recently and one today within six miles of Henry.

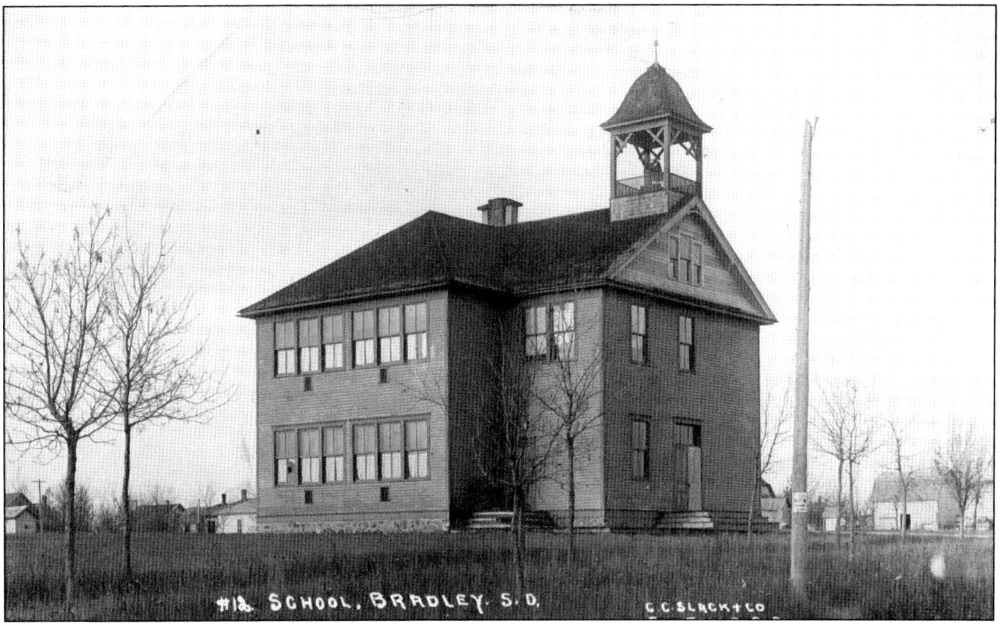

This was the third Bradley school building. It was dedicated in 1904 after the second one had burned in 1903. This structure was used for 19 years until it was condemned by the state in 1923. It was a four-room two-story frame building, measuring 30 feet by 56 feet. This card was mailed from "Papa" in Bradley in 1914 to Dorothy Peck at Willow Lakes, South Dakota.

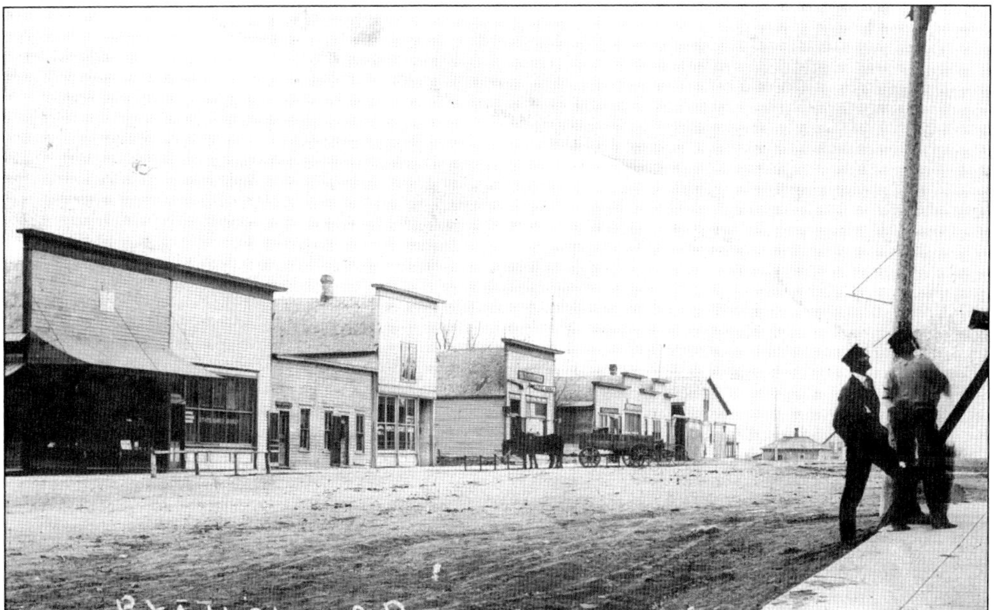

The State Bank of Bradley and the Peoples State Bank with the post office sitting in between are just three of the places identified on this card postmarked in 1909. The horses and buggies are tied up in front of the J. M. Rasmusson Store.

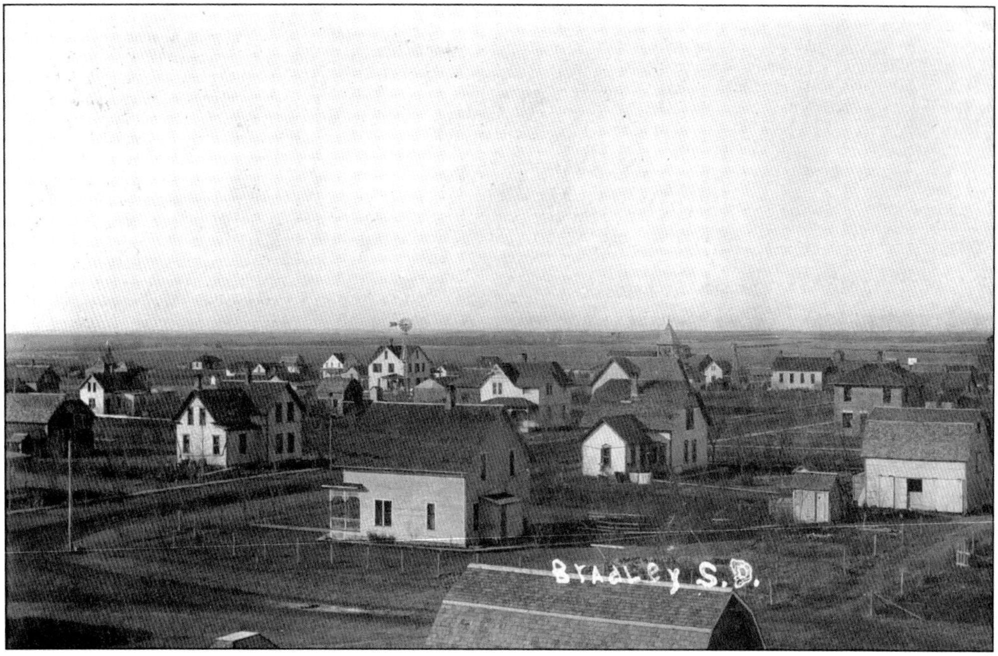

This view of Bradley is northeast looking southeast. The D. Perry (Monson) house is in the middle with the Baptist church just west of it. The original Bradley school (now the Senior Citizens' building) sits just further west. This card was sent to Cecil Cook in Janesville, Iowa, in 1908.

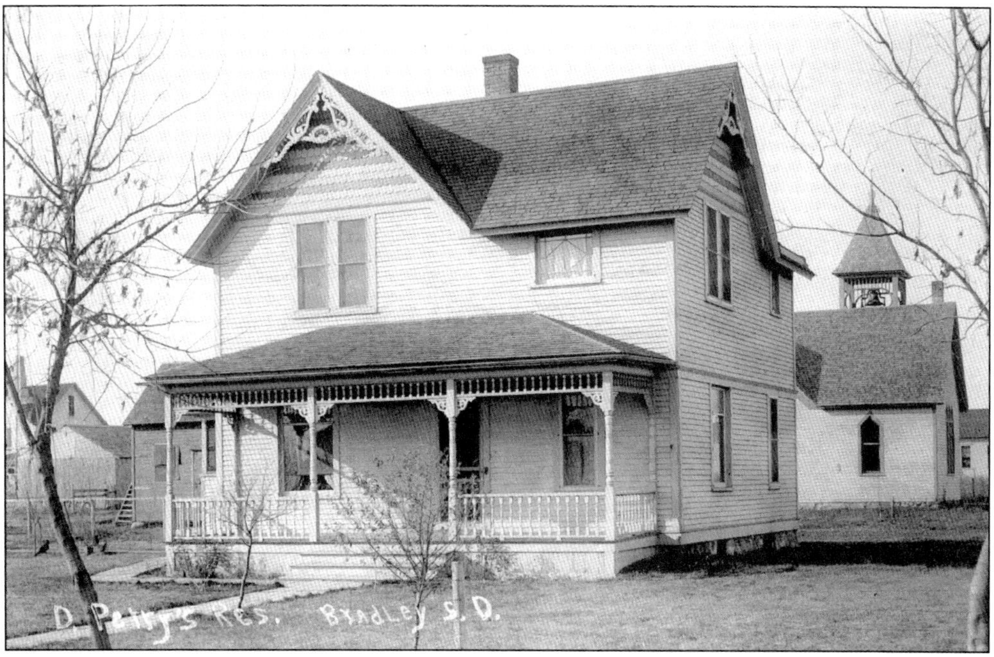

Here is a close-up view of the Dan Perry residence, local undertaker after Frank Kinyon, and in recent years this house was known as the Munson house. The card sent in July 1910 states: "Had a fire last night, Granges barn burned with 9 head of horses, no ins. on the horses, 800 on building. The wind did not blow or the whole town would have burned, Love Inga Perry."

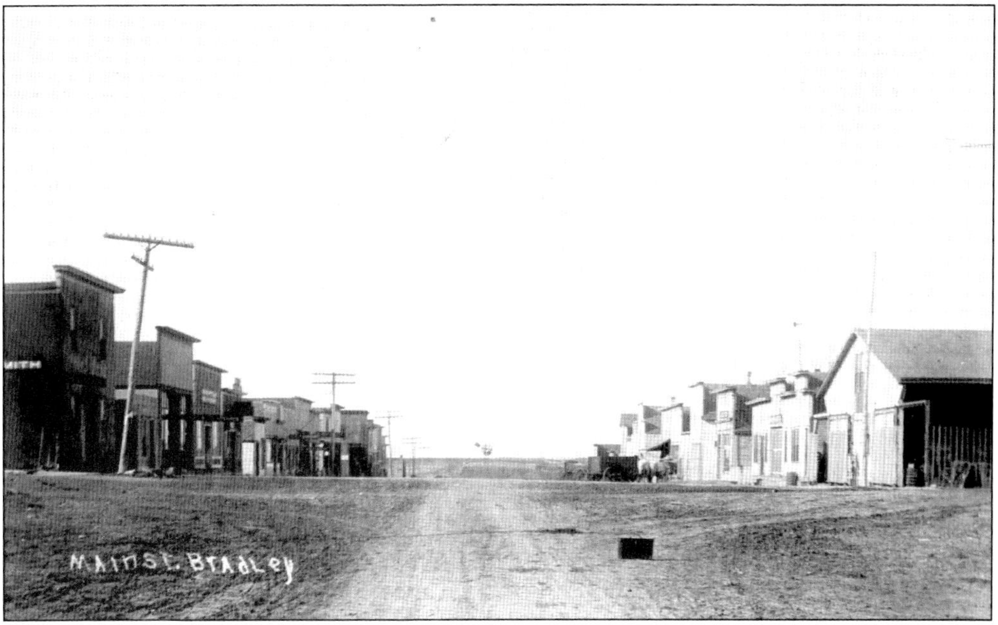

Looking west in Bradley, this is another nice Main Street view. This is a real photo postcard. On the back is written: "Part of Main Street which built up after fire, 1891. Cora Sjolie—Bradley."

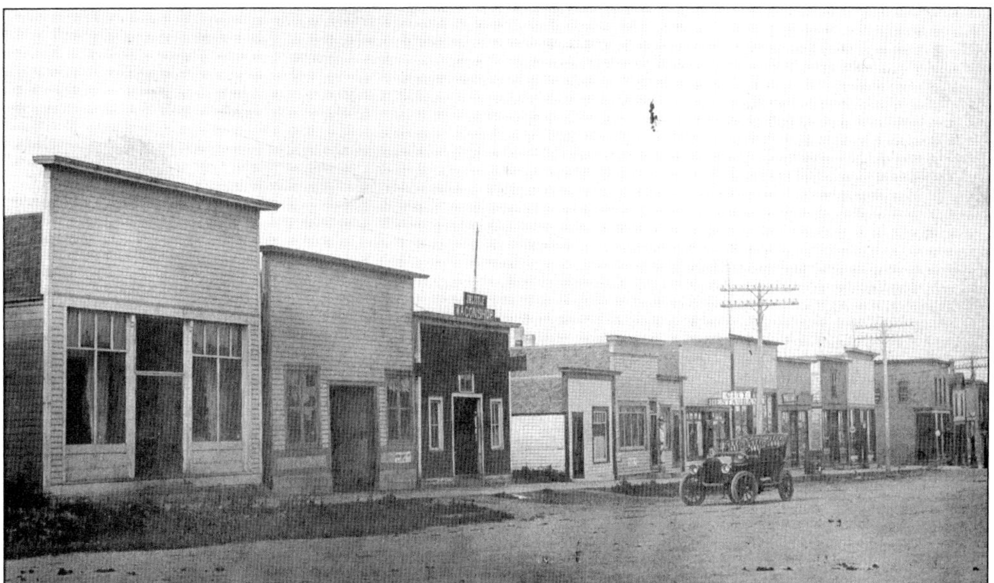

Did the car run out of gas, or did the driver park here while they went in for breakfast at the City Restaurant? The J. Little wagon shop sits in front of where the car is also. This card was sent in 1911, from Bradley to Wisconsin.

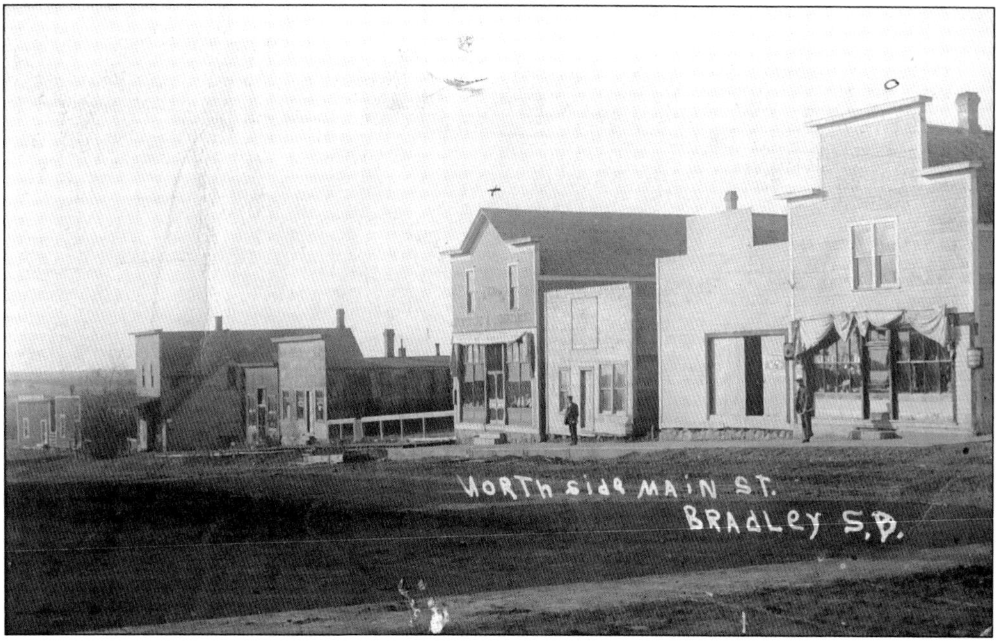

This photograph, taken between 1908 and 1910, shows the F. D. Kinyon Furniture and Undertaking business in the middle. Note that both men in the photograph have conductor type hats on. The writer of the card, Jennie Kinyon, placed an "X" over the Kinyon Building and the "O" over the Hart Building, which she states was recently purchased by Colgate.

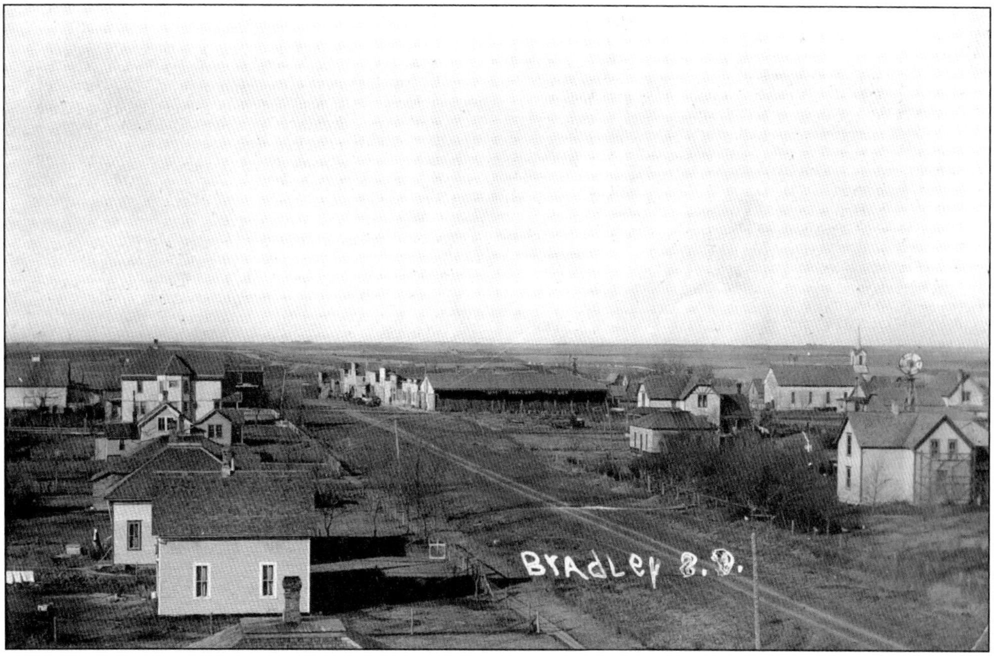

This view must have been taken from atop the school building, looking due west. The "big house" stands then and now so proudly. The first business on the left, just west of the house, states blacksmith. The Bradley Christian Church stands proudly on the right.

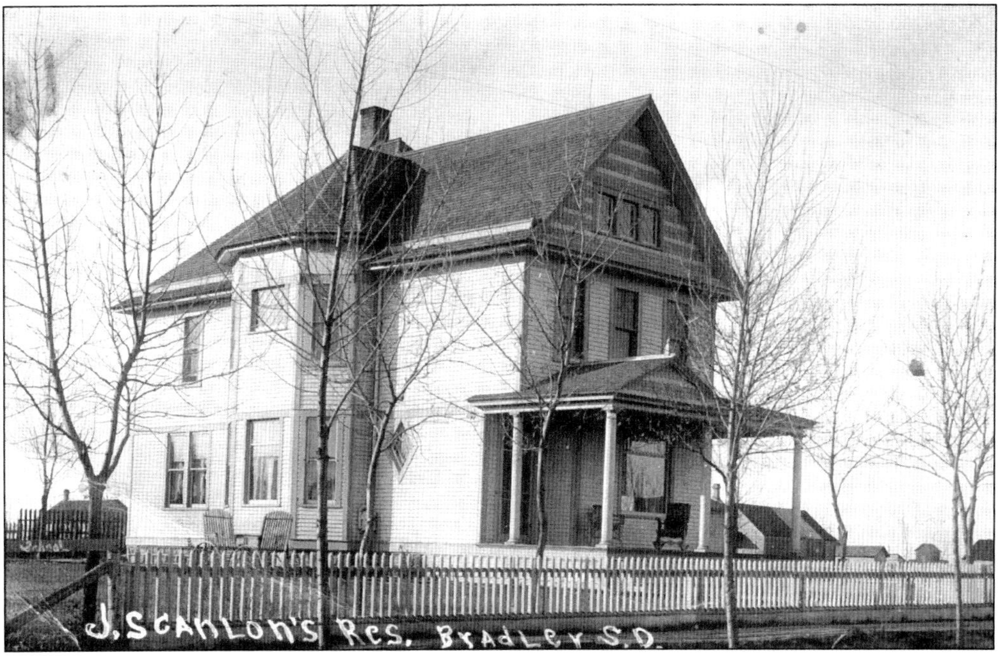

This is the John Scanlon residence in Bradley. John Scanlon and his wife, Emma (Perry) Scanlon, were the owners of the State Bank of Bradley. John was also a partner in the Scanlan, McKenny, and Perry Lumber Company. He came to Bradley in 1887 from Iowa.

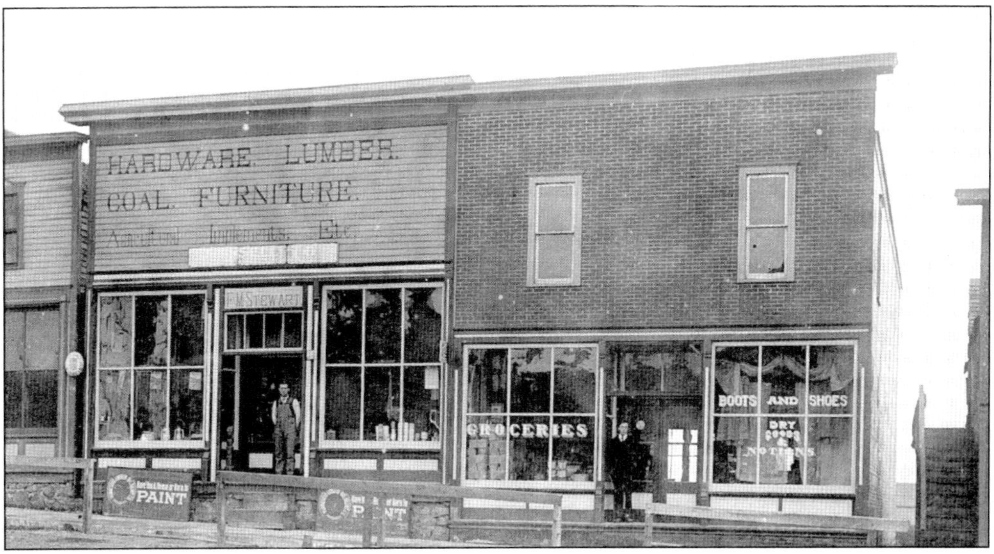

Shown here is a nice close-up view of two early Bradley businesses, the F. W. Stewart Hardware and General Store, and the Anton Peterson Grocery and Dry Goods Notions store. This card was sent from Bradley in 1907 to Iva Webb in Spirit Lake, Iowa.

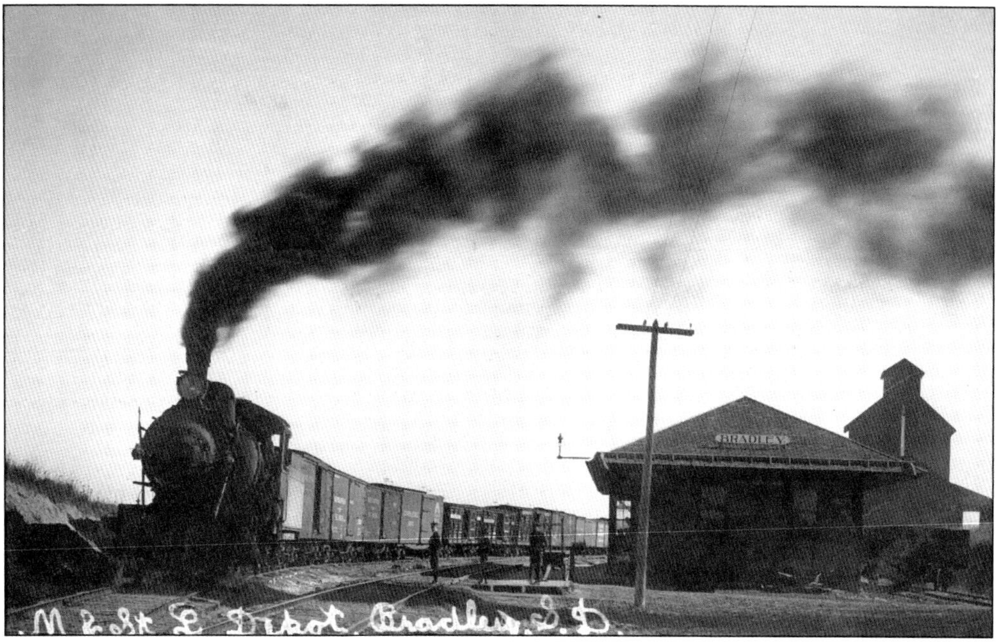

The Minneapolis and St. Louis Depot is seen here. What a beautiful sight and sound it must have been in the community. This card was sent by Emma (Perry) Scanlon from Bradley in December 1909, to Olive Perry.

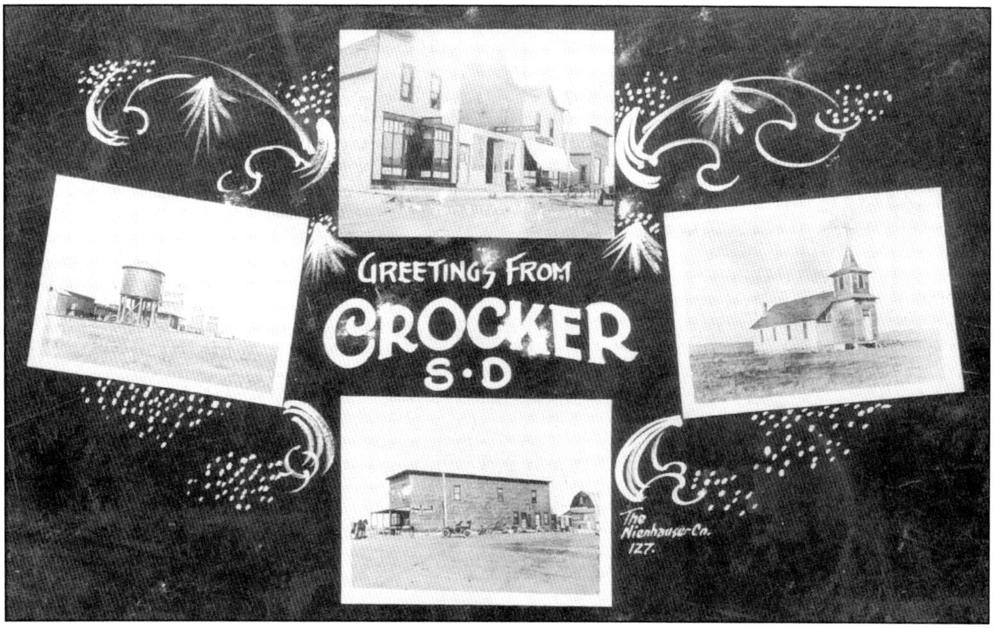

Postcards of Crocker are very rare, the author knows of only one other card, and that is of the elevator and depot, which he does not have. On this card is the train water tower, three elevators and depot along the track, the Catholic church, pool hall, lunchroom, and the west side of Main Street showing four businesses. Enjoy!

Two

Garden City and Elrod

The Garden City community is located in the northeast part of Clark County, with the town located on the northeast one-fourth of Section 8 of Eden Township. Records show this area was first settled in 1882. Locaters and railroad workers stayed in the home of R. S. and Cynthia J. Carpenter when they were platting and building the railroad. The story is that they so enjoyed Cynthia's hospitality, and especially her cooking, that they gave her the privilege of naming the new town. Apparently, she thought it was a veritable "Garden of Eden," for she chose "Garden City" for the name of the town, and the township was called "Eden."

Elrod's original name was Ida, but Elrod was soon adopted in 1883. Some believe it was named for Sam H. Elrod, who was a disbursing agent for the Sisseton Indians. He became an attorney in Clark and later served as governor of South Dakota from 1905 to 1907. Others say the town was named for W. S. Elrod, who bought grain there, and still another account is that actually two towns started at this spot, one on the Chicago and Northwestern Railroad called South Elrod and one on the Milwaukee and St. Paul Railroad, called Ida. The rivalry ended successfully for the East Elrod, which was shortened to the name Elrod. Ida's post office name changed to Elrod in 1884. Elrod Township was organized in 1885. Martin Larson was the first white child (male) to be born in 1881, and Emma Schaaf was the first white child (female) born in 1883. The Elrod Post Office closed on August 31, 1954.

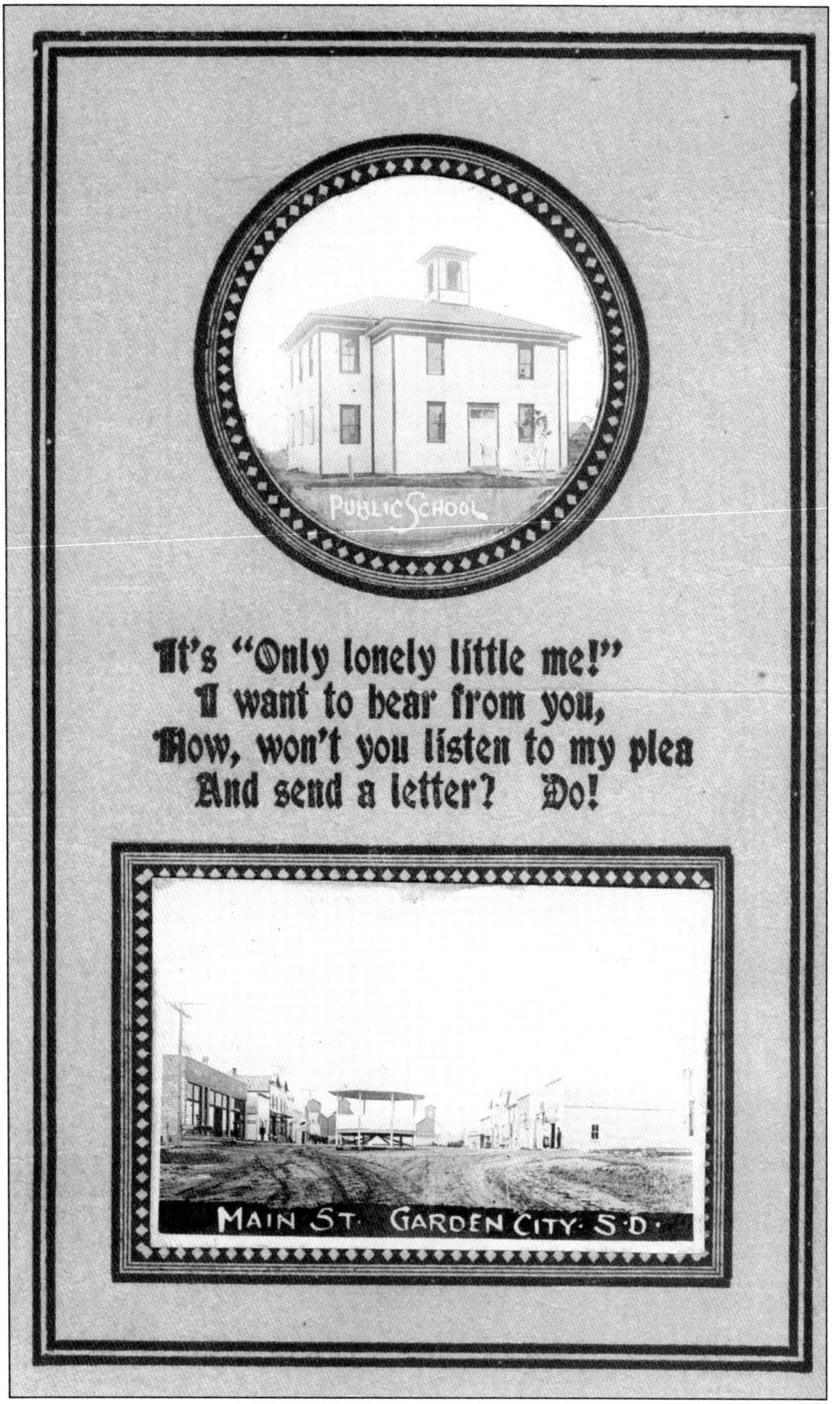

This is the author's first postcard of Garden City, in fact, nearly the first postcard of his entire collection. The author bought it in Davis, California, in 1998 while on a vacation with Martin Metzler, one of his foreign-exchange students from Germany. He paid $5 for it. It shows the public school and Main Street with the bandstand. It was sent from Clark in 1912 to Moline, Illinois. It is truly a great find to bring back home to Clark County.

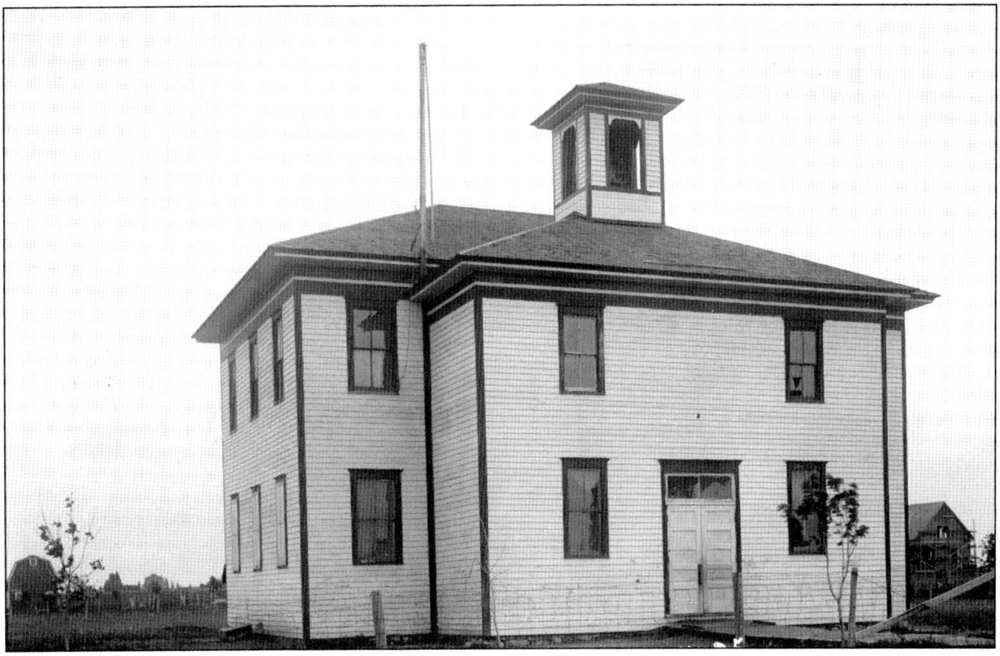

The Garden City Public School, a two-story frame building built in 1900, was built on the north side of the main road. The building was replaced by a brick school around 1914. A school building no longer exists in the community.

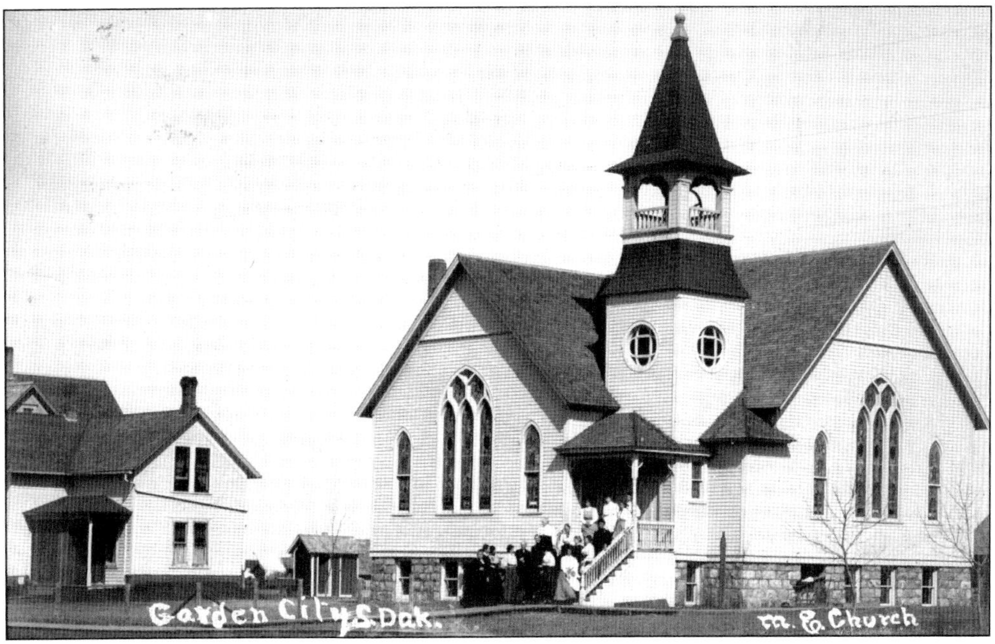

It must have been United Methodist Women's day in the church. It says on the back of this card that the social was a decided success. The card was sent from Garden City in 1909. This building was dedicated in 1906. It was destroyed by fire on January 1, 1977.

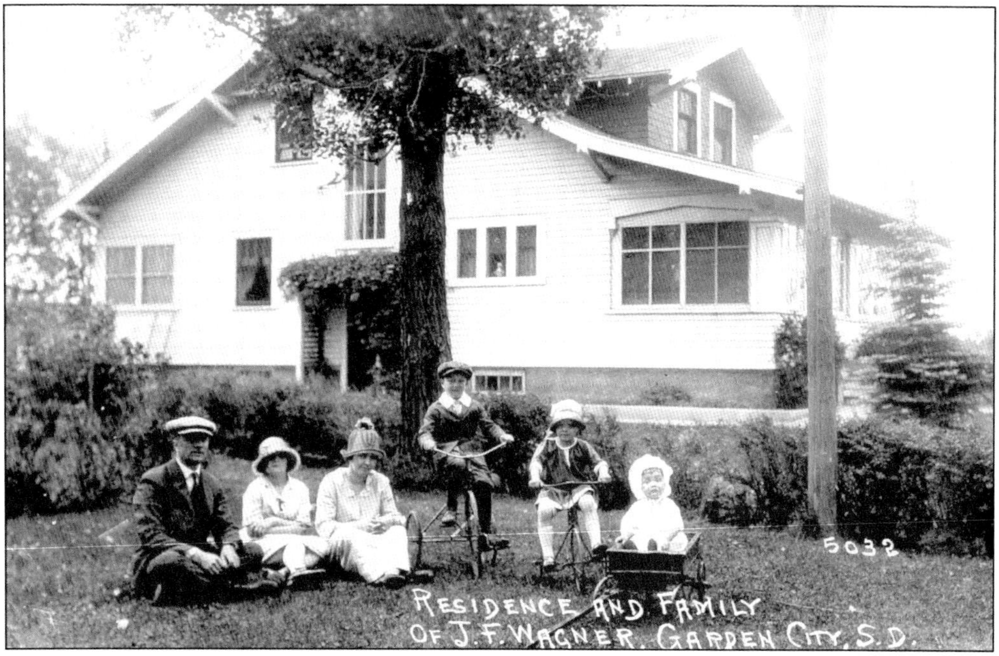

This is the Joe "J. F." Wagner family and its residence in Garden City. J. F. Wagner was a businessman of many hats, so to speak. He was a druggist/pharmacist, an undertaker, and the town bandleader for many years. (Courtesy of Darlene "Dolly" Peterson.)

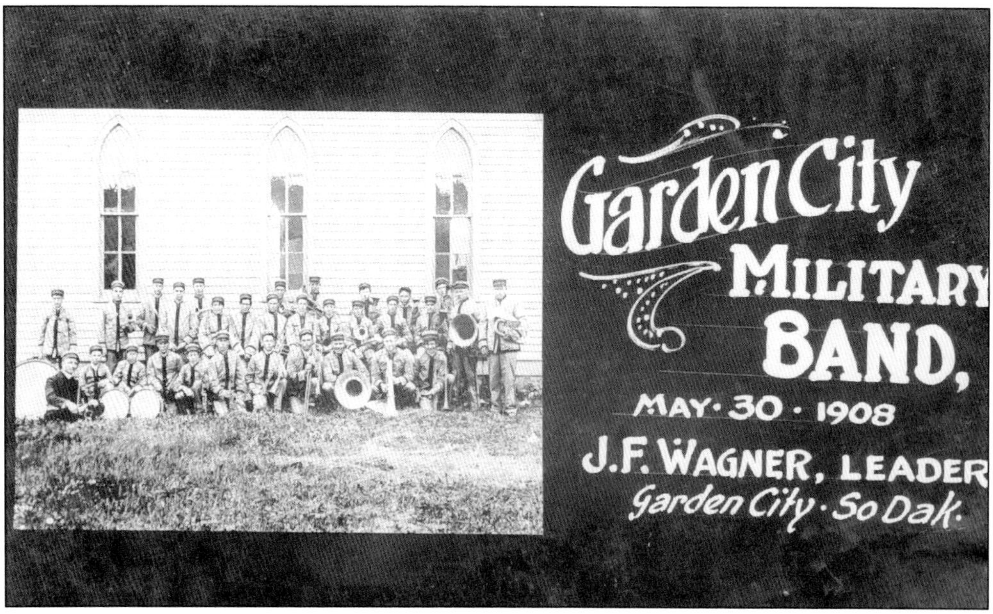

Shown is a nice view of the Garden City Band and its leader, J. F. Wagner. The photograph was taken on May 30, 1908, while performing in Bradley, South Dakota.

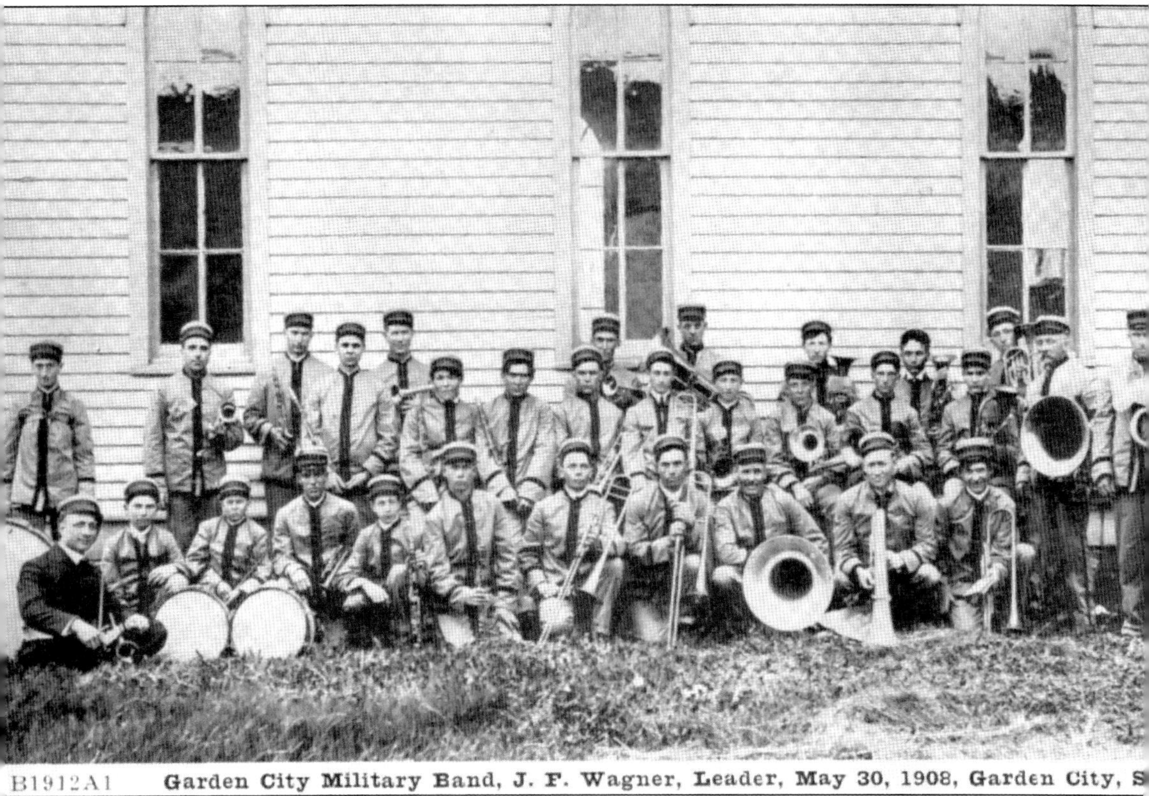

The Garden City Band was organized in the fall of 1905. This early view of the band has been identified by Everett Fletcher and Charlie Barkley, both longtime residents of Garden City and now both deceased. From left to right are (first row) director Josiah F. Wagner, Bob McKay, Frank Phipps, Archie Harding, Claude (Jake) Rhodes, Carlys Lyke, Willie Bell, Earl Brewer, Chase Bailey, Ole G. Haugen, and Bernie Shannan; (second row) Archie Feldmeyer, Frank Huffman, Herb Belcher, Ed Taylor, Clint C. Bailey, Frank Bailey, Charlie Barkley, Artie Ritchie, Edsel Barkley, Phil Feldmeyer, Milt Harding, Francis Shannon, Clarence Rea, Roy Young, Mat Miller, Elmer Fairbanks, Clyde Mankey, Harry Bailey, Andrew N. Rea, and Bert R. Barkhuff.

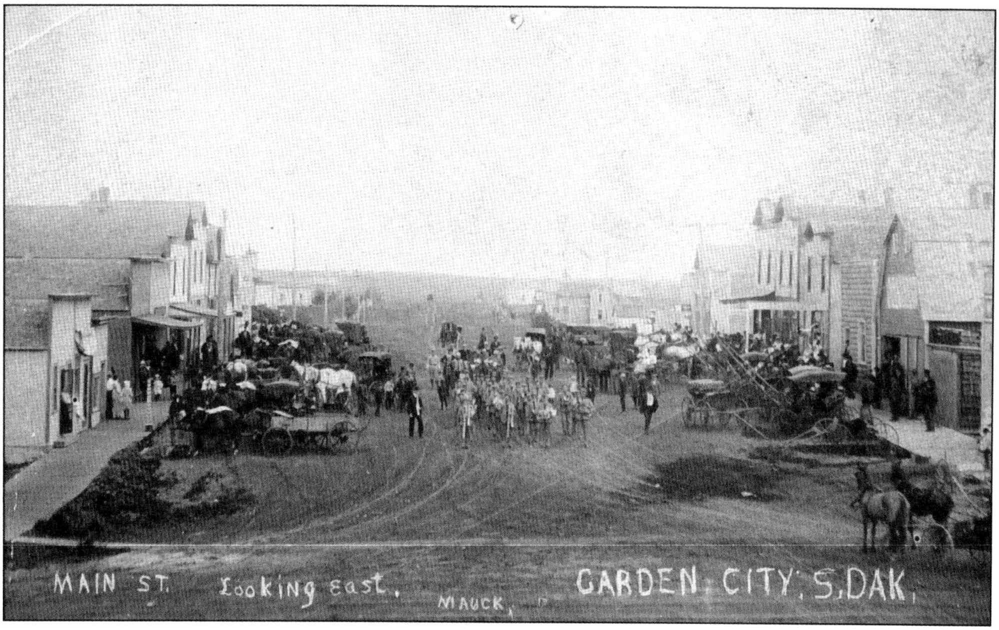

Here comes the Garden City Band and its leader, J. F. Wagner, during Gala Days, dated August 22, 1908 (written on the back of this card). Gala Days was a two-day event held annually in Garden City that attracted a large crowd in the neighborhood of 2,000 people. Besides horse races, it included a parade, baseball games, greased pig races, Model T races, and other events. The last Gala Day event was held in 1964.

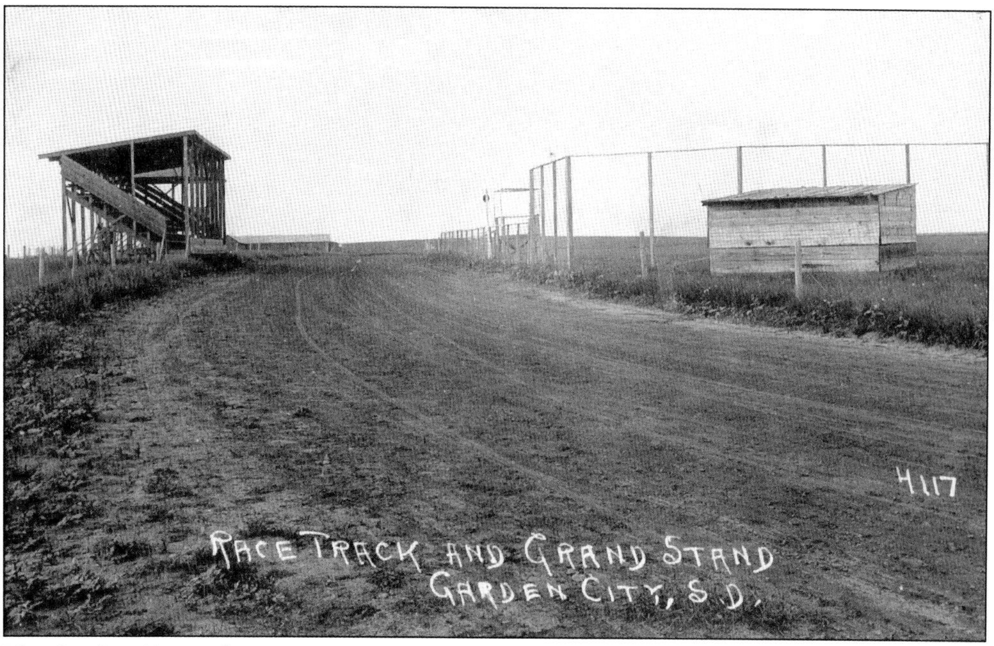

The Garden City Park Association was organized in 1914. The racetrack was built on 20 acres of land purchased from William J. Fletcher. John Zugschwerdt handled the blade while one of his sons, Lee, drove the team on the blade to shape the half-mile oval track. If this track could only talk, oh for the stories! Nothing much of the track exists any longer.

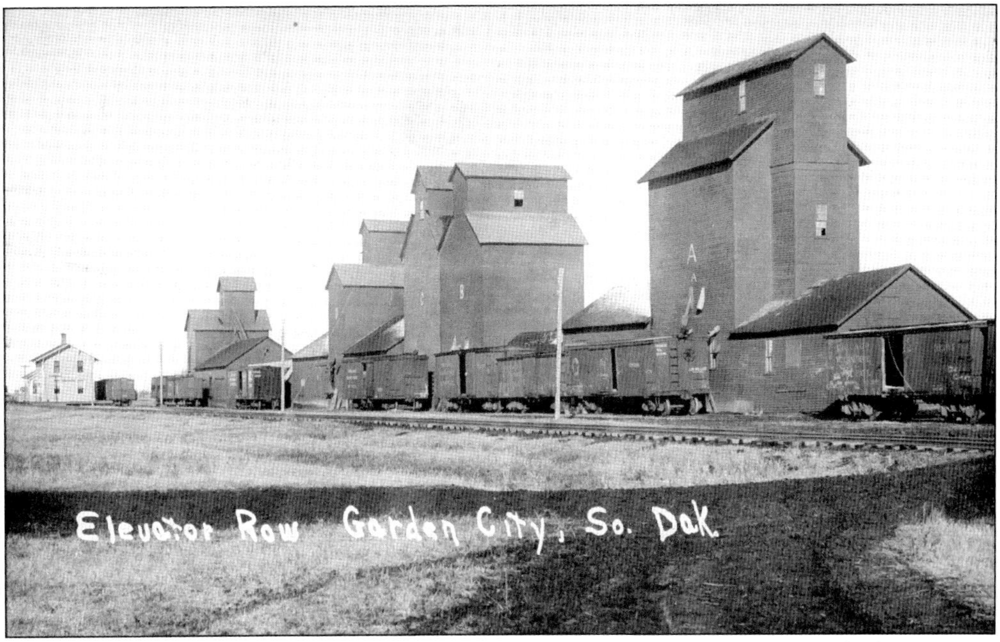

Here is the elevator row with the Chicago, Milwaukee and St. Paul Depot on the left. Notice all five elevators are lettered, A, B, C, D, and E respectively. The first elevator was constructed in 1903.

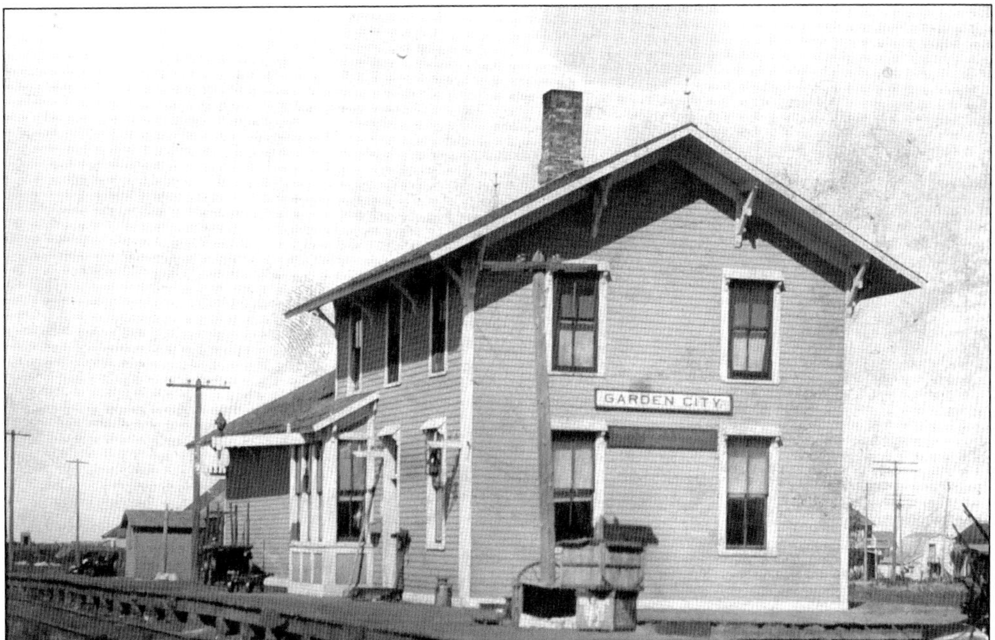

This first depot, for the Chicago, Milwaukee and St. Paul, was built along the tracks in 1887. It was a two-story frame building with living quarters for the depot agent upstairs. In about 1911 or 1912, the depot was destroyed by fire.

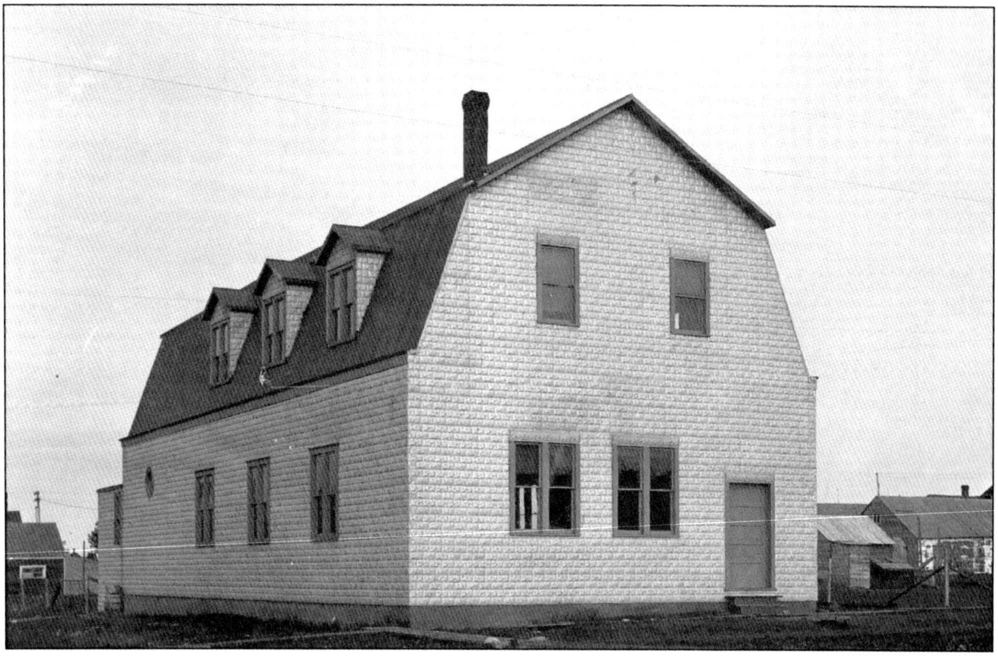

The Garden City Opera House and Hall was built in 1908. Not only was it a place for great plays, drama, and the Garden City Band concerts, it served for many years as the home of the Garden City Dragons. This real photo postcard was taken by Johnson and Olson of Alexandria, Minnesota.

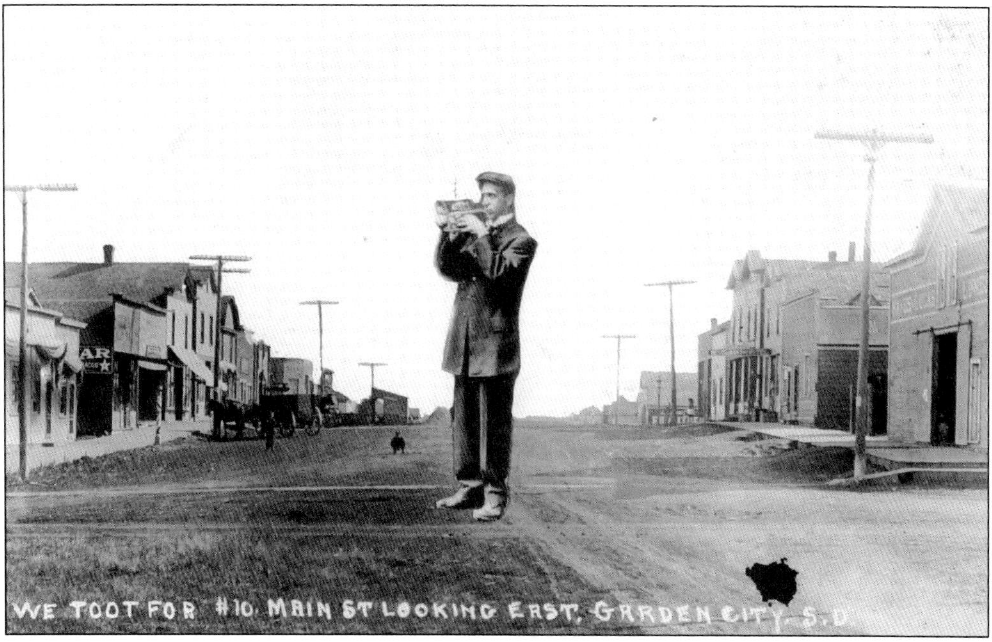

"We toot for $10." Whom or whatever was the $10 for? Maybe a train ride? This imposed bugler card also shows Main Street. This is a Slack and Company, Sioux Falls, South Dakota postcard.

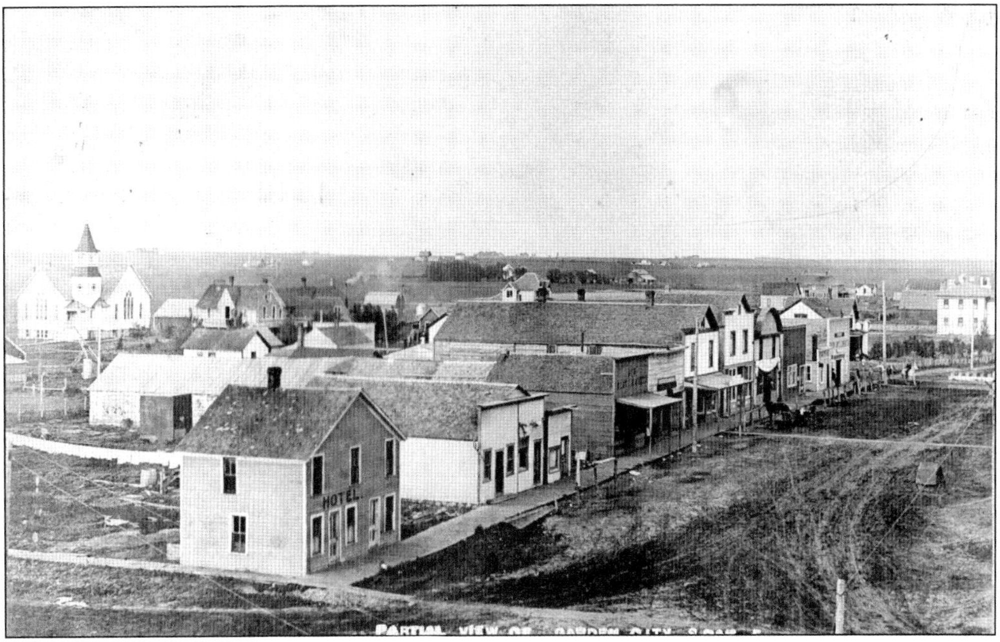

This real photo postcard of Garden City must have been taken from one of the elevators on the west side of town looking east. The Hankey House Hotel is in the foreground (the present post office location), the Methodist church is off to the left side, and the Garden City School is on the right. Other businesses included McCloskey's Brothers Farm Implements at the far right on the northeast side of Main Street.

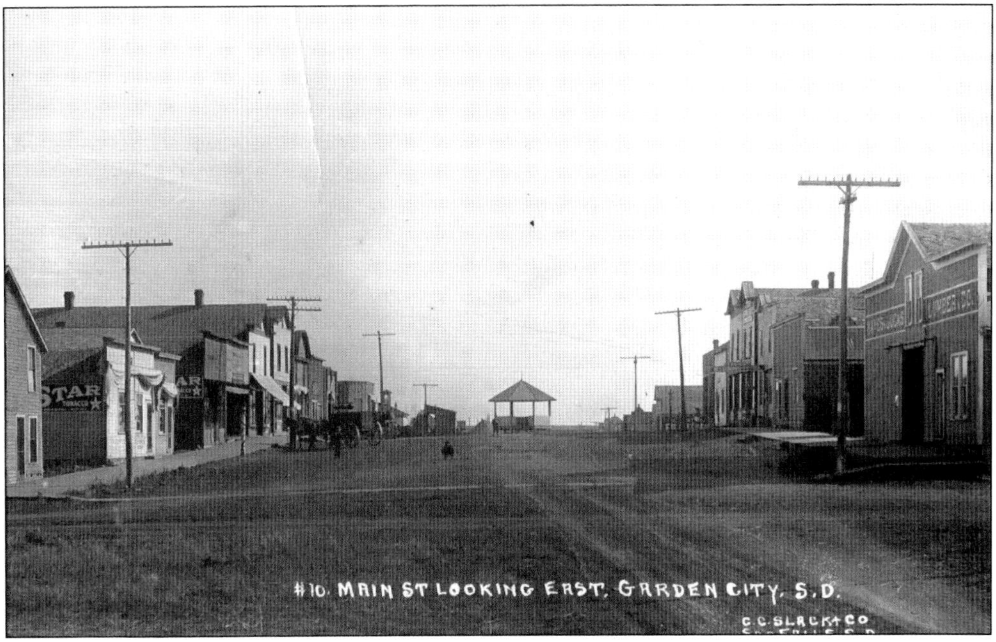

In another view of Main Street looking east, the Arcade Restaurant and Hotel and the Hayes-Lucas Lumber Company are on the right side. One can only imagine the bandstand filled with J. F. Wagner and the Garden City Band on summer nights!

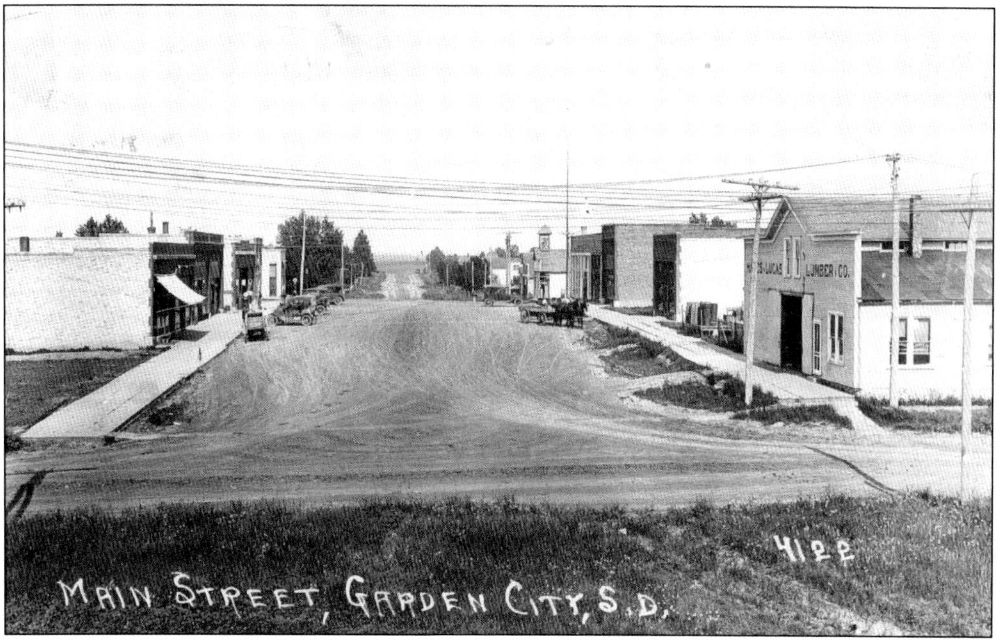

This card is a nice mix of the "horseless carriage" and the horse-drawn wagons on this Main Street view looking east. The bandstand is gone, as are other buildings on both sides. Most likely, this photograph was taken after the fire of 1917. It is postmarked from Elrod on October 2, 1930, and was sent to Monroe, Wisconsin.

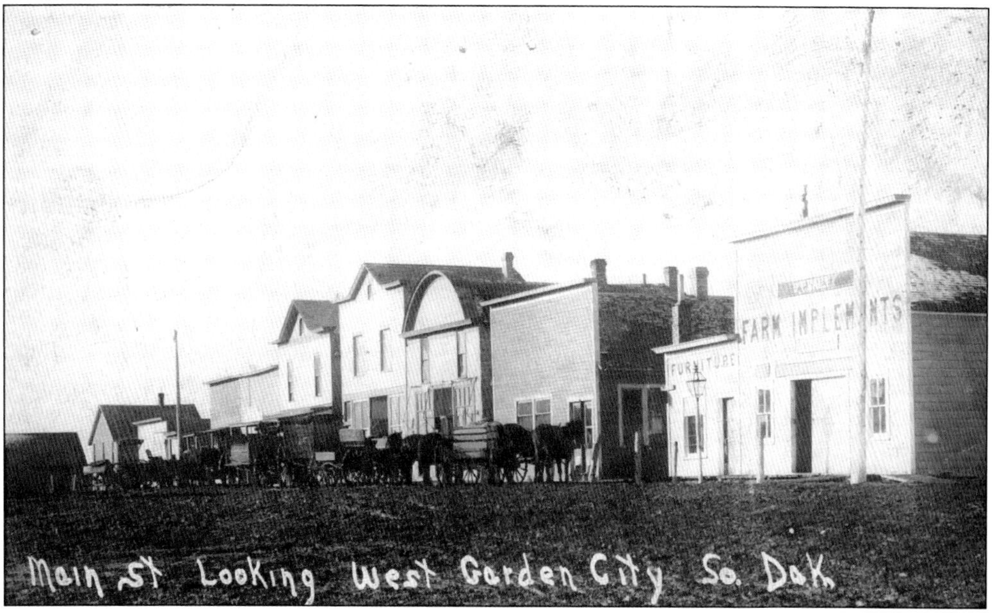

This was the O. E. Bailey Farm Implements building, a furniture store, and then the building that housed the Garden City State Bank (the shadow of the old sign indicates this). The bank moved across the street in 1908.

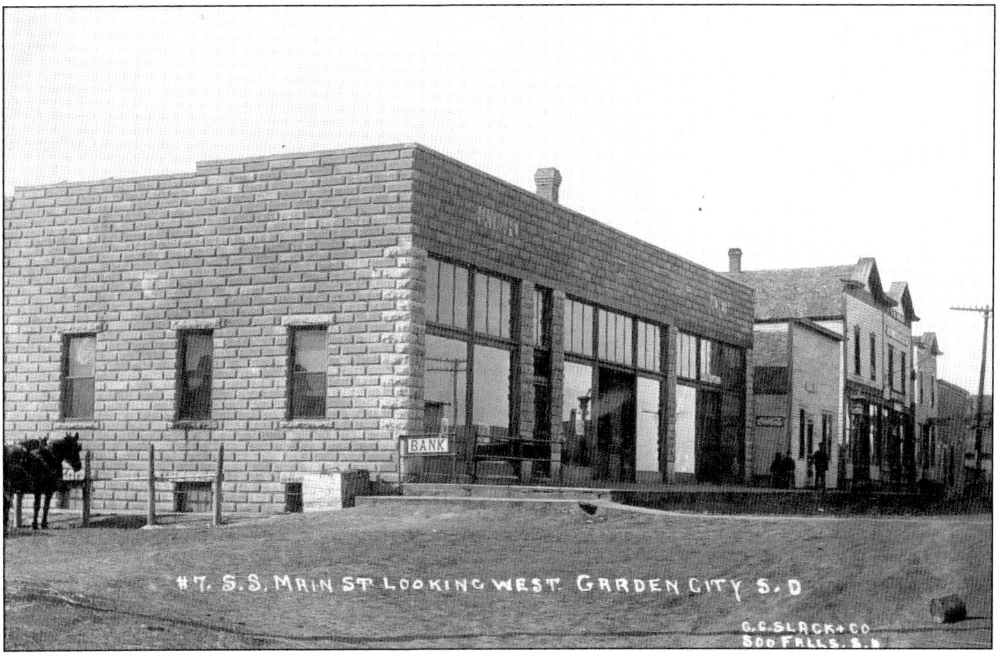

Here is a very nice real photo postcard showing the new Hayward and Wagner building, built in 1908. The Hayward building housed the Garden City State Bank. Did the teller/cashier ride the horse to work?

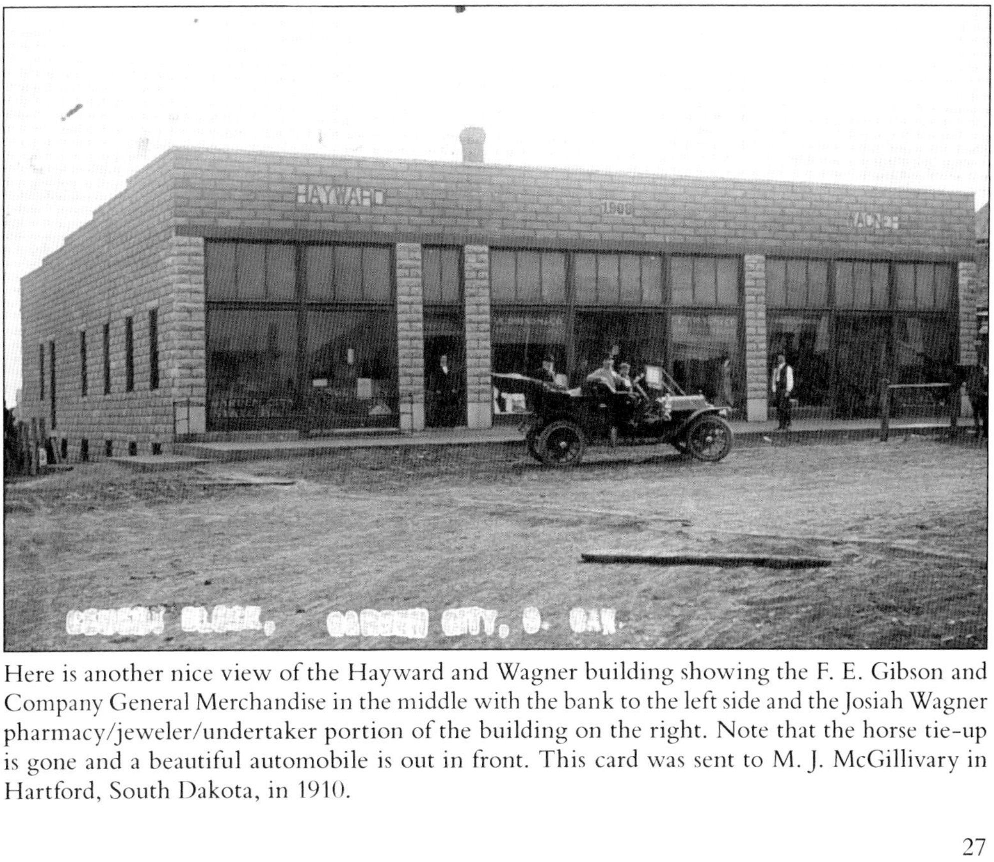

Here is another nice view of the Hayward and Wagner building showing the F. E. Gibson and Company General Merchandise in the middle with the bank to the left side and the Josiah Wagner pharmacy/jeweler/undertaker portion of the building on the right. Note that the horse tie-up is gone and a beautiful automobile is out in front. This card was sent to M. J. McGillivary in Hartford, South Dakota, in 1910.

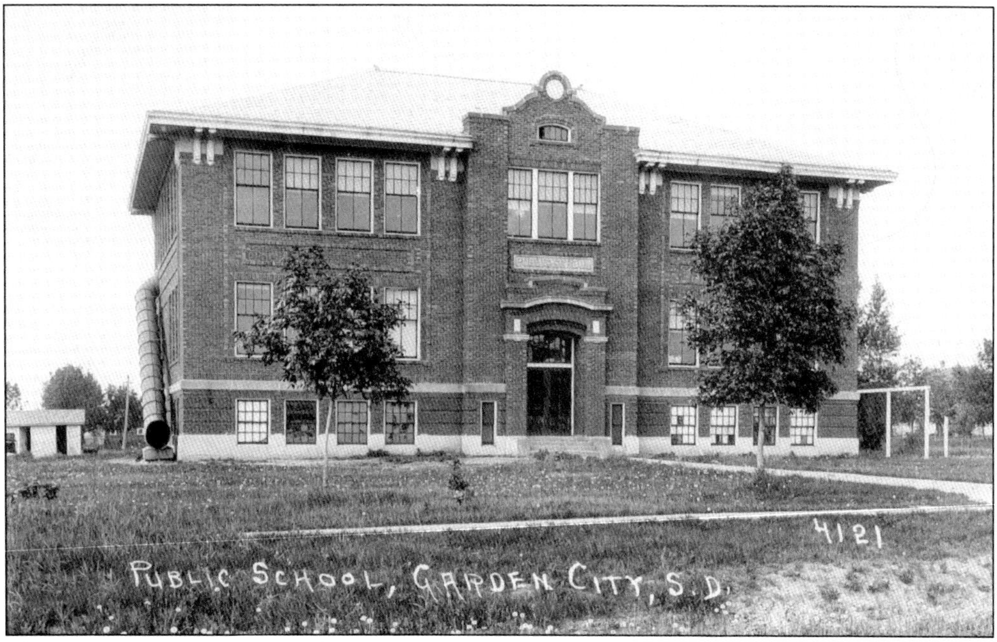

The Garden City section would not be complete without this view of the Garden City School built in 1914. In the fall of 1966, the Garden City High School closed and the students went to the Clark School. Grades one through six continued to be in Garden City for a while and later also became a part of the Clark School. This building no longer stands. (Courtesy of Darlene "Dolly" Peterson.)

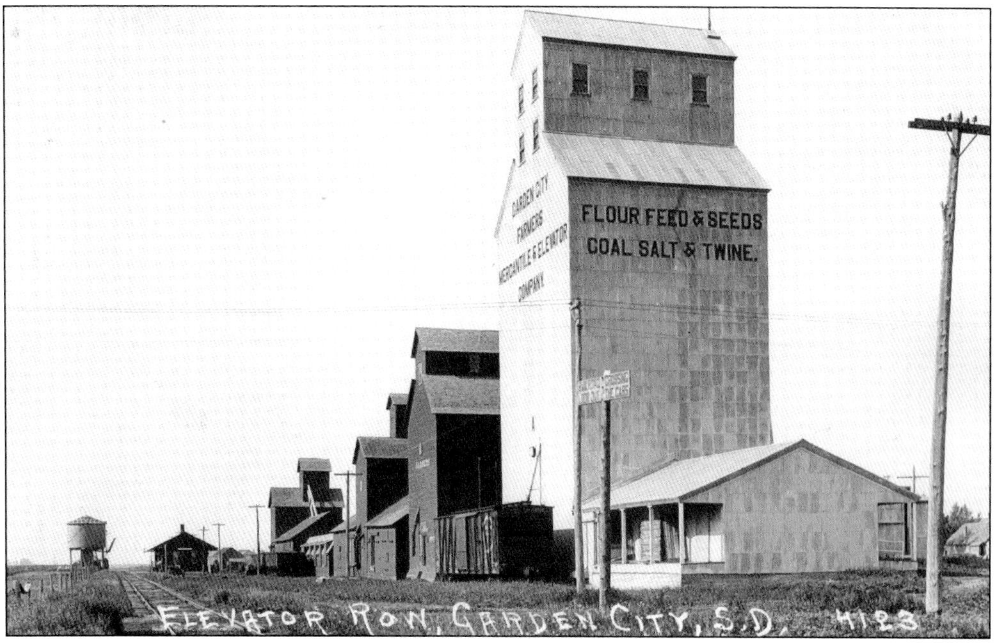

After a fire destroyed the old depot in 1911, this new depot was built alongside the tracks. The author included this card not only to show the new depot, but also take a look at the Garden City water tank, or "Petticoat Junction" as it was known to many. It was torn down in 1976. (Courtesy of Darlene "Dolly" Peterson.)

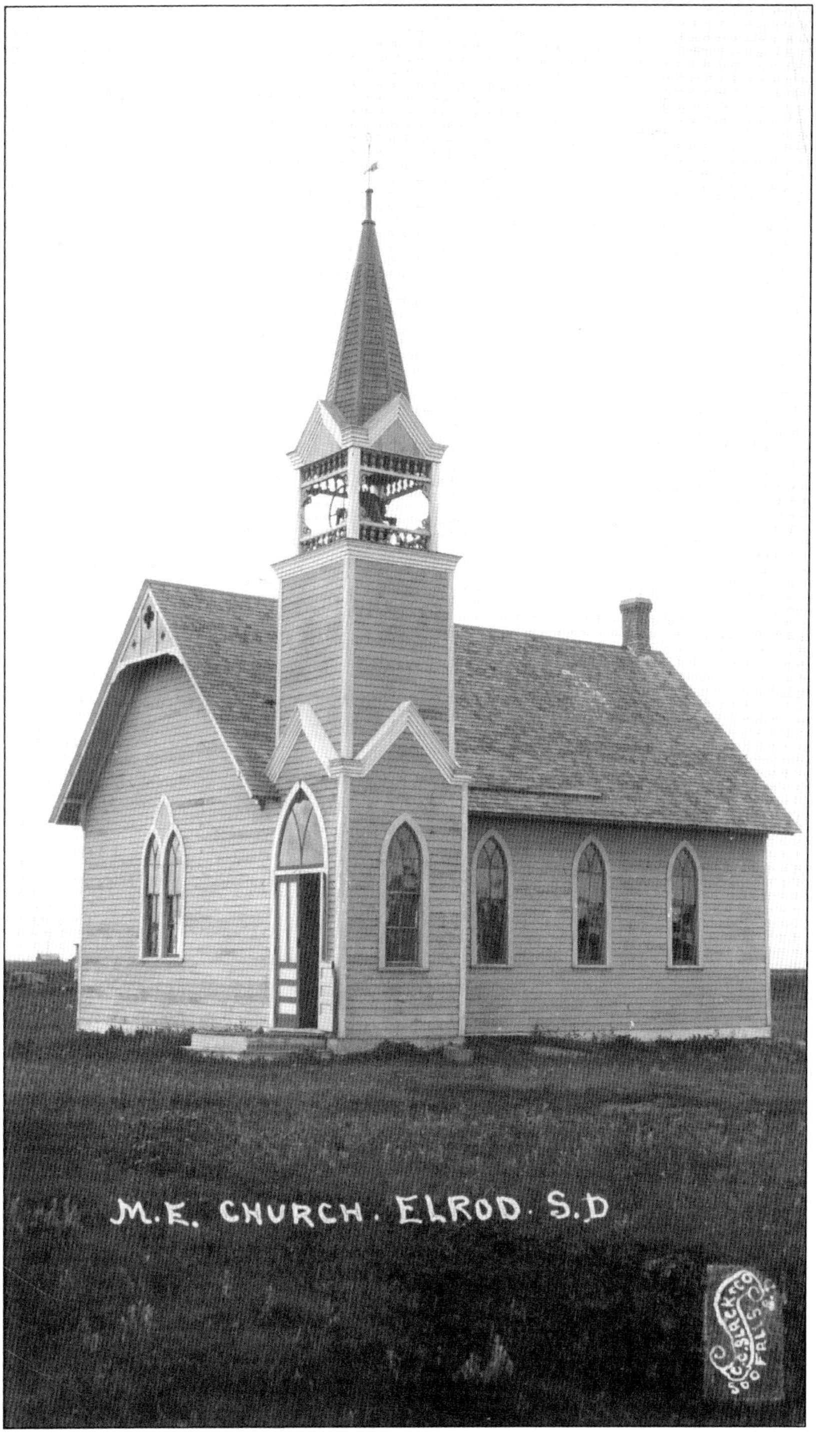

A beautiful prairie church building, the Methodist Episcopal Church at Elrod was the original Methodist church in Garden City. Built in 1889, it was moved to Elrod in 1905 by a team of four horses. It was sold in 1933, and moved to a Kloster farm northwest of Clark. This card has a very nice Elrod cancellation from March 22, 1913.

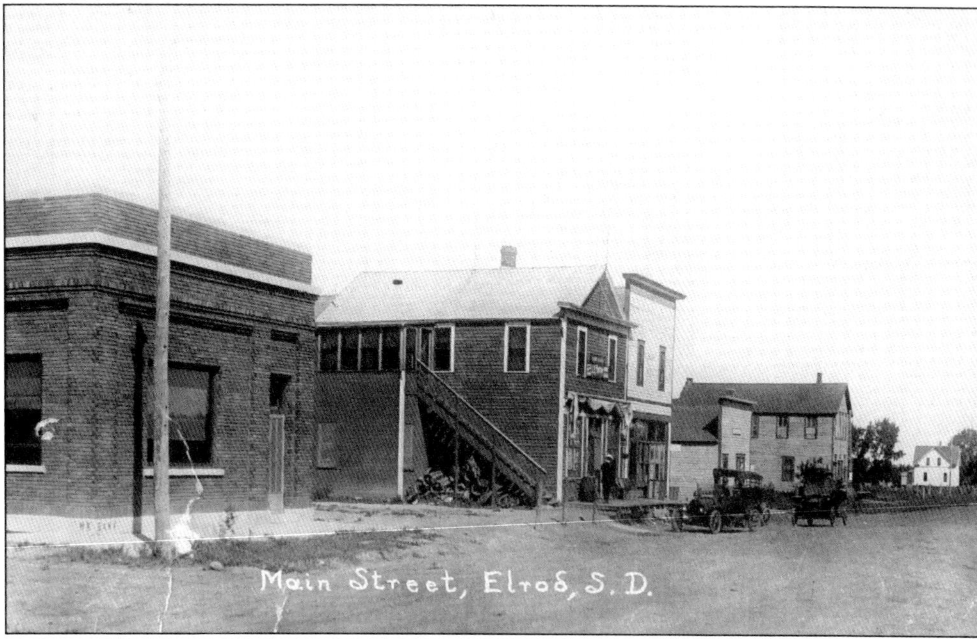

Main Street in Elrod, South Dakota, shows a bank building on the corner (which went broke in 1924), the Elrod Store that was operated by Joe Maltby, a cream station, a land office, and a hotel. Elrod once was a crossroads for railway travel, the Chicago, Milwaukee line running north and south and the Chicago, Northwestern running east and west.

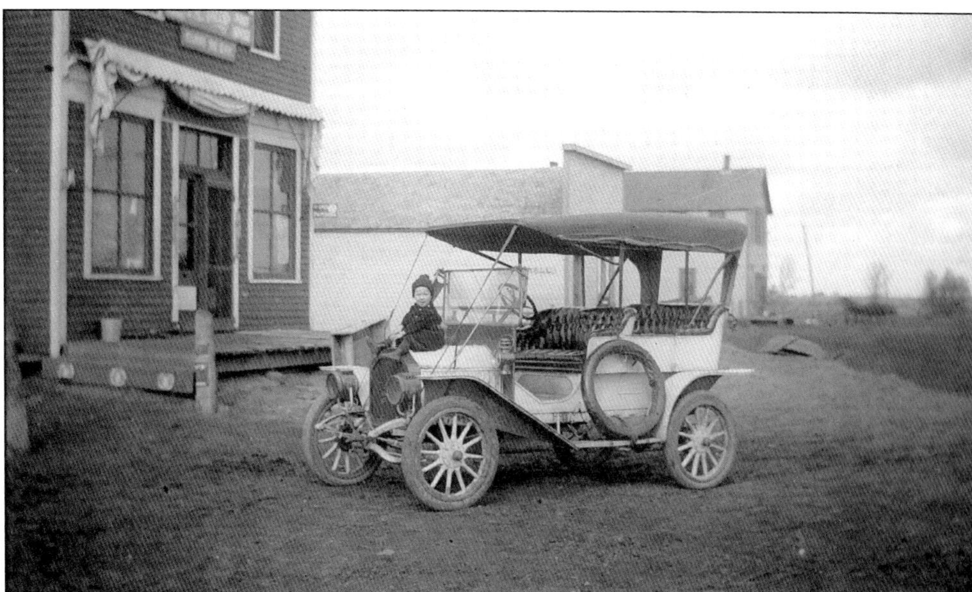

"Vivian on Joe Maltby's car at Elrod, SD," is what is written on the back of this never-used card. The author also owns a token good for 25¢ in merchandise from the Thomas and Sons Big Store in Elrod. It may have operated in the former bank building after the bank went broke. The owners also operated a store in Worthing, South Dakota. The author wonders who Vivian was.

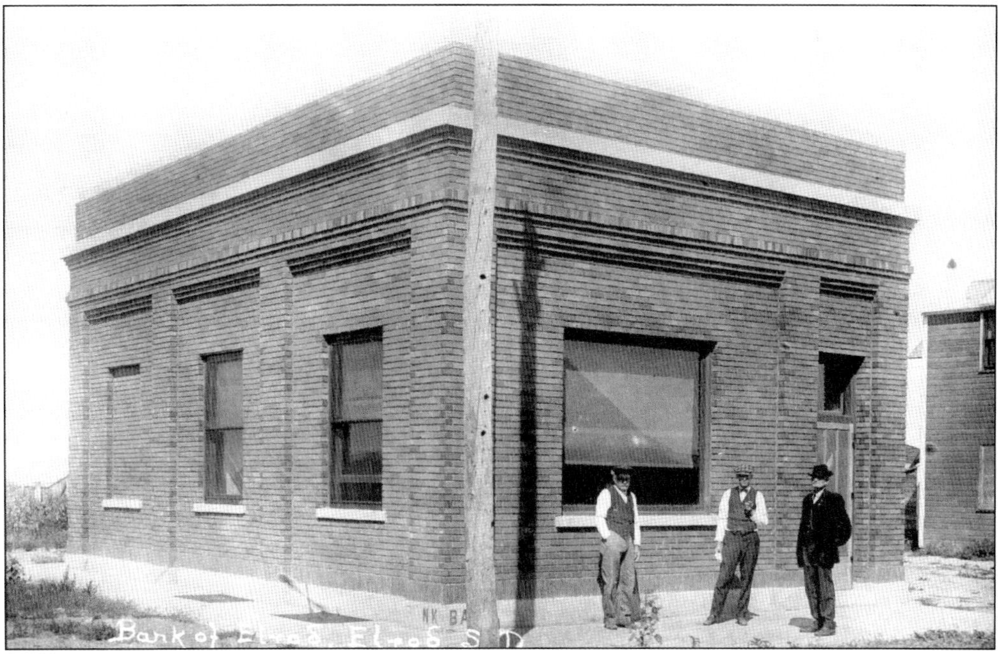

The Bank of Elrod has some interesting history written about it. One day the bank was robbed at high noon, and the robbers were never caught. After the bank went broke in 1924, it was used for a restaurant operated by Gladys and Lud Nelson, later a dry good store and millinery shop, and possibly the Thomas and Sons Big Store, run by Jack Reinhart. Imagine buying a hat in Elrod!

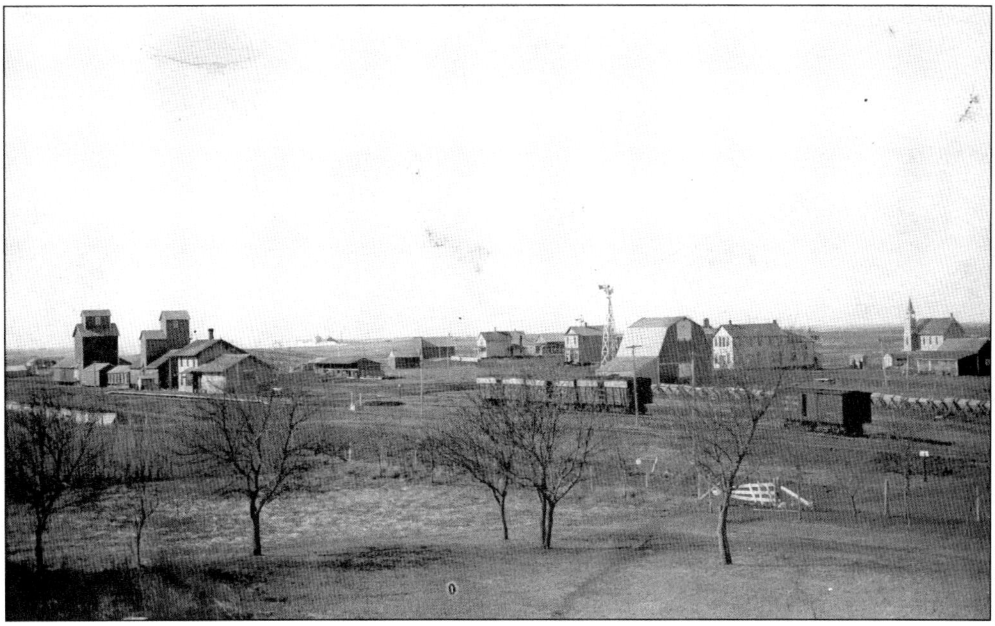

This view of Elrod looks to the south, showing the Elrod Depot and elevators, the church way off to the right, and way off on the horizon is the current home of Clifford and Boots Dekker. This card has a postmark from Elrod in May 1909, and was sent from Nettie to Johanna Dekker in Austinville, Iowa.

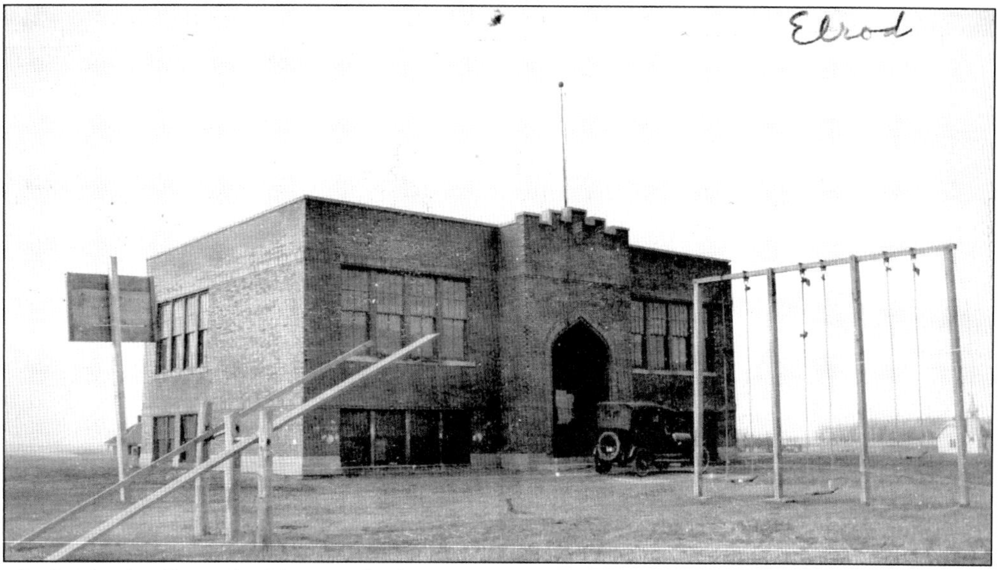

This brick schoolhouse building was built in Elrod in 1917 and was known as the Elrod Consolidated School. The school had all eight grades plus two years of high school. It was a meeting place for many social events, the Community Club among these. The school closed in 1967. It was razed in the past few years. (Courtesy of the Clark County Historical Society.)

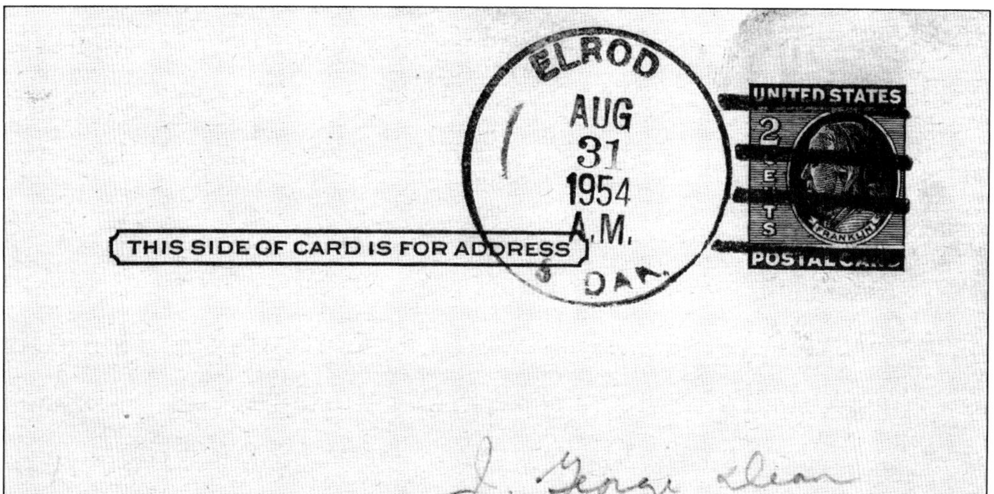

Yet another chapter closes on a Clark County community. This card was postmarked from Elrod on August 31, 1954, the last day the post office was open. Only small remnants remain of any building in Elrod.

Three

Clark

The city of Clark began as Clark Centre, situated at the center of the four townships—Garfield, Mount Pleasant, Lincoln, and Day—which at that time were one township named Clark. This was also the center of Clark County. Mattie Greenslet erected a hotel called the Clark House at this point; it stood on the corner where the Catholic cemetery is. The first mail was brought here in 1881. Such was the beginning—a few more settlers came in 1881 and the county was organized, but the big settlement of Clark came after the railroad reached it in 1882. After the railroad filed their plat of Clark, the present town began taking shape south of the original Clark Centre. The first passenger train arrived on July 4, 1882.

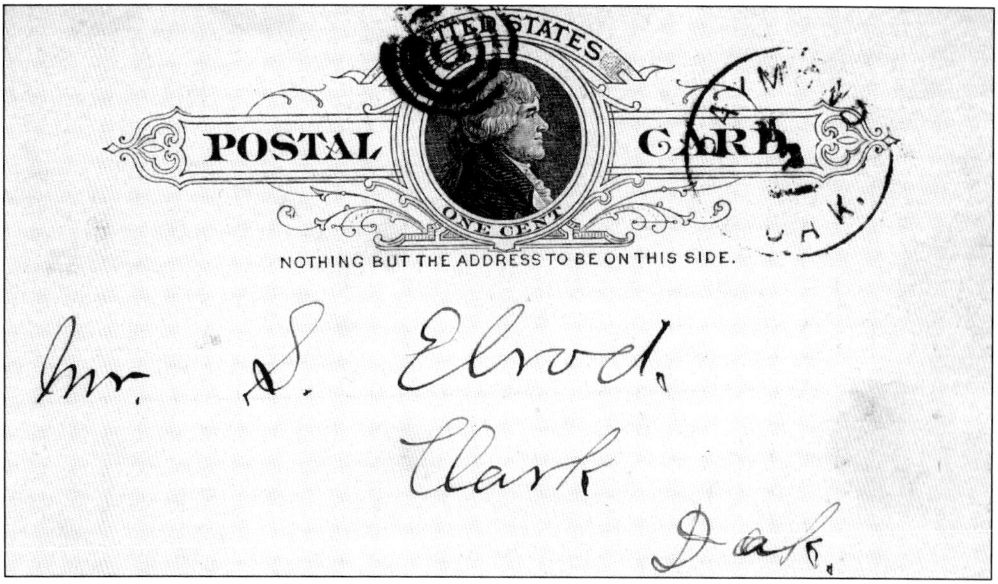

This is the oldest postcard in the author's collection. It was sent from Raymond, Dakota, on May 2, 1888, by William Resser, a blacksmith in Raymond. It is addressed to a Mr. S. Elrod, who was an attorney in Clark. Resser wants to know if his bill against the Harding estate had been filed. Elrod went on to be governor of South Dakota.

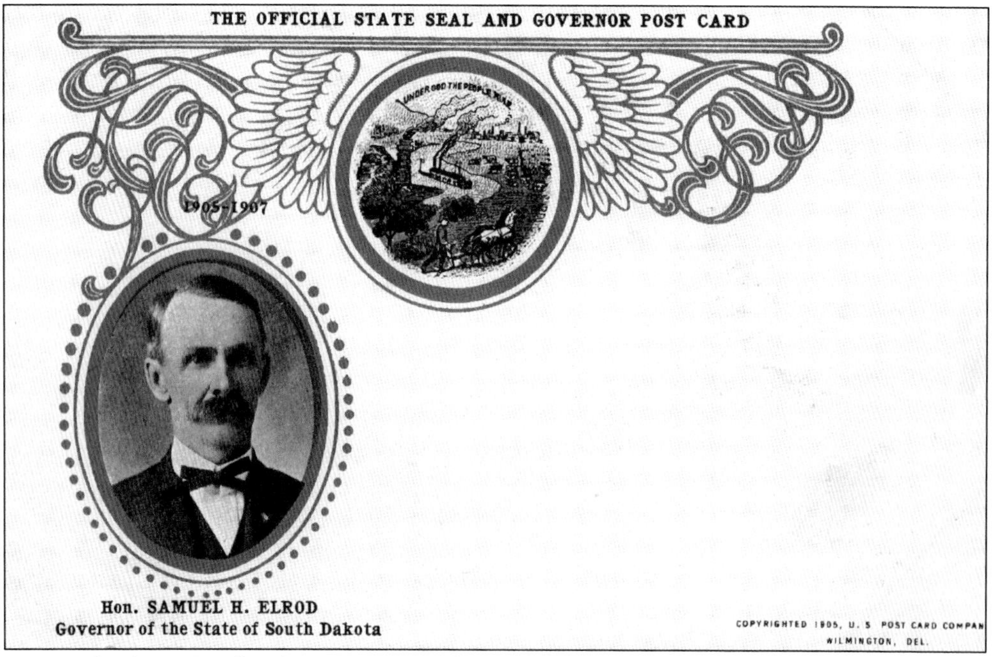

Copyrighted in 1905 by the U.S. Postcard Company in Wilmington, Delaware, this was a political advertising card sent out by the Hon. Samuel H. Elrod of Clark, governor of the state of South Dakota. He arrived in Clark on July 4, 1882, in time to deliver a speech for territorial Gov. Arthur Mellette. He was a native of Indiana.

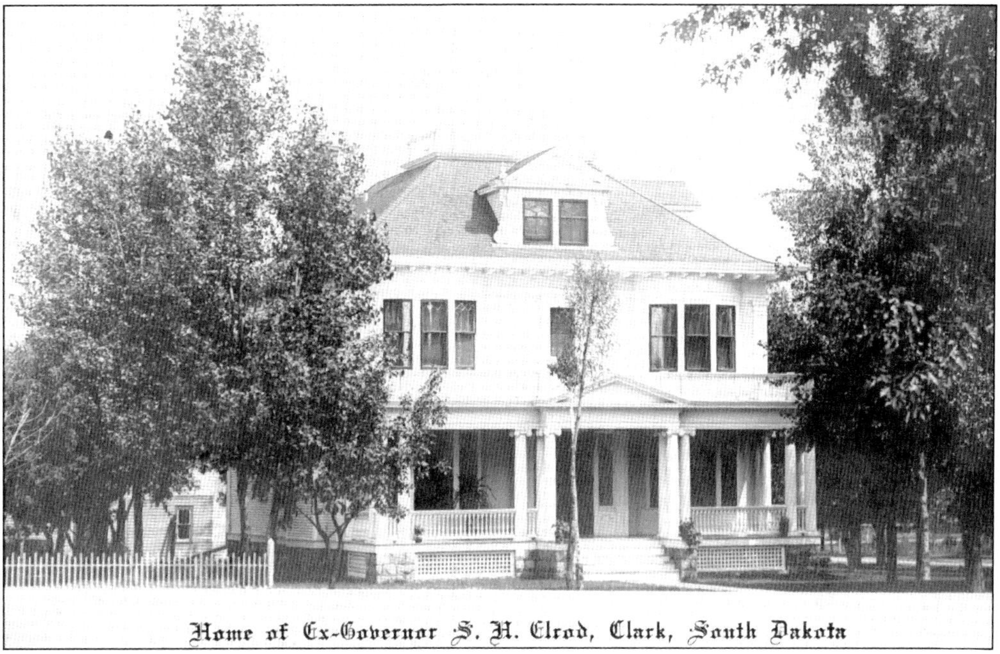

S. Elrod hired the architect who had drawn plans for the state capitol building in Pierre to design his home in Clark. The house was built between 1907 and 1908, and on Christmas Day in 1908, Governor Elrod and his wife served a seven-course dinner to guests from Watertown. Today, the home is a private residence.

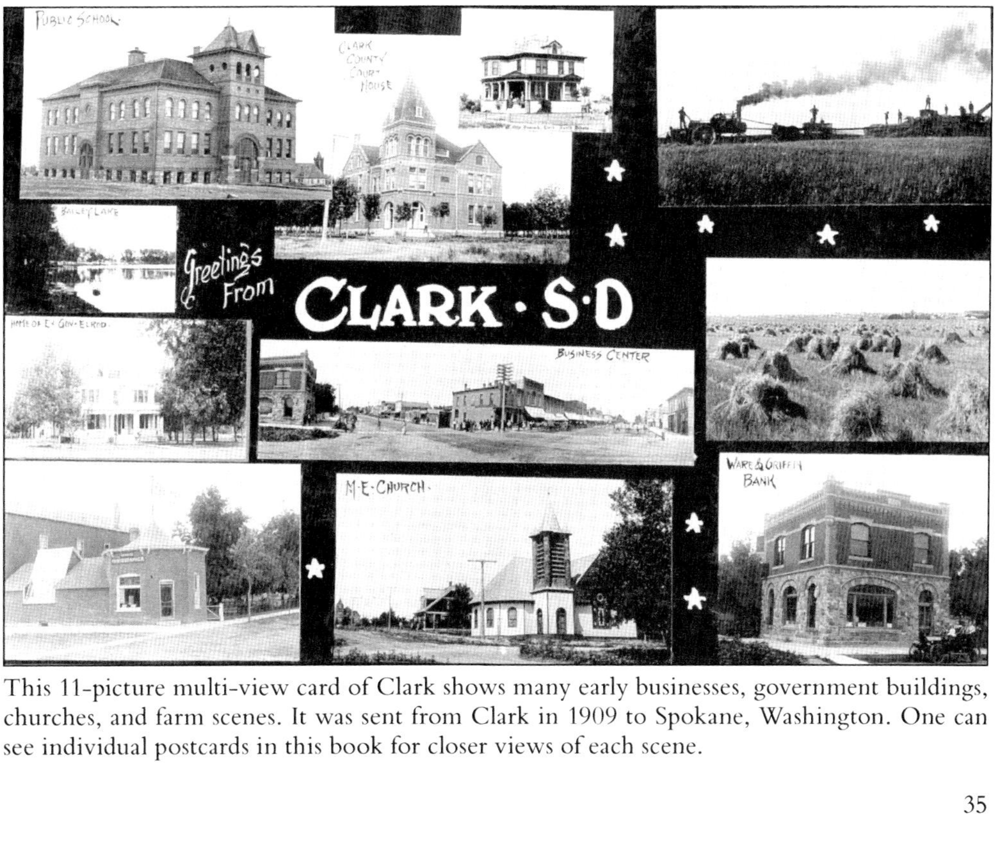

This 11-picture multi-view card of Clark shows many early businesses, government buildings, churches, and farm scenes. It was sent from Clark in 1909 to Spokane, Washington. One can see individual postcards in this book for closer views of each scene.

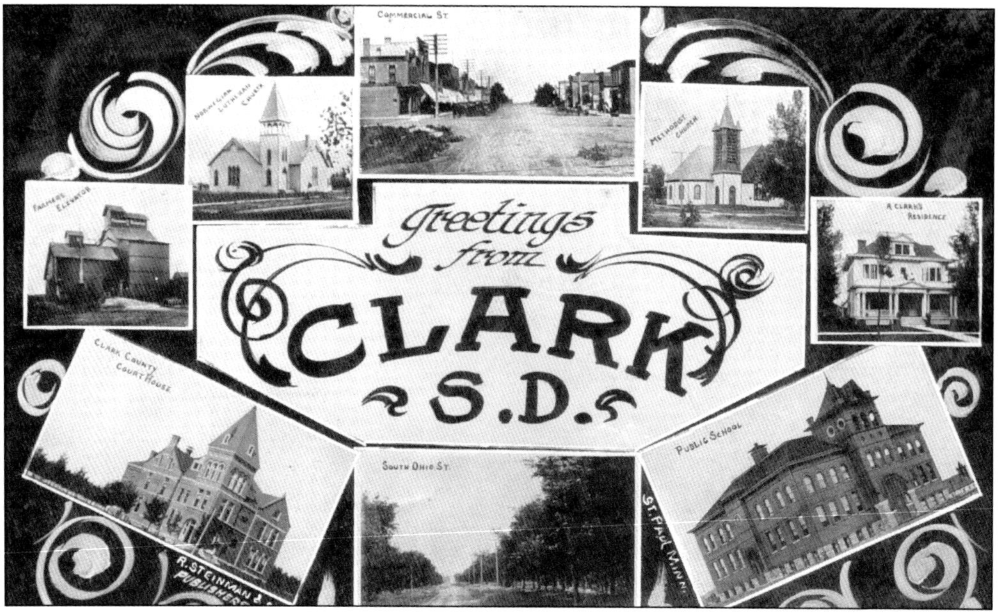

Shown are eight views around Clark. South Ohio Street is now called South Cloud Street. With the exception of the Elrod house, the elevator, and a couple of buildings on Commercial Street, all the others are gone. This card has a very nice Clark cancellation from 1910.

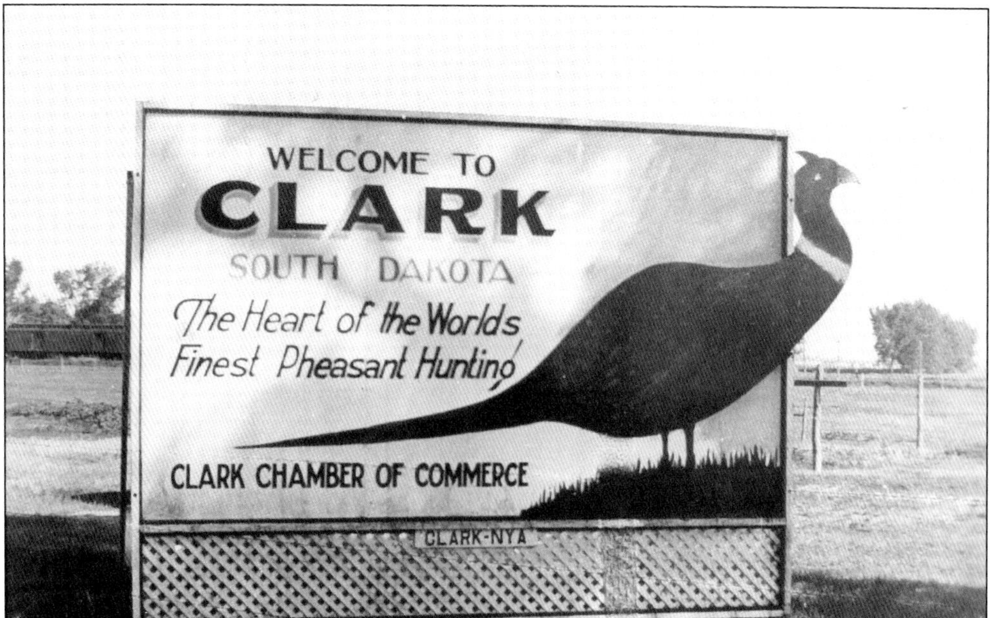

This is a 1940s "Welcome to Clark" sign that was located on the east edge of Clark. To the left side of the fence, a train car can be seen. The sender of this card was on her way to Hobo Day in Brookings. It is postmarked October 27, 1945.

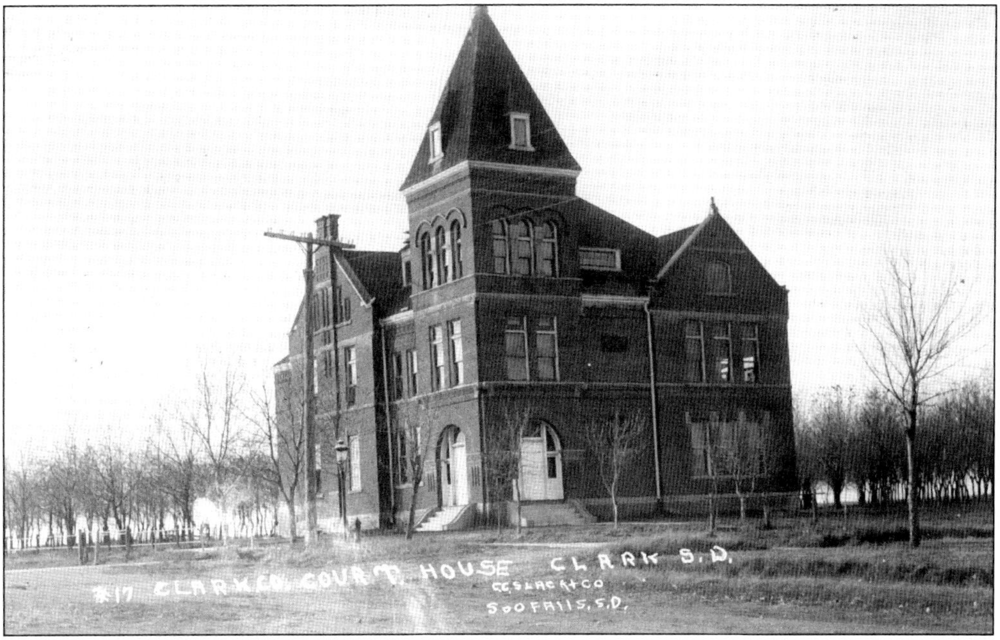

This first courthouse building was constructed in Clark County in 1888. Clark, the county seat, is the largest town in Clark County, and is located in the center of the county. It was a beautiful brick building and was constructed for $15,000 including furnishings. It stood on the southeast corner of what is now called Swimming Pool Park. It stood on the hill so it was visible for miles around. It was razed in the 1930s.

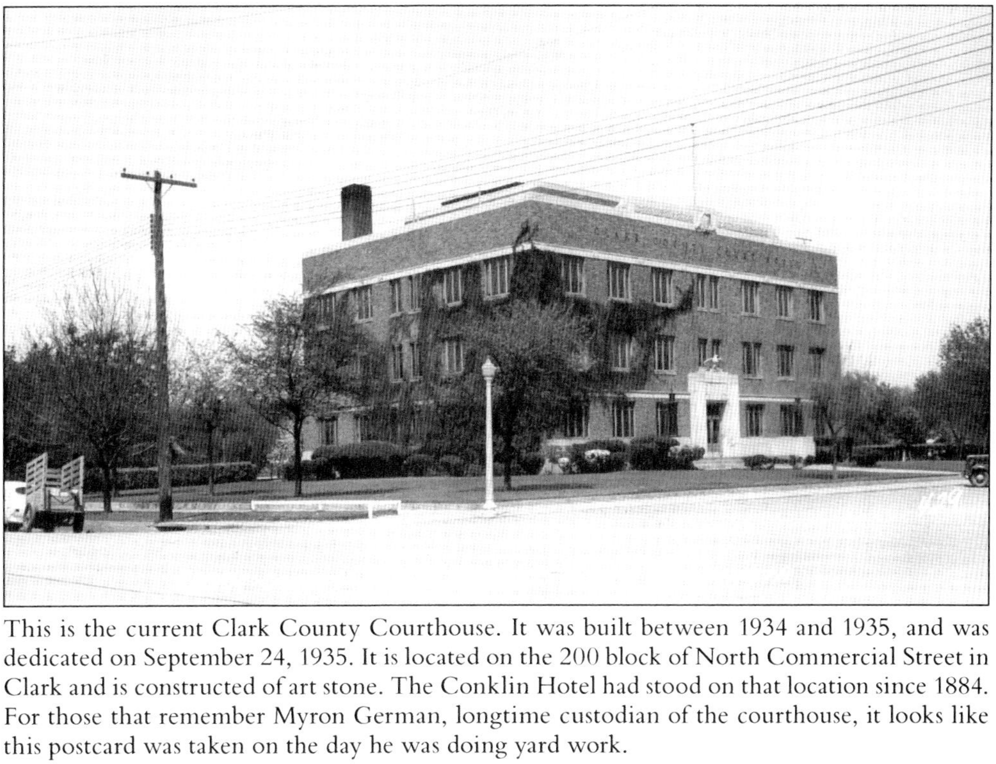

This is the current Clark County Courthouse. It was built between 1934 and 1935, and was dedicated on September 24, 1935. It is located on the 200 block of North Commercial Street in Clark and is constructed of art stone. The Conklin Hotel had stood on that location since 1884. For those that remember Myron German, longtime custodian of the courthouse, it looks like this postcard was taken on the day he was doing yard work.

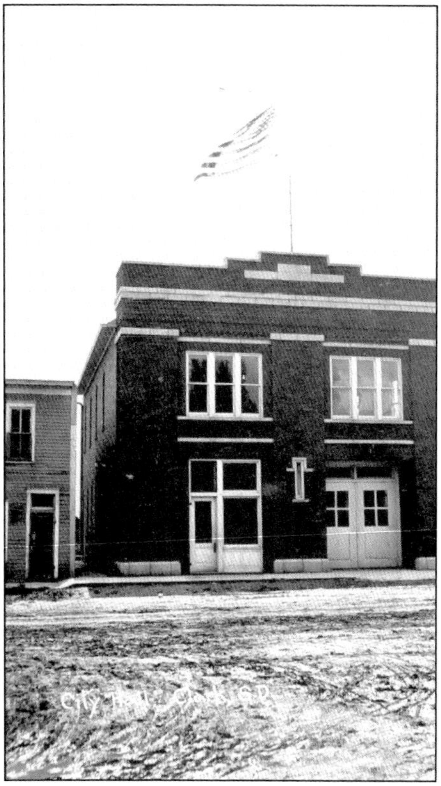

The former city hall in Clark was constructed in 1914, with the west part of the building housing the fire department. The building is located just west of the Adams Hotel, near the corner of Smith and First Streets. It serves as the law office of Chad Fjelland Esq. He is in the process of restoring the building.

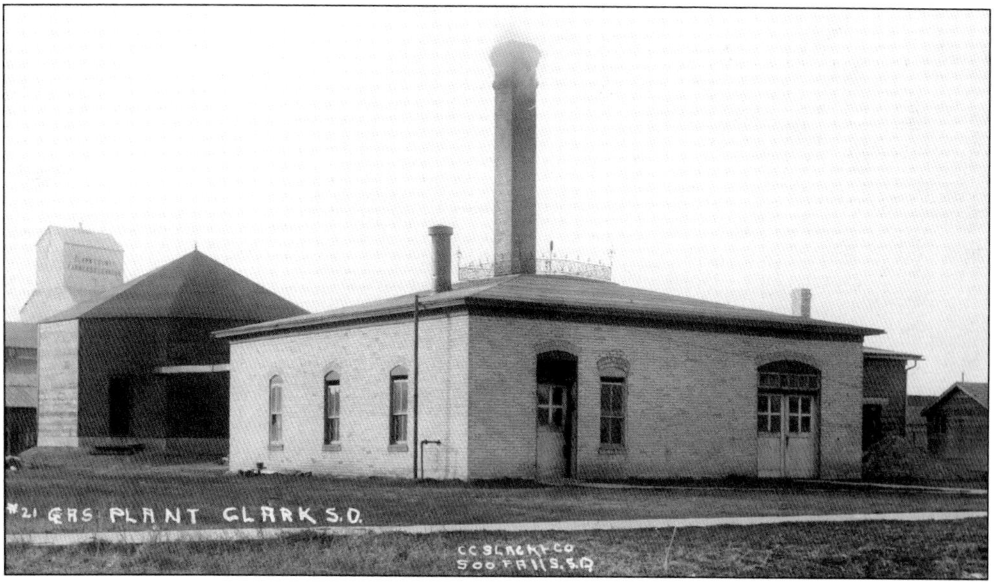

The first municipal illumination in Clark was from gaslights installed at each corner of the downtown district. They had to be lit by hand each night and put out in the morning, a task that was given to the city policeman Archie Dunlop. The gas was provided by this city-owned gas plant constructed by Will Dickey. This plant was located on the corner where the city-county ambulance building is now. Electric replaced gas downtown around 1920.

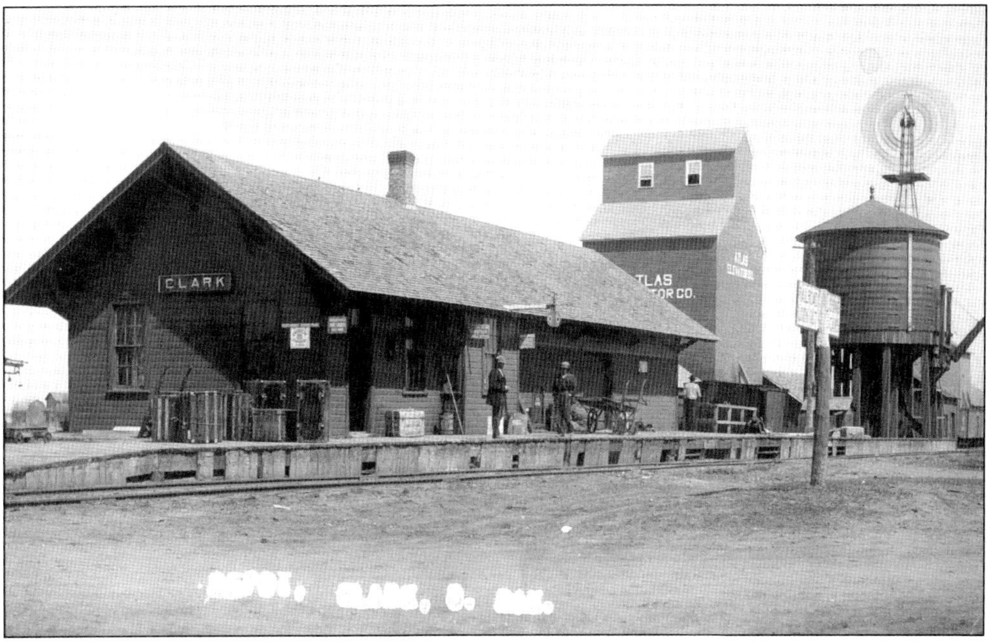

The Chicago-Northwestern Depot was built in Clark in June 1882. The depot was a hub of activity in the early years. By 1911, the depot facilities were considered inadequate and a new building was a remodeled version of the first one with 60 feet added to the east side for freight. In the 1970s, the depot was moved to the site of the Clark Historical Society, and is housed with many items from former depot agent Perry Goth.

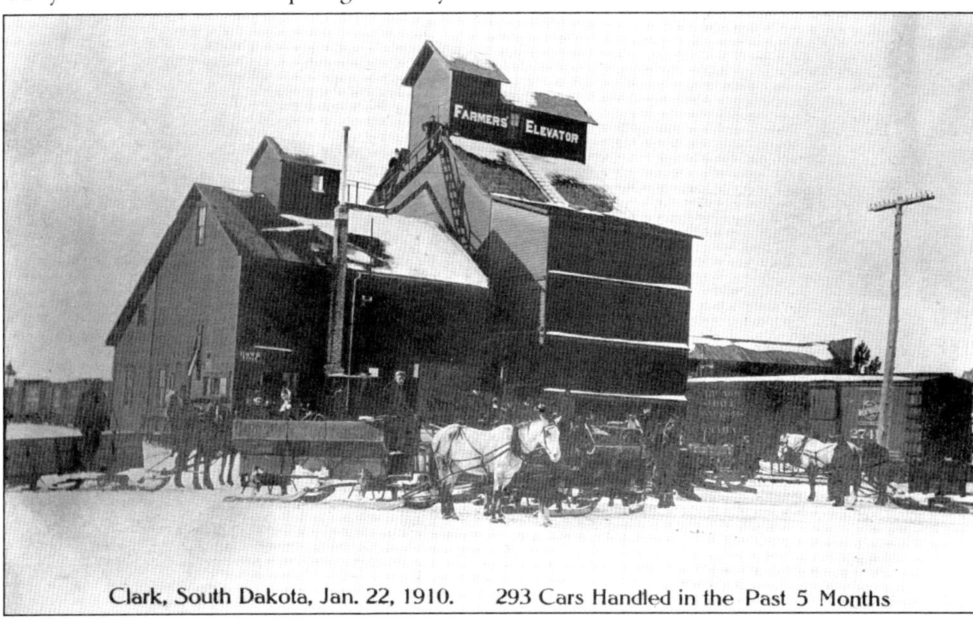

This is the Clark County Farmer's Elevator on January 22, 1910, with nearly 60 cars a day being handled in the past five months! Most of this structure was destroyed by fire in mid-1910, and by the fall of that year the grain-buying plant was operating again. Only seven managers have served this operation since it began in March 1904: Merton L. Yeamans, Charles Richmond, E. J. Keenan, Jim Keenan, Boyd Guffey, Dialo Schmidt, and currently Bruce Yanish.

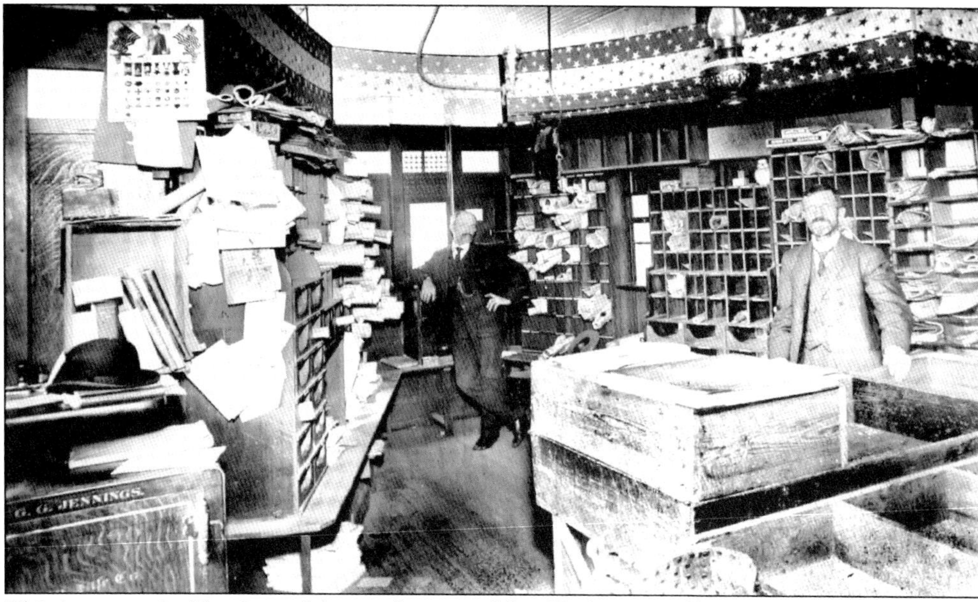

This is a great inside view of the workroom of the Clark Post Office in 1907. The post office was located at the northeast corner of First and Commercial Streets, where the Pantry Café, Donna's Café, and other businesses have stood. Current businesses are Hidden Springs Java Shoppe, Clark Tae Kwon Do, and Hair-n-Stuff. The two gentlemen in this real photo postcard are postmaster Orator H. LaCraft (left) and assistant postmaster Judson E. Smith. (Courtesy of David and Bert Moritz.)

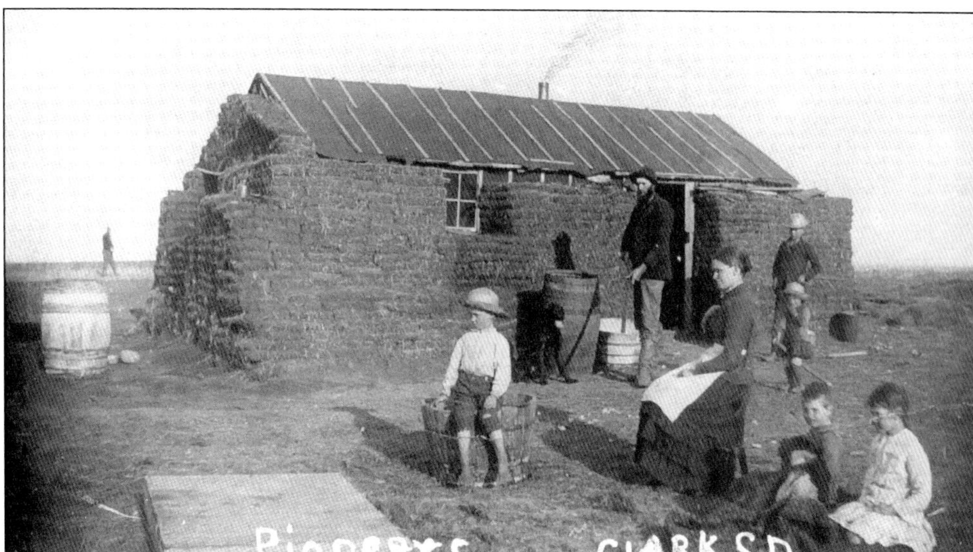

This printed card of Pioneers near Clark clearly shows the sod type shanty over the tarpaper shack. There are no other identifying marks on this postcard. (Courtesy of Darlene "Dolly" Peterson.)

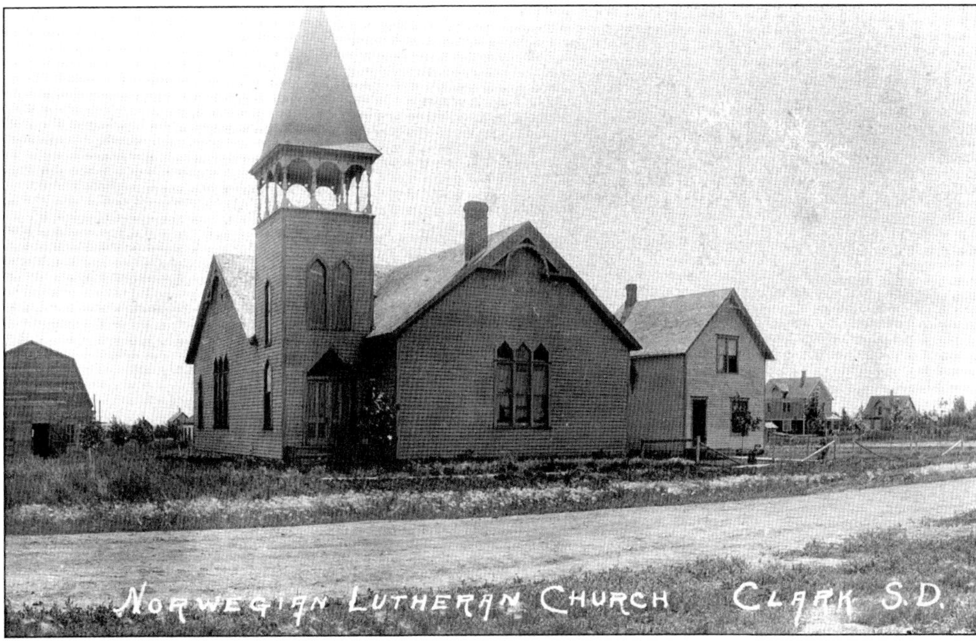

The Norwegian Lutheran Church and parsonage was located just to the north of where the present St. Paul Lutheran Church parsonage now sits. It was originally built and used as a Baptist church. The St. Paul congregation used this building after its new building was erected in 1952. Later it became the Masonic hall, and in recent years was razed.

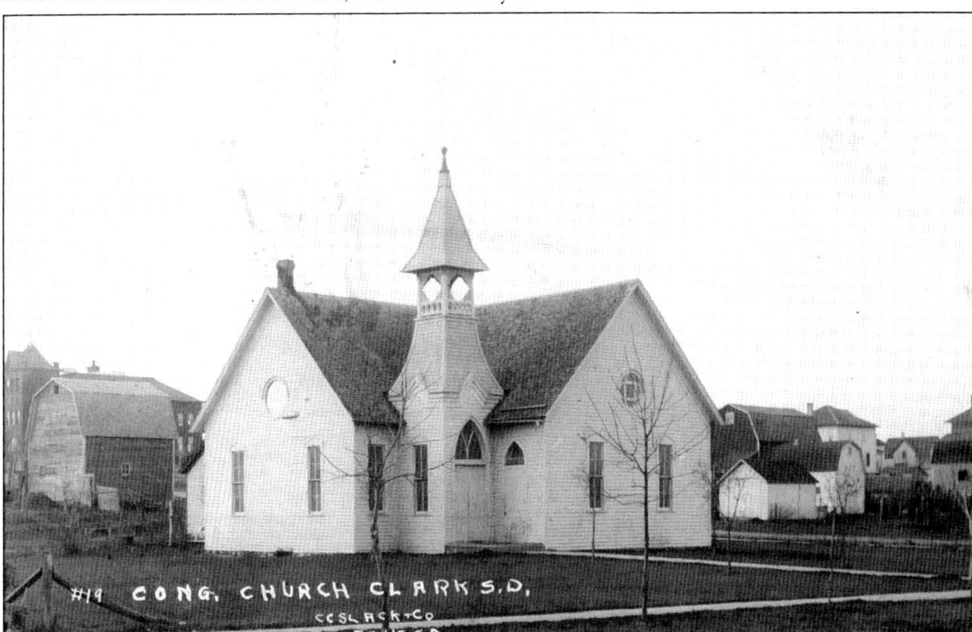

The history of the Congregational Church dates from the beginning of the county. The church was organized on October 2, 1881. The building of the church took place in 1883 and was located near the old railroad tracks. In 1899, the church was moved to the lot where this photograph was taken, at Second and Smith (Iowa) Streets, where the Plymouth Congregational United Church of Christ Church now sits.

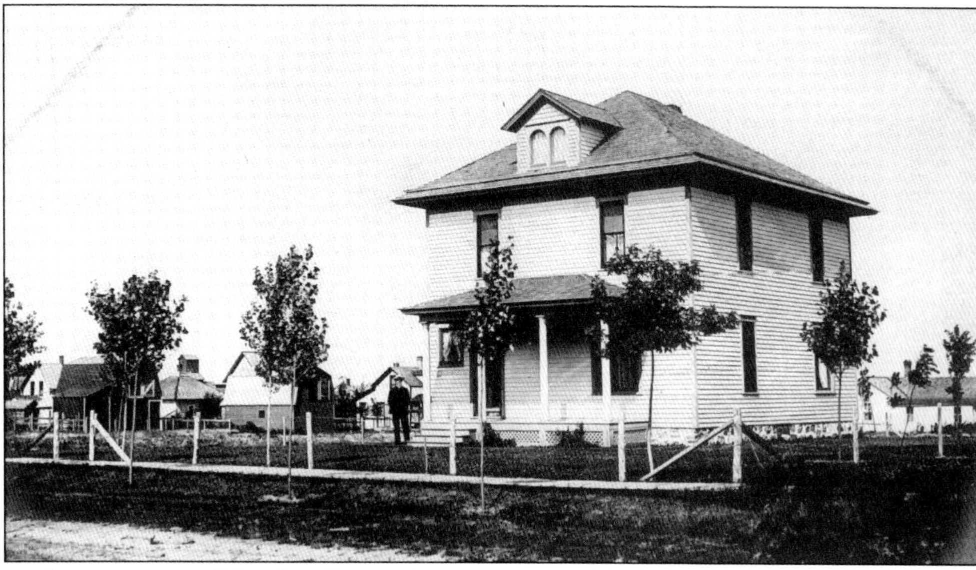

As the city grew and developed, so did the size and needs of the congregation. It was decided to build a congregational parsonage in 1908 while Reverend Oldfield was minister. It was constructed on South Smith Street, south of the present St. Paul Lutheran Church. C. H. Miller is the photographer of this Clark, South Dakota, postcard.

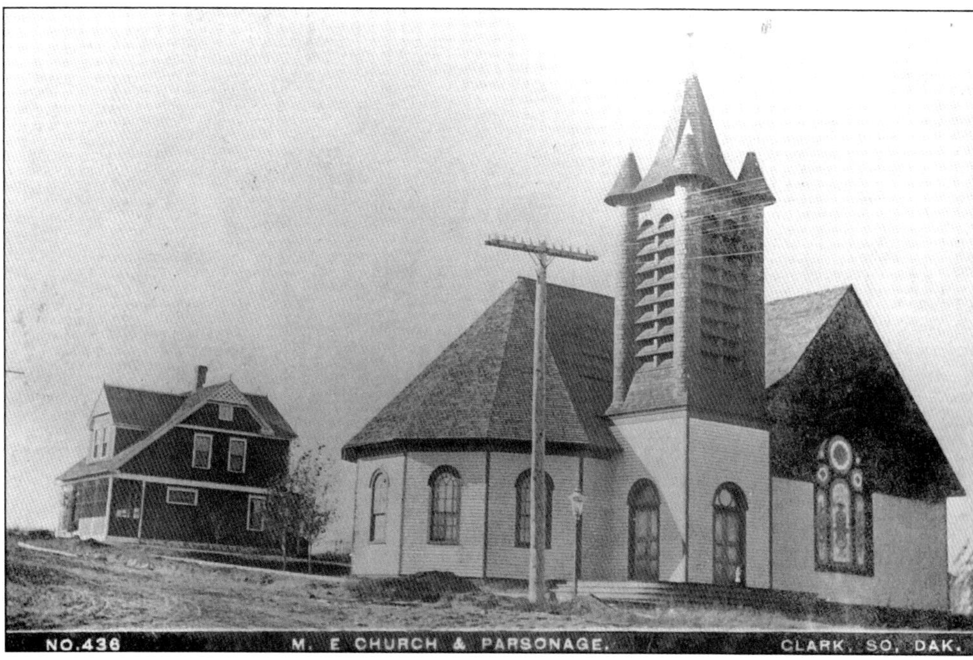

This view of the M. E. (Methodist Episcopal) Church, later called the United Methodist Church, and parsonage, was taken in the early 1900s. The church was completed and dedicated on June 8, 1902, and was located at the corner of Third Street and Smith Street, formerly 300 North Iowa Street. Around 1914, the church was lifted and a basement was dug under it. This building was razed in the late 1960s, and a private residence was built on the lot.

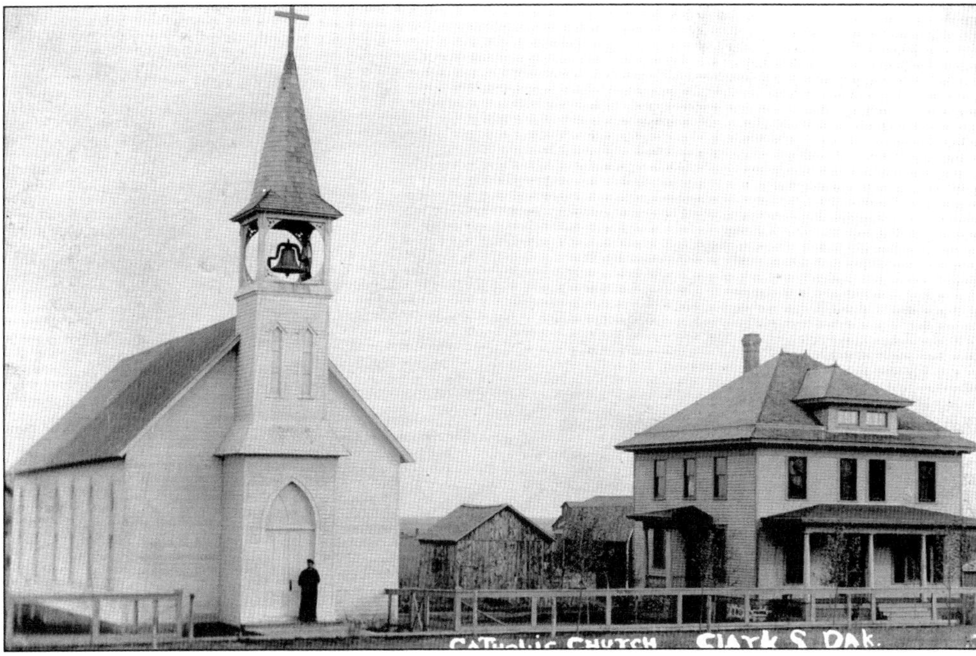

This real photo postcard was taken just after 1902, when contractor Fred Diehl cut the wooden church in half and moved it east and added to the middle, nearly doubling the size of the original Catholic church, as can be seen on the roofline. The rectory stood to the south side and has since been moved to another location in Clark. In front of the church the first resident priest is standing, the Reverend E. Bonneterre.

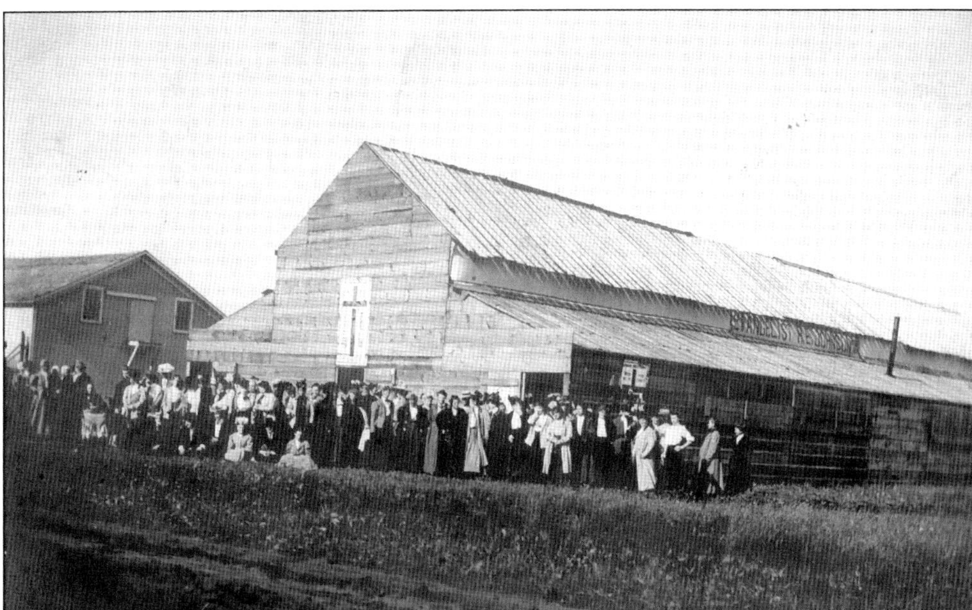

It seems that 1908 was a very good year to take photographs and make them into postcards; here is another real photo card taken in June 1908. This was a revival meeting by Evangelist R. E. Johnson at the "Tabernacle." Some say they used one of the lumberyard buildings.

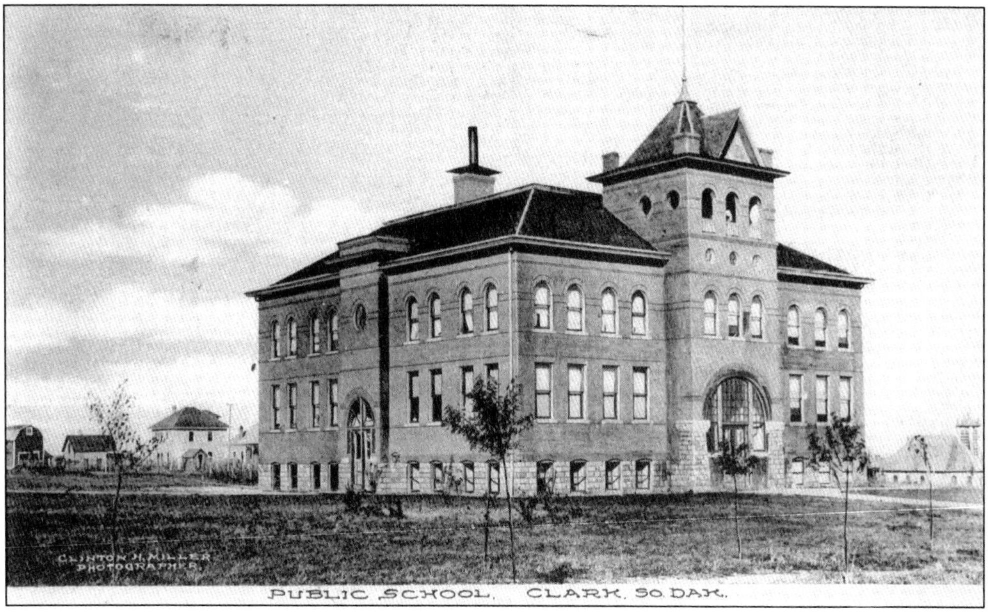

The public school building was erected in 1906 (razed in 1969) and was made of red brick. There were actually four stories at first, counting the basement as one. To the left side is the current home of the author's parents, Gene and Joan Furness, the former John and Eva (Ullyot) Rasmussen home. So not only was it a surprise to have the home the author grew up in on this card, but the postmark was the real jewel as seen below.

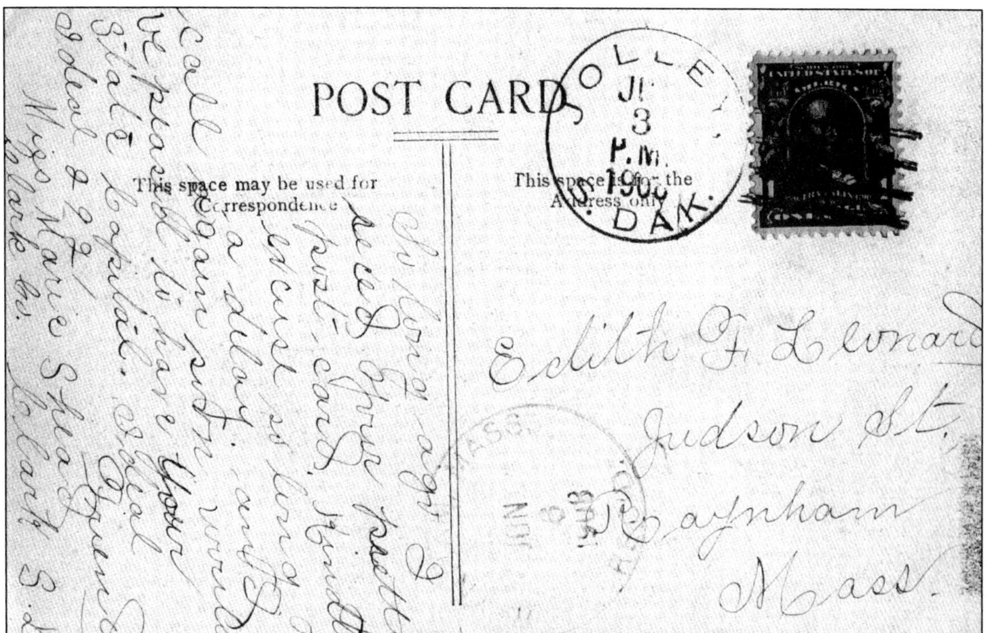

As mentioned above, the postmark was the real jewel of this card. It was mailed from Jolley, South Dakota, on June 3, 1908. Jolley was a very small post office northeast of Carpenter, in southwest Clark County. It was just northeast of the Jerry Wicks farm site. The post office closed on August 30, 1911.

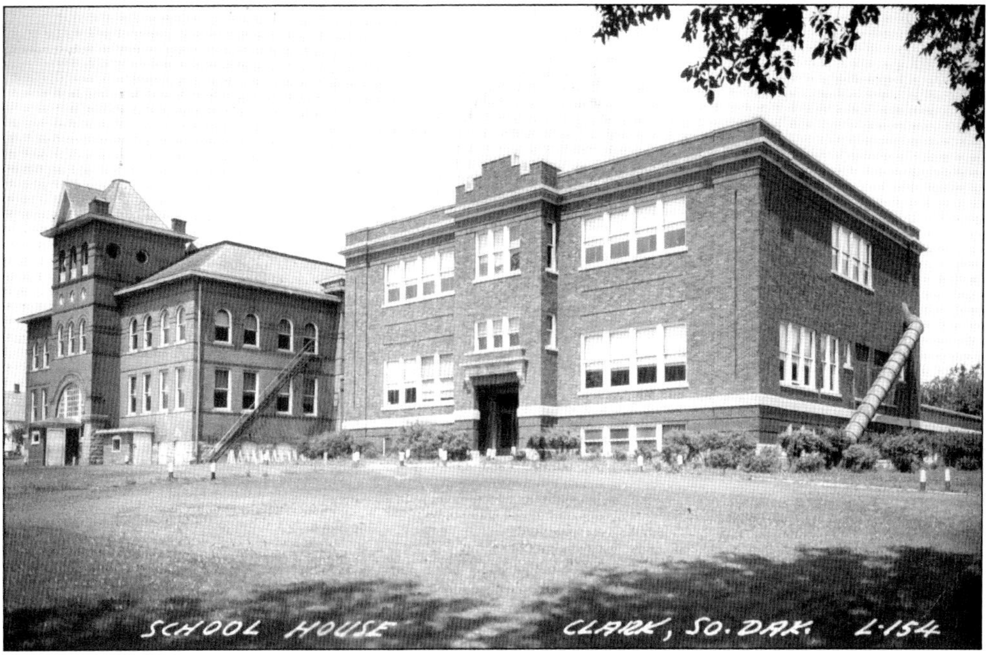

The new schoolhouse building on the right side was built between 1916 and 1917. It served as a high school and in later years a junior high school. The author attended sixth, seventh, and eighth grade in this building. It was razed in the late 1990s. Oh how the author remembers the fire escape slide.

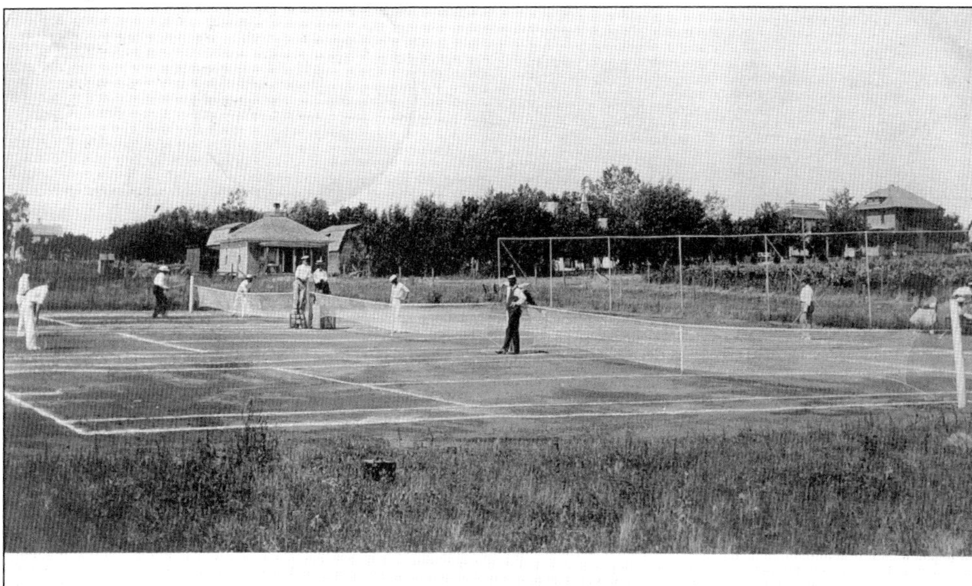

Tennis Court, Clark, South Dakota

The *Pilot Review*, from May 1908, (thanks to Ailene Luckhurst for digging this up) states that the new tennis courts are almost complete, and the *Pilot Review* in August 1908 states that the annual State Tennis Tournament is to be held on August 18, 1908, on the new courts. As near as anyone can recall (thanks to Winnie Ackerman and Max and Gen Benson), the courts were located just south or east of the swimming pool block area.

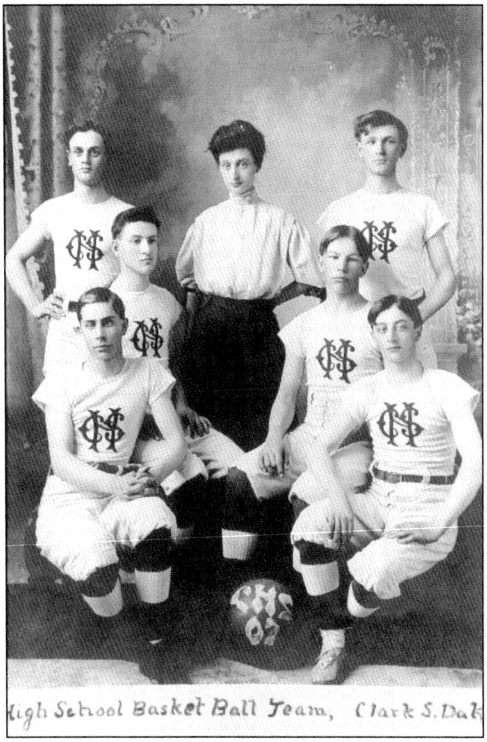

The 1907 boys basketball team from Clark included a female coach and these six fine young men in great uniforms.

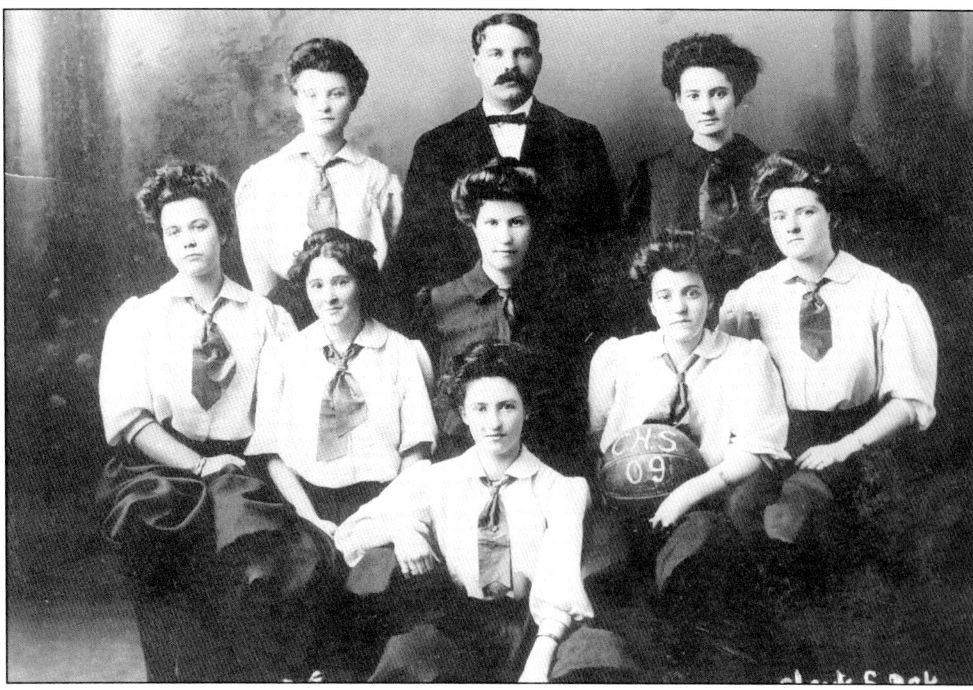

In 1909, the Clark girls basketball team consisted of, from left to right, (third row) Emma Cochran Sherwood, coach George B. Otte, and unidentified. Only two others could be identified in the remainder, Irene (Rasmusson) Geise on the far left and Ruth (Hyde) Pankonin to the far right. Olga (Rasmusson) Bailey sent this to Will Hawkins in Top Bar, South Dakota, in May 1909.

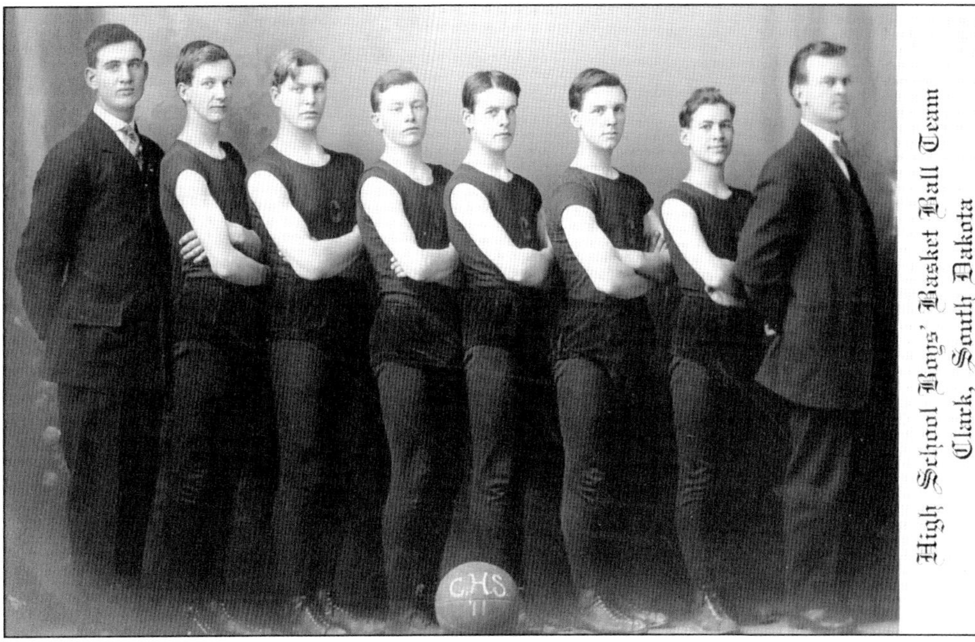

Shown here is the 1911 Clark High School boys' basketball team. The coaches on each end are unidentified. Players, from left to right, are George Cagley, Floyd Cook, Harold Sprague, Charles Gilbert, unidentified, and Claude Noel.

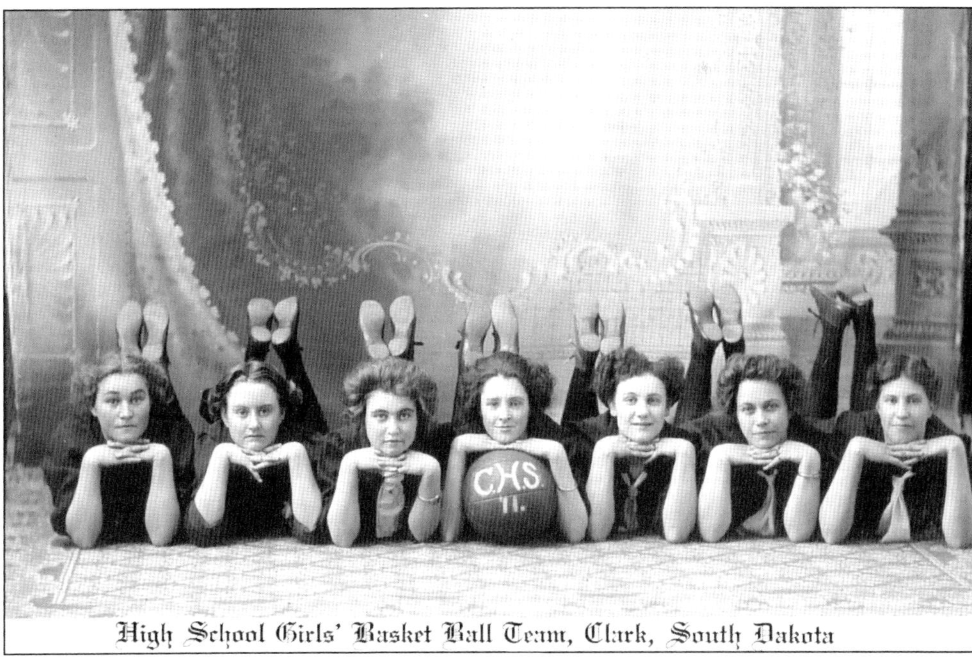

The 1911 Clark High School girls basketball team, from left to right, included the following: Perie Bickel, Mabel Larshbough, Wilda Dickey, Ruth Hyde, Ruth Geise, Irene Rasmusson, and Minta Thorp. Wow, what a line-up!

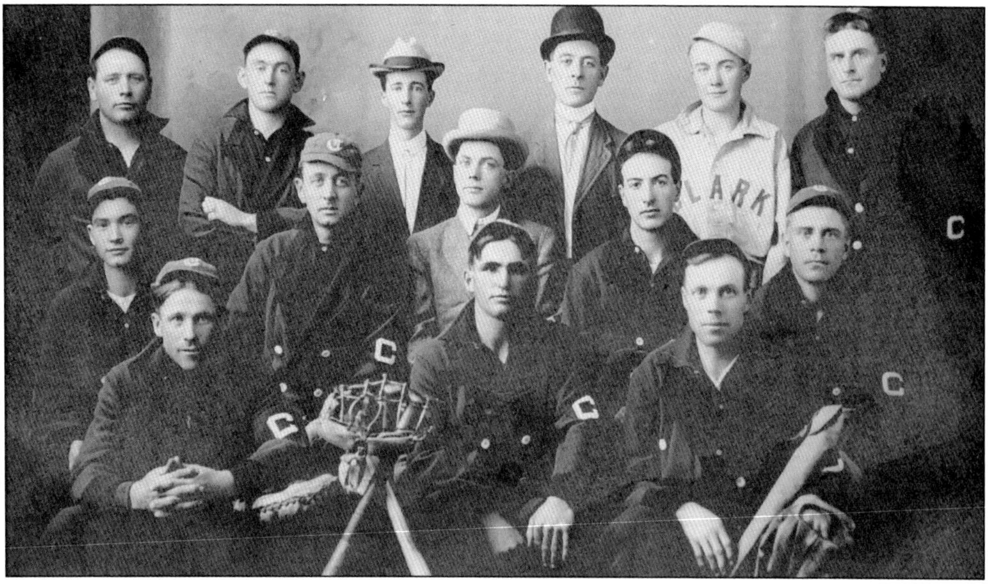

Another 1911 Clark sports team, this one is the baseball team, most of whom only identified by their last name. Pictured from left to right are (first row) Klock, third base and center; Morey, right field; and Peterson, center; (second row) Hyde, center fielder; Gale first base; Jacobs, manager; Bast, second base; and Olverson, short stop; (third row) Murphy, pitcher; Noel, pitcher; Frank Bockoven, secretary-treasurer; George Bisel, president; Dickey, substitute; and Johnston, catcher.

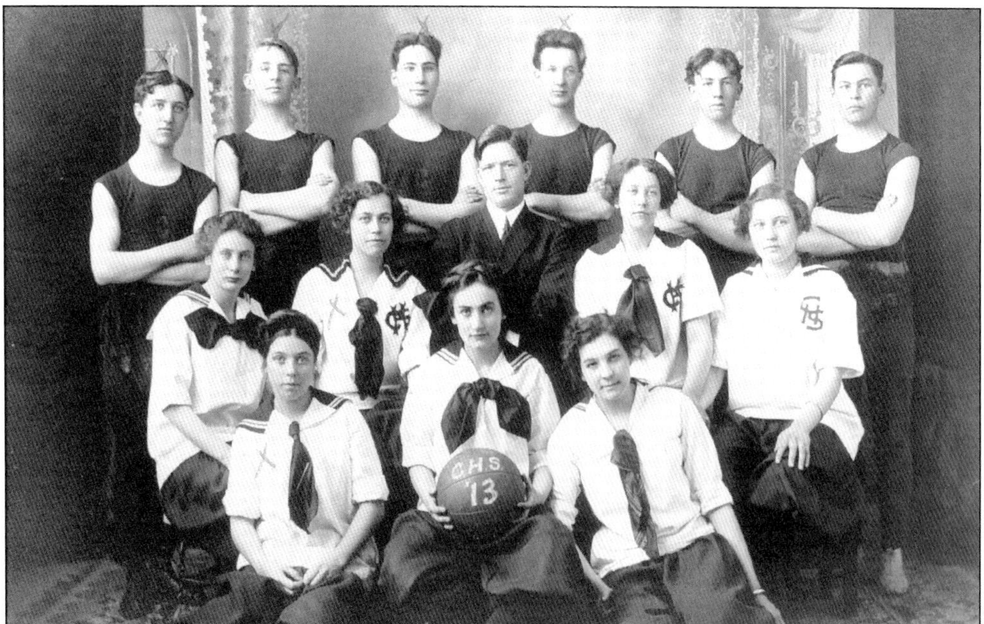

This is a nice view of the 1913 Clark High School boys and girls basketball teams. By the way, the girls team went undefeated! Pictured from left to right are (first row) Helen Griffin, Winifred Keenan, and Flora Zimmer; (second row) Ruth Keenan, Irene Rasmusson, coach Guy Goddard, Olga Rasmusson, and Edna Page; (third row) Lyn LaCraft, Harold Sprague, Charles Gilbert, George Cagley, Roy Hurlbert, and Claude Noel. The home games were all played at McClelland Hall on First Street (Highway 212). (Courtesy of David and Bert Moritz.)

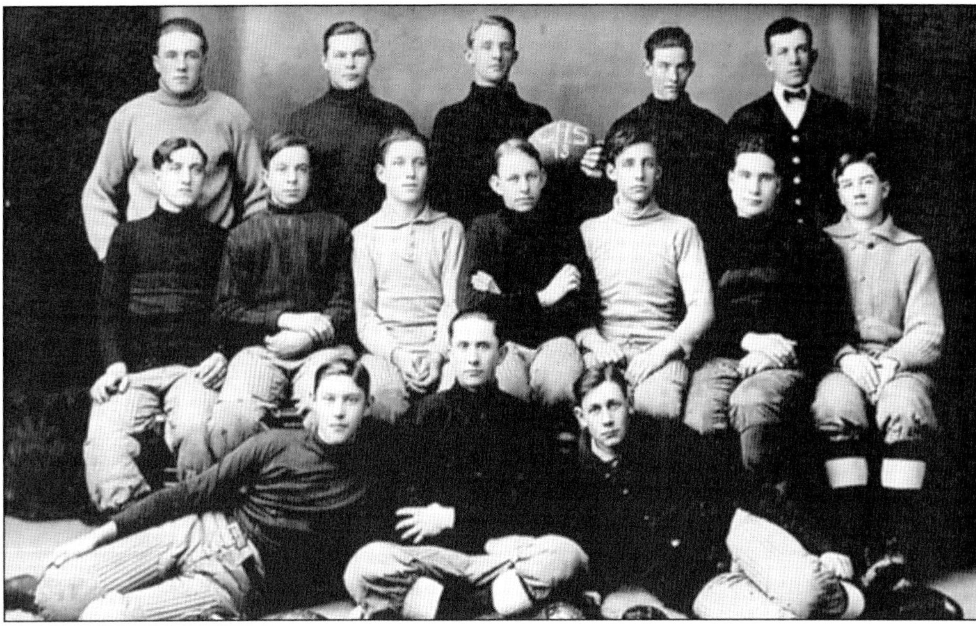

In 1913, the Clark High School football team, from left to right, consisted of (first row) Clay Noel, Wendell Sellers, and Phil Titus; (second row) Lynn LaCraft, Ralph Brown, unidentified, Elmer Kirkeby, Leon McCarthy, Charles Gilbert, and Clarence White; (third row) Arthur Elrod, Claude Noel, Harold Sprague, Lawrence Whitmer, and coach Guy Cook (also superintendent of schools). (Courtesy of David and Bert Moritz.)

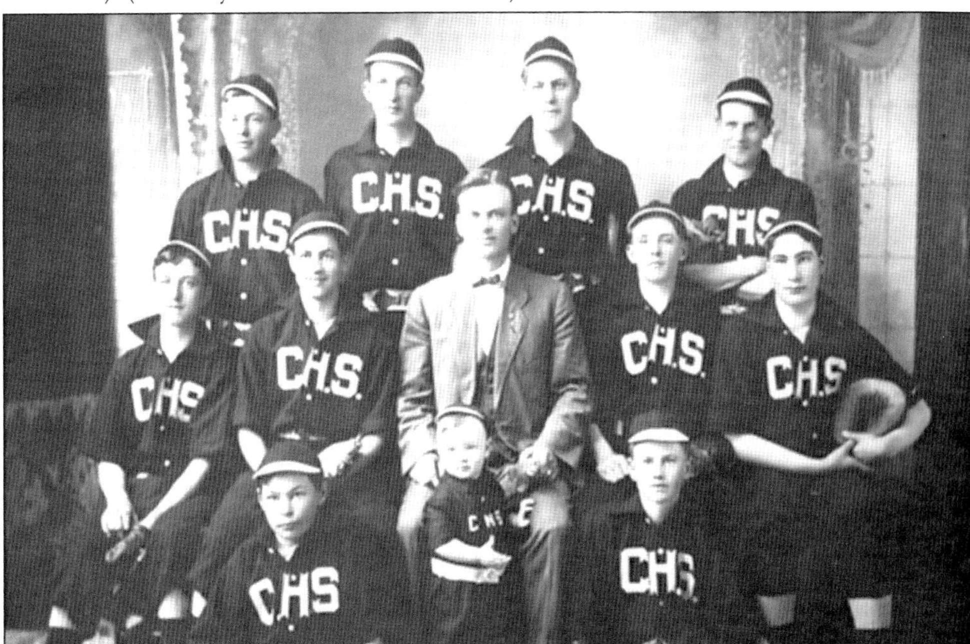

Seen here, from left to right, this is the 1913 Clark Baseball team, consisting of these 10 players: (first row) Claude Noel, unidentified, and Clarence Donahue; (second row) Lynn LaCraft, Clay Noel, coach Hatteberg, Kenny Sprague, and Charles Gilbert; (third row) unidentified, George Cagley, Floyd Cook, and unidentified.

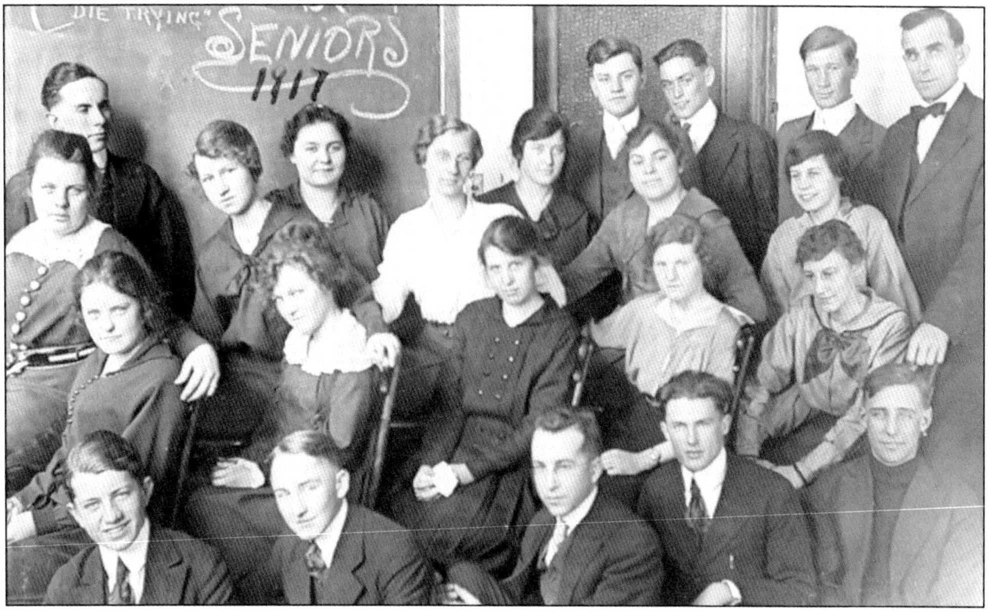

Clark High School's class of 1917 had the following members, from left to right, (first row) Leon McCarthy, Alphonzo Jungbluth, Henry Desnoyers, Forest Ullyott, and Wallace Craney; (second row) Verna Batien, Manilla Pederson, Helen Thoreson, Iola White, and Lola Cochrane; (third row) Clara O'Brian, Esther Murphy, Anna Bickett, Pauline Peterson, Moretta Ullyott, Alice Harris, and Zola Cochrane; (fourth row) Mr. Heimiller, Ben Graves, Frederick Goodrich, Raymond Rohrback, and Worth Titus.

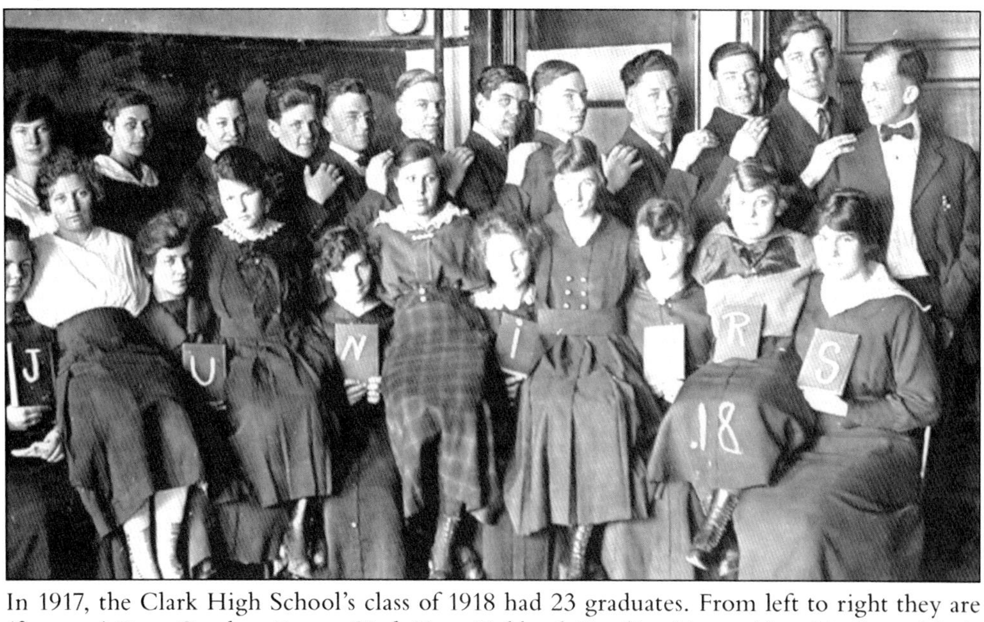

In 1917, the Clark High School's class of 1918 had 23 graduates. From left to right they are (first row) Rose Crocker, Emma Gisel, Vesta Hubbard, Emeline Mann, Alma Lindberg, Marie Shirk, AnnaBelle Skidmore, Helen Hyde, Bernice Moffitt, Ruth Ullyott, and Marie Baker; (second row) Bernice Richmond, Ethel Smith, Victor Jones, Ralph Harvey, Frank Exline, Glen Donahue, Clifford Williams, Carter J. Huber, McKinley Bonfoey, Lawrence Whitmer, Chearles Emmett Smith, and Guy Cook.

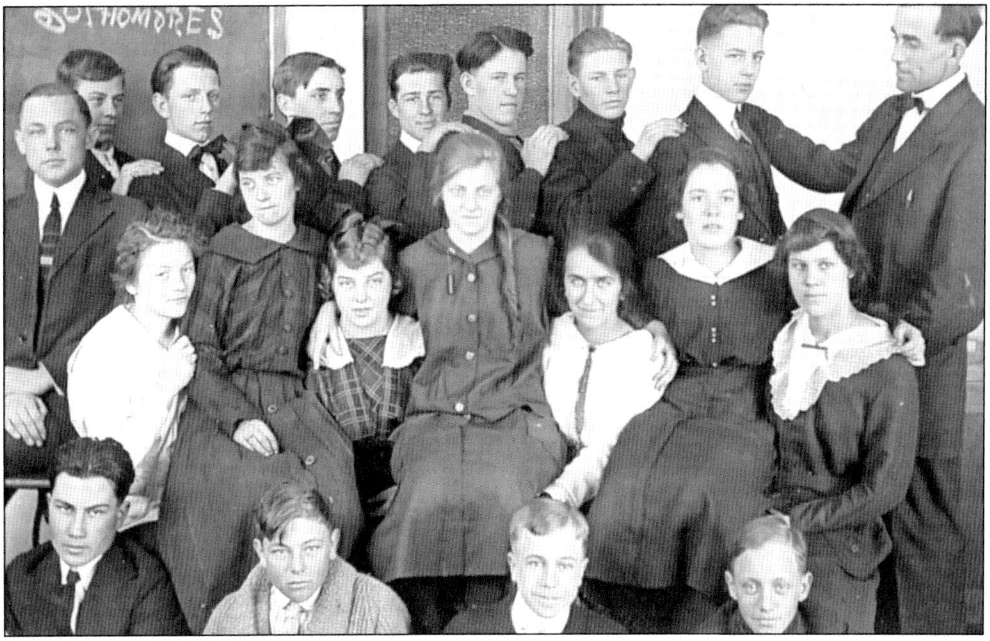

In 1917, the class of 1919 at Clark High School consisted of, from left to right, (first row) Sigurd Haugland, Charles Bohri, Fred Geise, and Alvin Day; (second row) Esther Foss, Ruth ?, Alice Henry, Alice Hofstad, Alberta Pederson, Audrey Beatty, and Ruth Peterson; (third row) Roy Cradit, Ray Donahue, Clifford Craney, Ralph Audus, Willis Manning, Caswell Bryan, Wilbur Sprague, Truman Rutherford, and Mr. Heimiller.

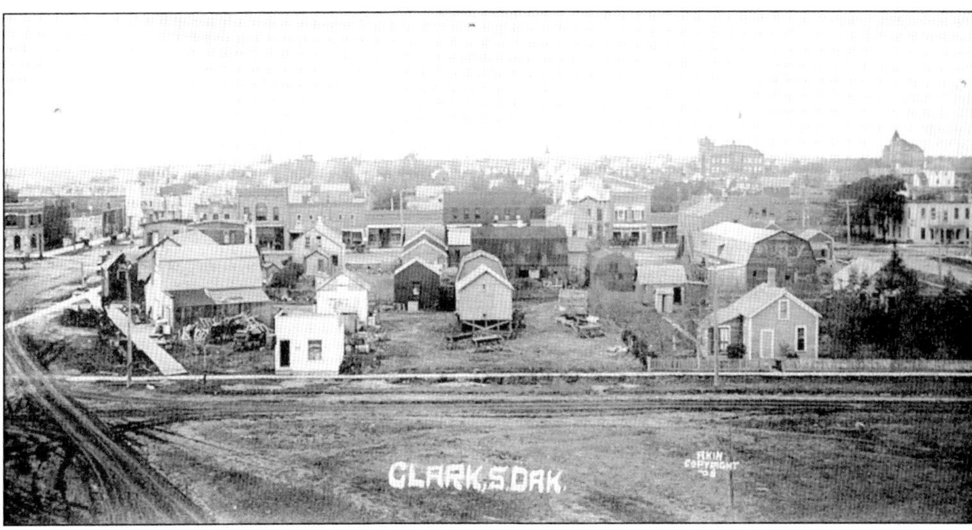

Seen here is a nice view from the top of the water tower near the railroad depot, looking west, sometime after 1904. The Conklin Hotel is the white building on the right; the old courthouse sits proudly on the hill to the right, just as the builders intended it to. The school was built in 1906.

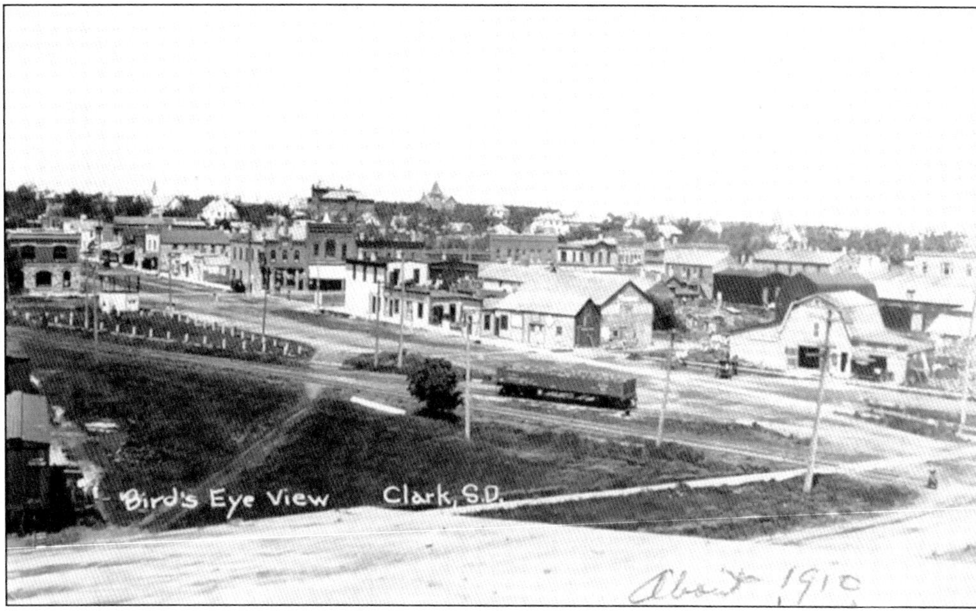

This bird's-eye view of Clark, taken around 1910, which must have been from on top of the flour mill, clearly shows where the railroad tracks came through town, just south of what is now Flat Iron Park. The downtown business district is really being built up. The bandstand sits on the corner of Commercial and First Streets. The soldiers' monument has not been placed.

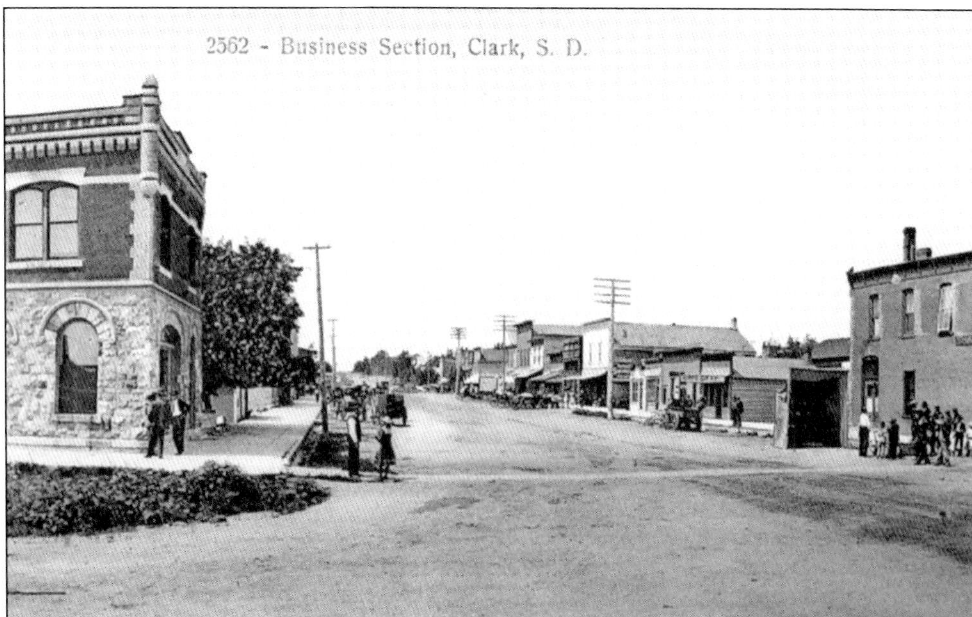

What a great panoramic view of the business section of downtown Clark. This is actually a folding card; the other part of it is to the right (bottom of page 53). The author bought this card in Spirit Lake, Iowa. It was sent to a William Bobzien in Clark in 1910. The view on this side shows the corner building, now Clark Liquors, and First Street looking west. See the photographer set up at the right-hand side.

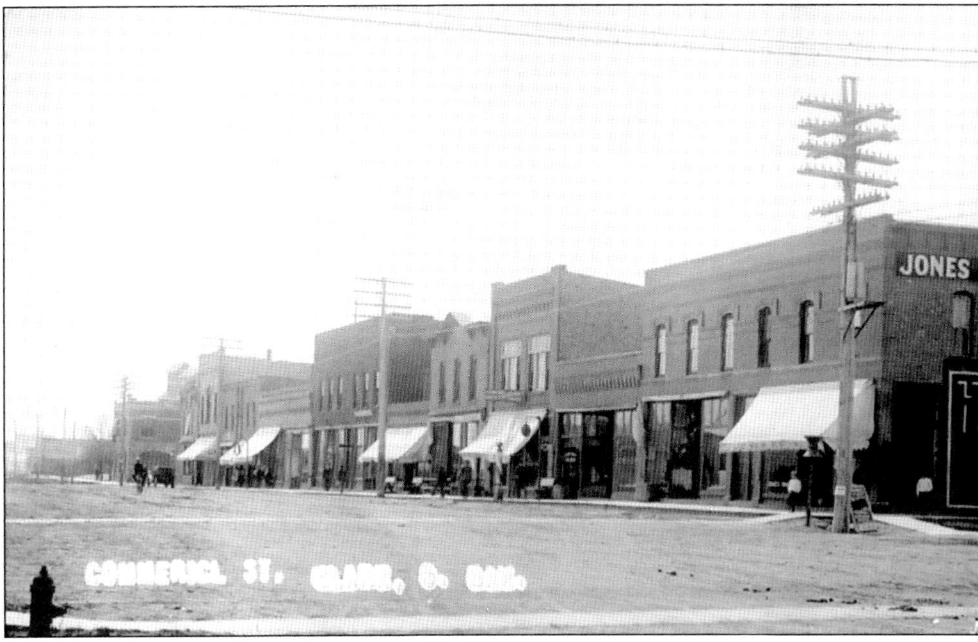

This is a view of the west side of Commercial Street looking southwest. On the corner stands a Clark landmark, built in 1883, by O. E. Dewey and Ferdinand Desnoyers. In 1900, E. M. Jones purchased the business, and in 1903, he bought the building. In 1938, the Wilkins family purchased it, and in 1948, Al and Faye Knutson became the proprietors. The Ullyott Building, city hall sits on the site now.

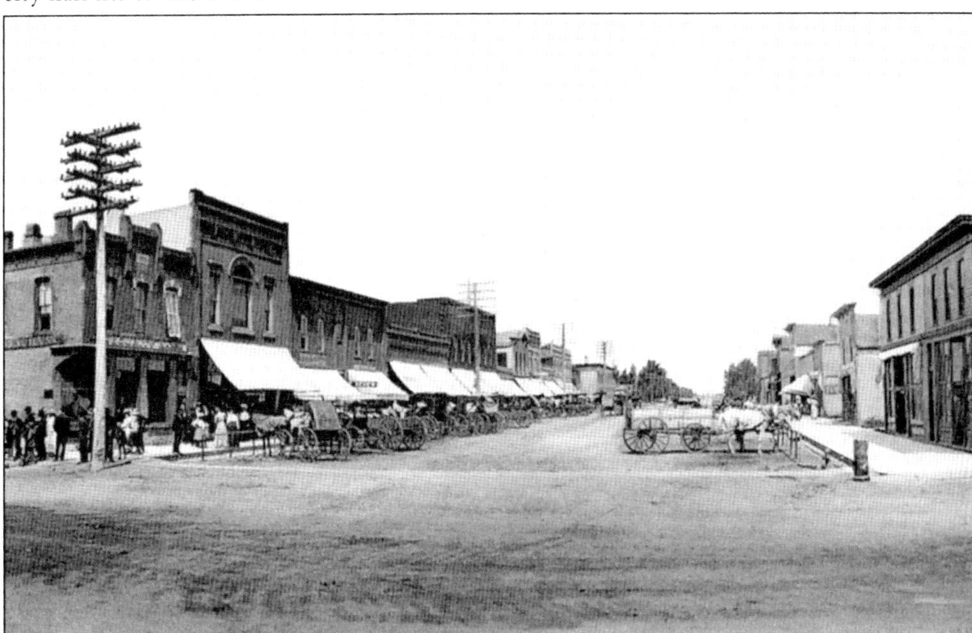

The other half of this panoramic view of downtown Clark shows Commercial Street looking north from the intersection of First Street (Highway 212) and Commercial Street. It appears to have been a very busy day in downtown by the looks of all the horses and buggies. The text on this card is all in German.

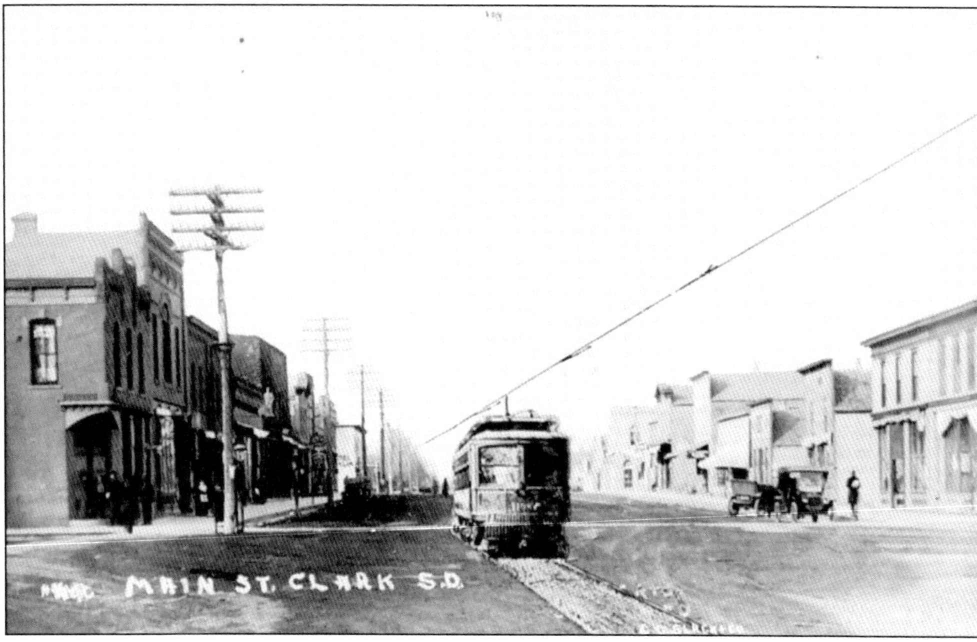

Seen here is a great view of the corner of Highway 212 (First Avenue) and Commercial Street (Main Street) looking north. The trolley car was in Clark, just like the "big towns." Actually, the trolley never ran in Clark, the photographer or publisher, C. C. Slack and Company in Sioux Falls, super-imposed the image of the trolley; it was done to rival the big towns.

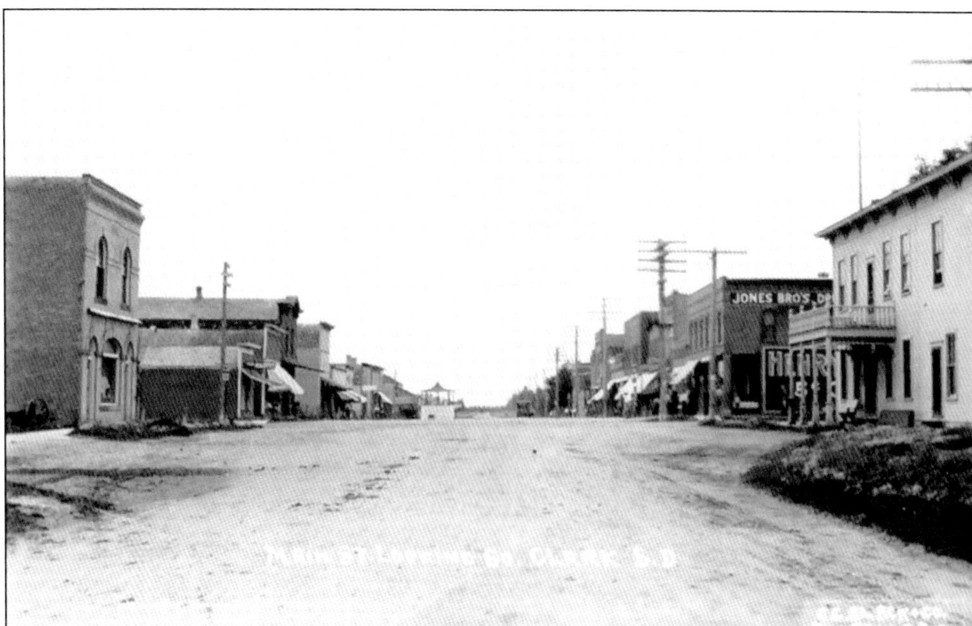

This view is looking south on Commercial Street (Main Street). The photographer was standing in front of the area that is now the courthouse. The Clark County National Bank is the first building on the left, and the Conklin Hotel is on the right. The bandstand is in the middle of the block, all ready for a Saturday night concert. The author imagines that "a great time was had by all!"

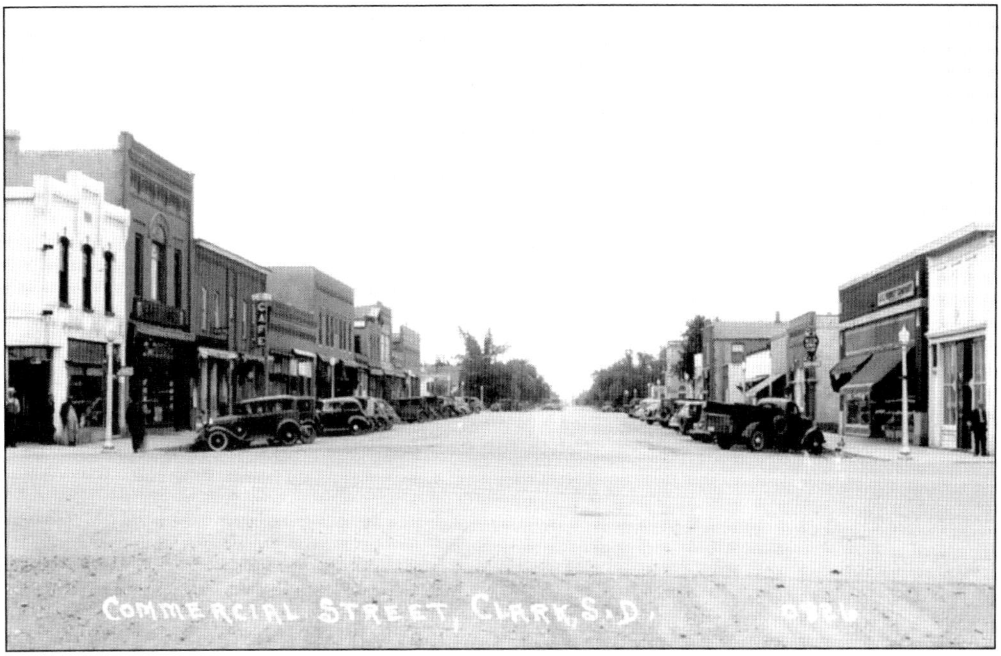

The transition from the late 1920s to the 1930s in downtown Clark also shows a full business district. This real photo postcard was taken in 1938, just after the Red Owl Store opened in the old Brown Brothers Auto building, now the American Legion Hall. The Bisel Café was open; it closed in the early 1940s. The Gamble Store was open where the Clark Flower and Gift Shop is now.

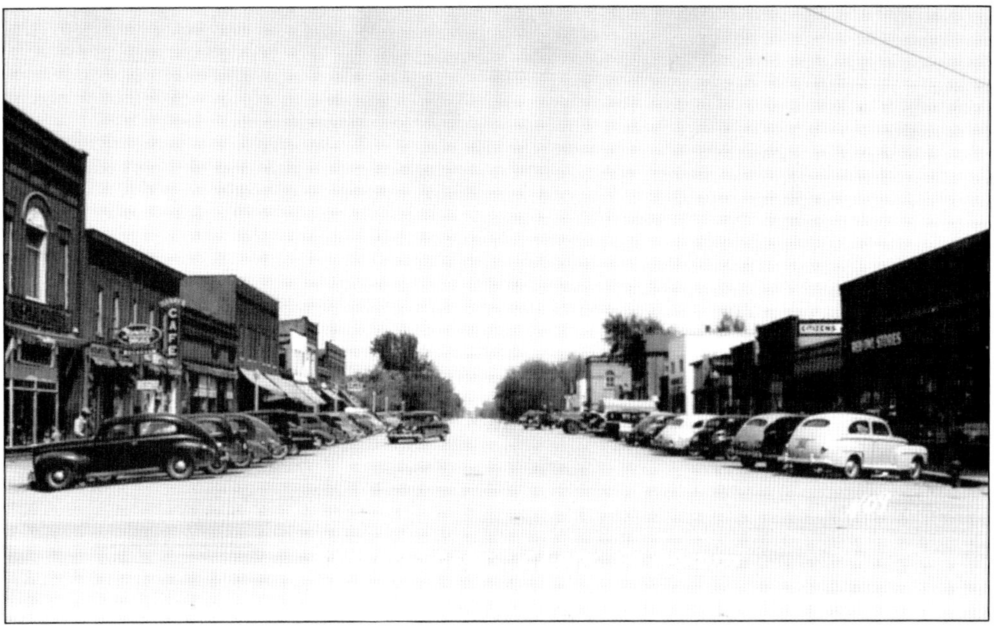

This view from the late 1940s shows Commercial Street in downtown Clark loaded to capacity with vehicles. Maybe they were in the Red Owl Store, Gambles, Harry's Café, Citizens Bank, Baldwin's, Bockoven's, Tom Thumb store, or any other fine establishment.

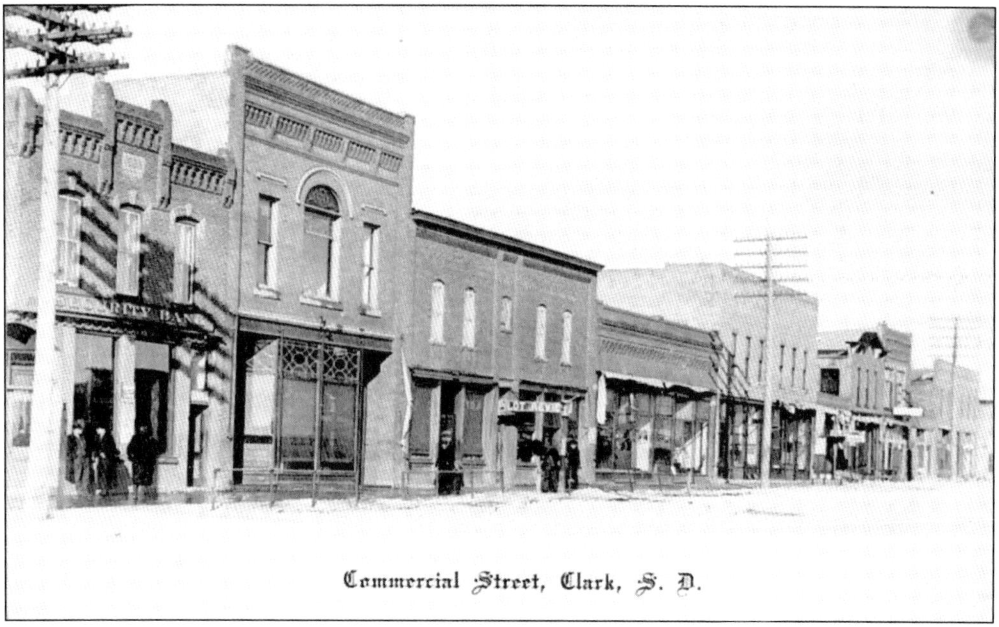

This undivided back card, postmarked on December 19, 1906, from Clark, was sent to Jessie Lamb in Naples, South Dakota, with a received postmark of Naples on December 20, 1906. This is a very nice look at the McGaan-Ware Building (now the Clark Flower and Gift Shop), which is currently under restoration by David Helkenn, an area pharmacist and Clark High School class of 1981 graduate. The *Pilot Review*, a local newspaper, was located in the upstairs of the Bockoven Building.

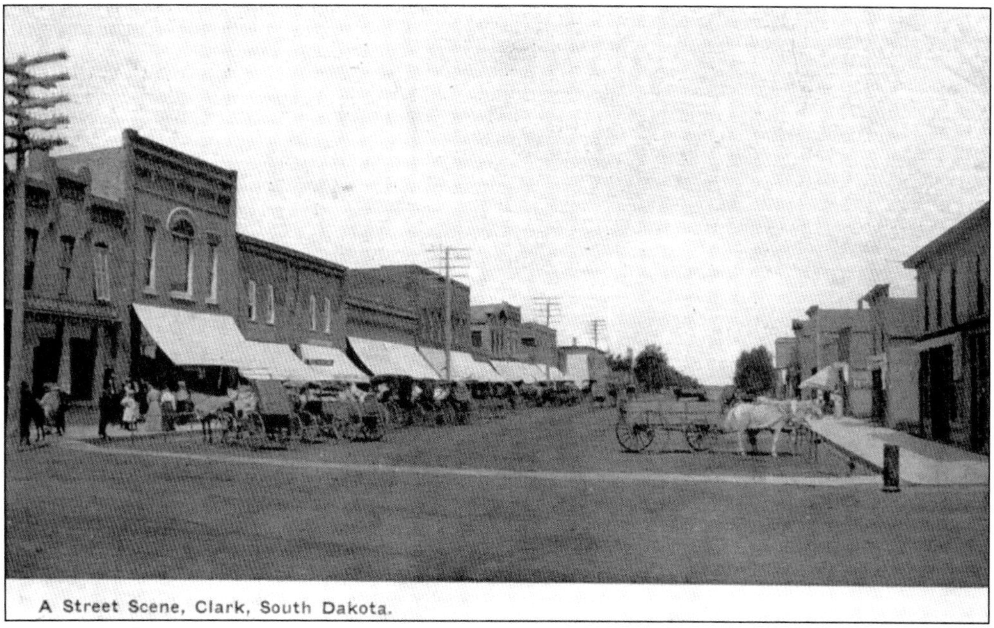

Another look at Commercial Street and the horse-and-buggy days is actually a view looking west on First Street (Highway 212). The west side was bustling and the east side looks like it is being developed. This card was sent from Clark on November 26, 1908, to Rose King in Conde, South Dakota.

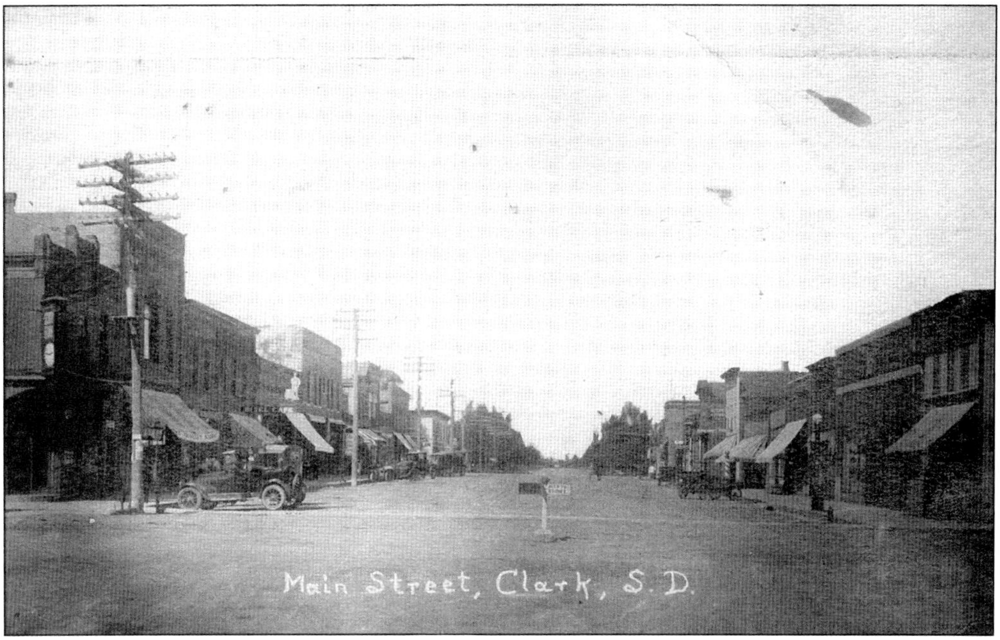

This is a view of Main Street (Commercial Street) looking north from First Street. Notice the electric clock on the Security Bank Building—it is 2:45 p.m. A sign in the middle of the street says, "Keep to Right." The Bisel Café, Johnson the Clothier, Brown Brothers Auto, and other landmark buildings line the street. This card was sent from Clark in 1924 to Nebraska.

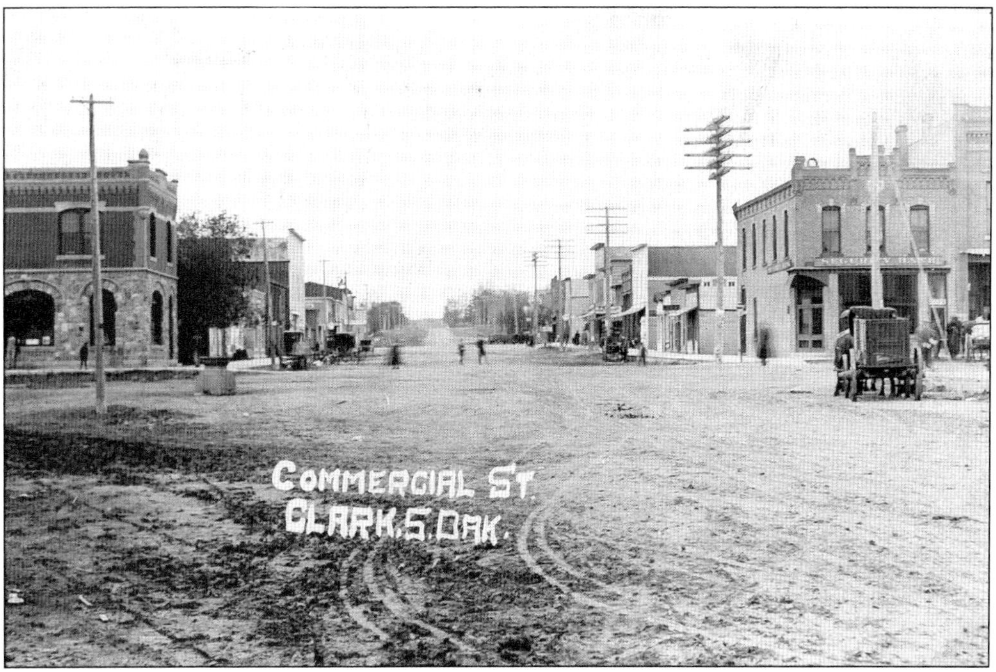

No license plates were needed on any vehicle in this real photo postcard, taken around 1909. The photographer, Earle D. Akin, of Hillsboro, Wisconsin, must have been standing in the middle of what is now Highway 212 looking west. It says Commercial Street, however, it is clearly First Street.

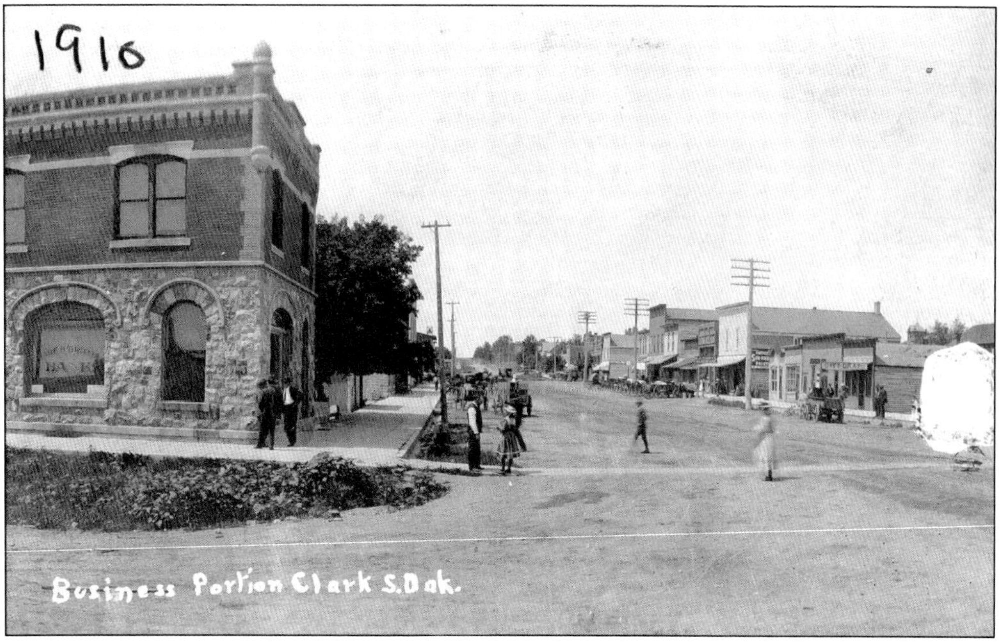

This card by photographer C. H. Miller was taken just shortly after the building on the corner, Ware and Griffin Bank, was built (between late 1909 and 1910). The City Dray building is the first building on the right side, in this view looking west on First Street.

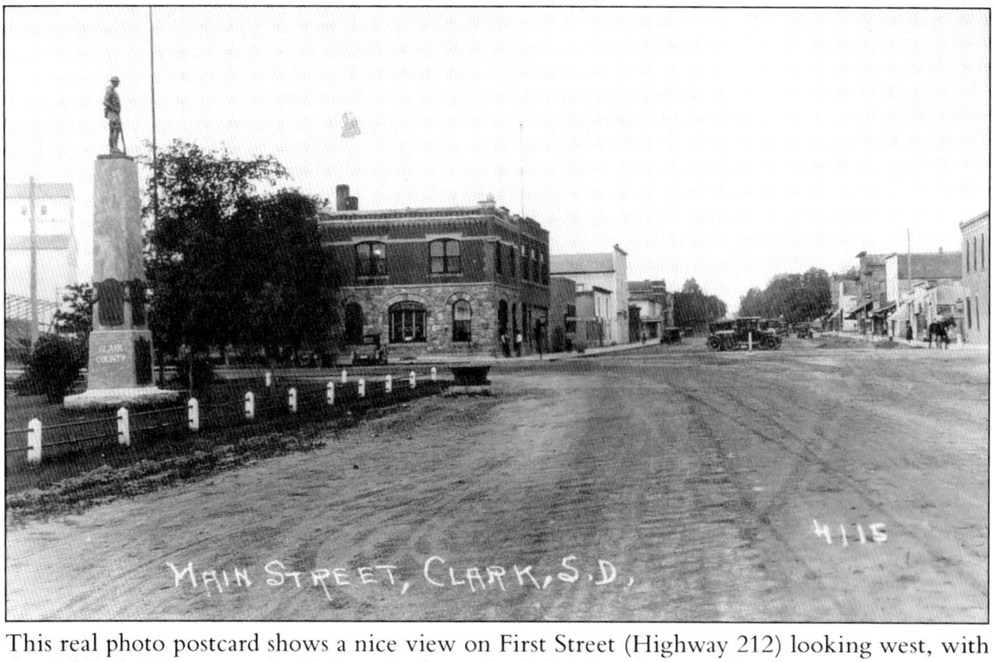

This real photo postcard shows a nice view on First Street (Highway 212) looking west, with the Soldier's Monument in Flatiron Park on the left. The photograph was taken in the early 1920s. Notice the cars parked in the middle of the road—must have been to let the horse go free on the right side!

S. H. E. (Samuel H. Elrod) delivered this postcard to Laura McEown. A very unique "find" in the author's collection of cards, if only Elrod had actually signed the card.

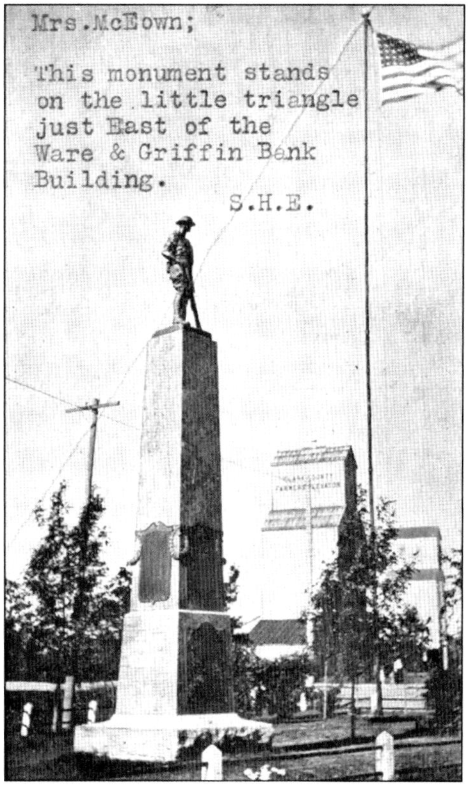

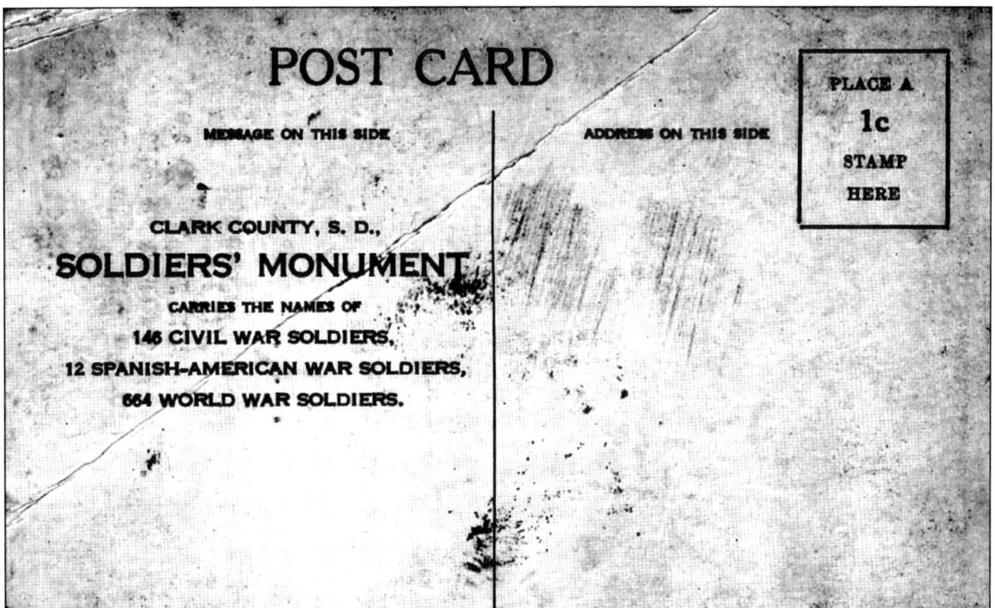

The author had to include the backside of this S. H. E. card because he has seen this monument since he can remember and never knew these facts, so he thought it would be good to have this included with these amazing statistics.

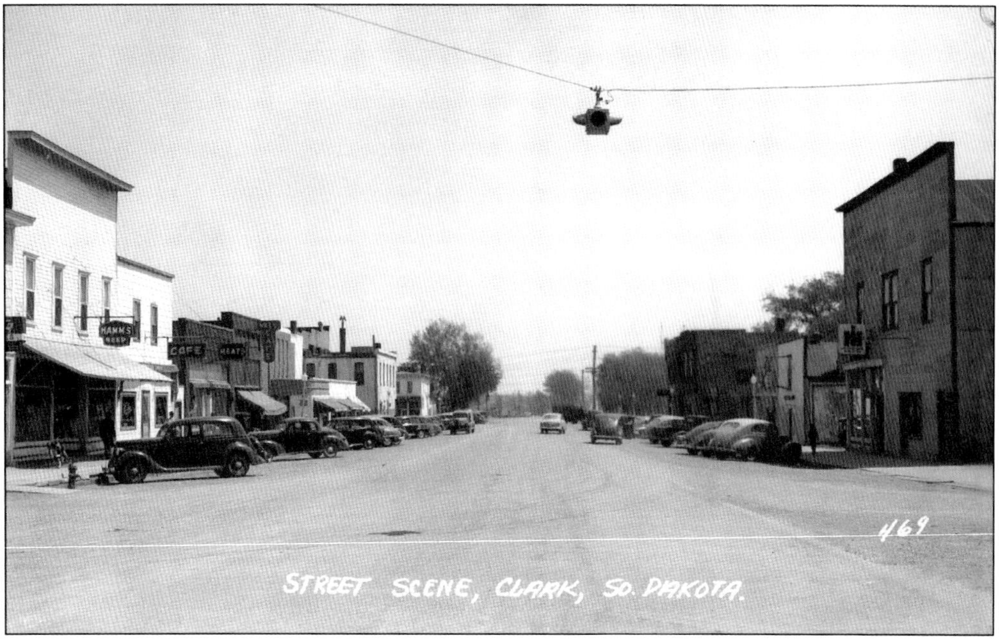

The author does not remember a traffic light in Clark, but as evidenced by this scene, a light was at the intersection of Iowa (Smith Street) and First Streets (Highway 212). It states in the centennial book that Bonfoey's opened a café to the west of the theater on the north side of First Street in 1940. McClelland Hall sits proudly on the right side. The hall was on the upper floor, where dances, high school basketball games, and graduations were held.

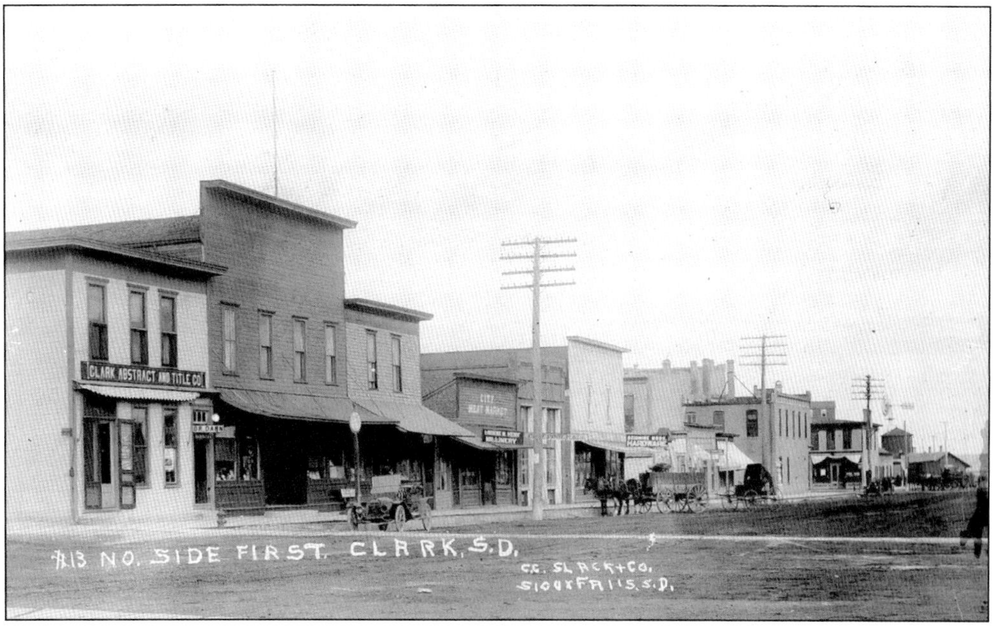

This is an early view, around 1908, of the north side of First Street looking east. Some of the businesses included the Clark Abstract and Title Company, Dr. E. F. Dann (A Civil War veteran), Gales Confectionery, City Meat Market, a millinery shop, City Pool Hall, Scidmore Hardware, Kurth Cigar Shop, a barbershop, and the Security Bank building.

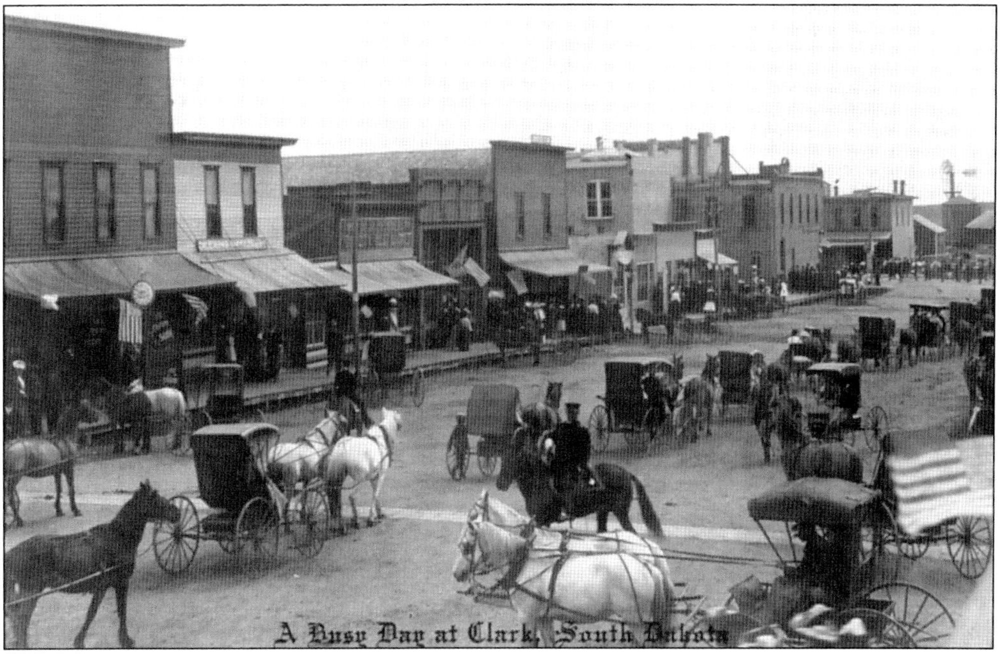

"A Busy Day at Clark, South Dakota" is how this card is entitled—and yes it was. This is an undivided back, C. H. Miller, real photo postcard, postmarked from Clark on May 1, 1907. The photograph was taken around 1904. Business places included Gales Confectionery, McClelland's Implement, Anderson and Arpin Barbershop, Zender's Meat Market, Scidmore Hardware, Bohri's Law Office, Kurth's Cigar Store, another barbershop, and Security Bank on the corner. Wow! What a Day!

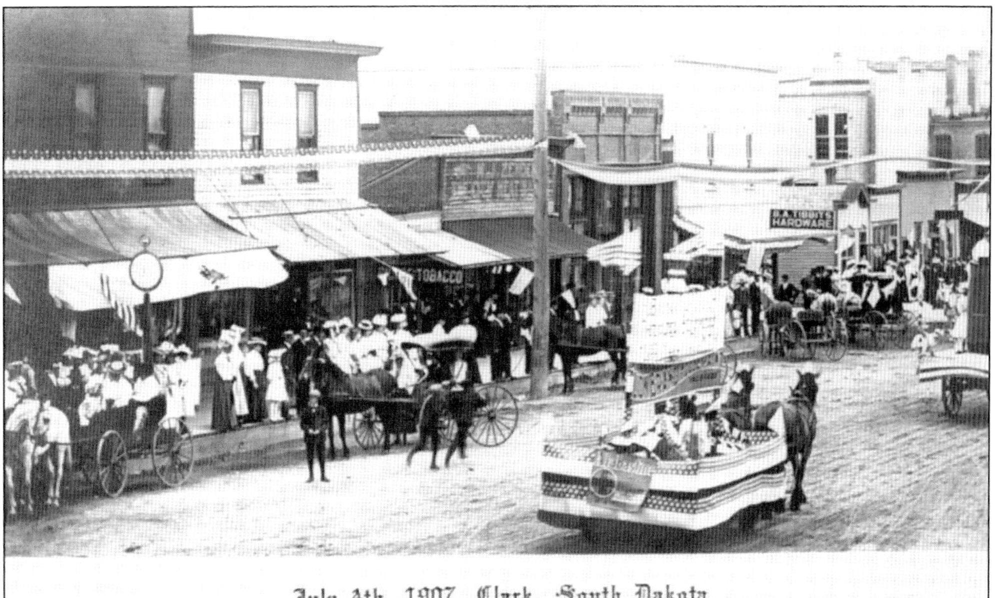

Three years later, on July 4, 1907, was a Fourth of July parade from Scidmore Brothers Hardware to B. A. Tibbets Hardware (some of the businesses have changed hands). Another tobacco store took over the Anderson and Arpin Barbershop location. This is another C. H. Miller photograph.

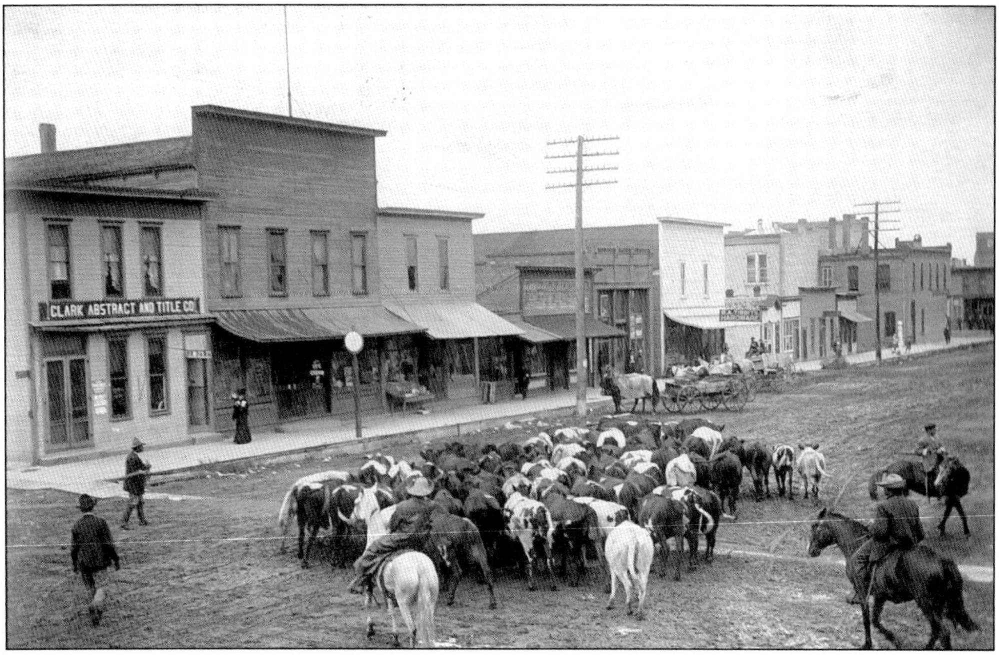

Imagine this happening on Highway 212 today. The above card was sent from Naples, South Dakota, (DPO) in 1910 by Earl Geise and was taken around 1907. Below is a load of 156 bushels of barley from the Buttrey farm, in a picture taken in 1907 in front of the Zender Meat Market and Tibbits Hardware. The Pilot Review was across the street, E. A. Buttrey probably stopped for a newspaper photograph. This is another C. H. Miller photo postcard.

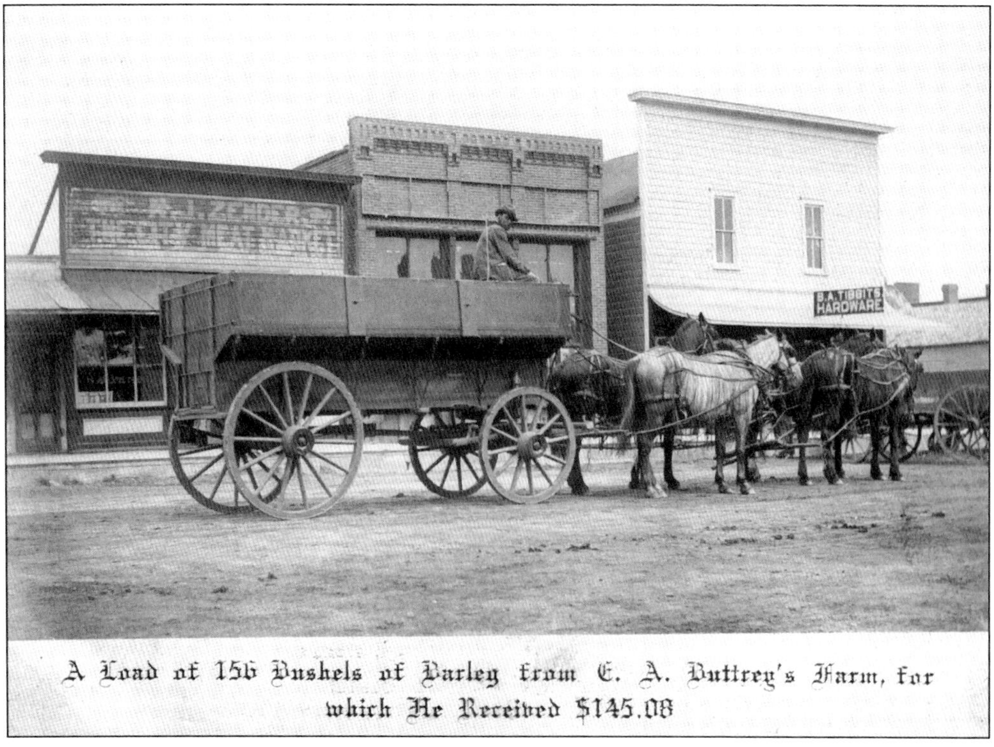

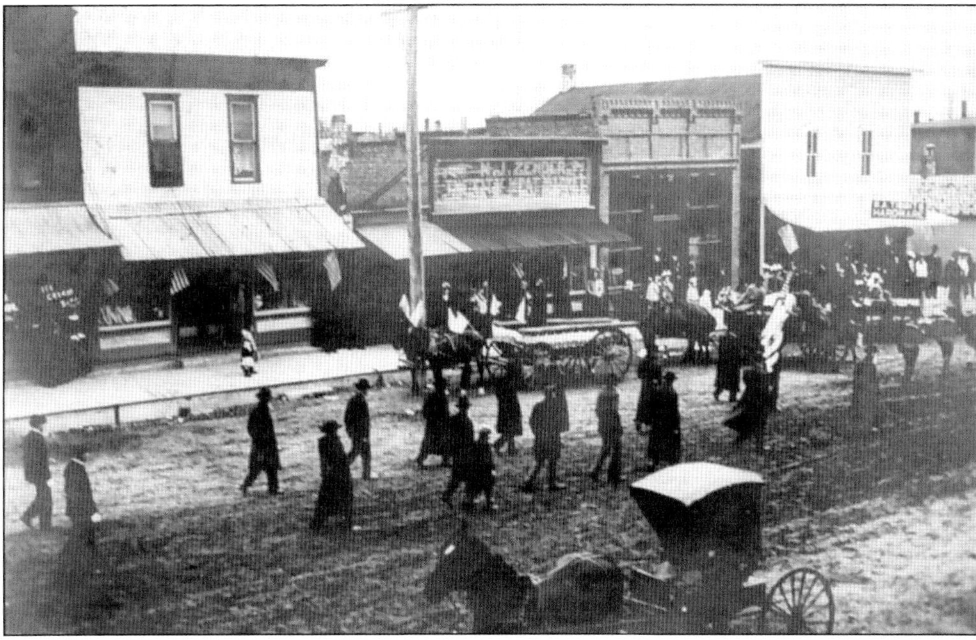

The Decoration Day parade in 1908 in Clark looks somber. Decoration Day is now called Memorial Day, a day for people to remember the veterans who have gone on before them. This card was sent in 1909 to Dear Grove, Illinois.

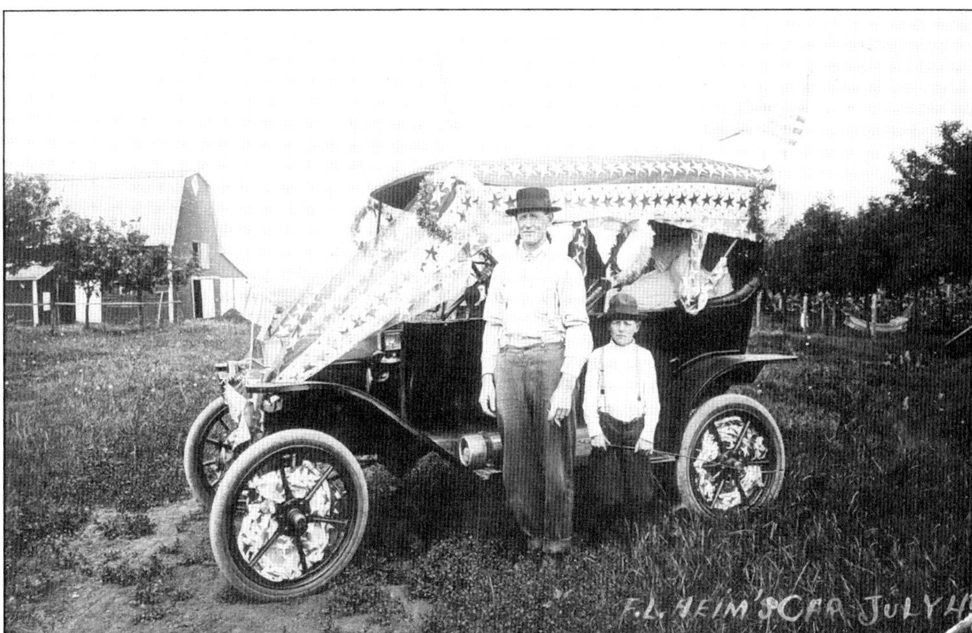

F. L. (Frank) Heim and his son Earl are getting ready for a Fourth of July parade. This real photo postcard was taken around 1910; Earl was born in 1905. The Heim farm was in Merton Township.

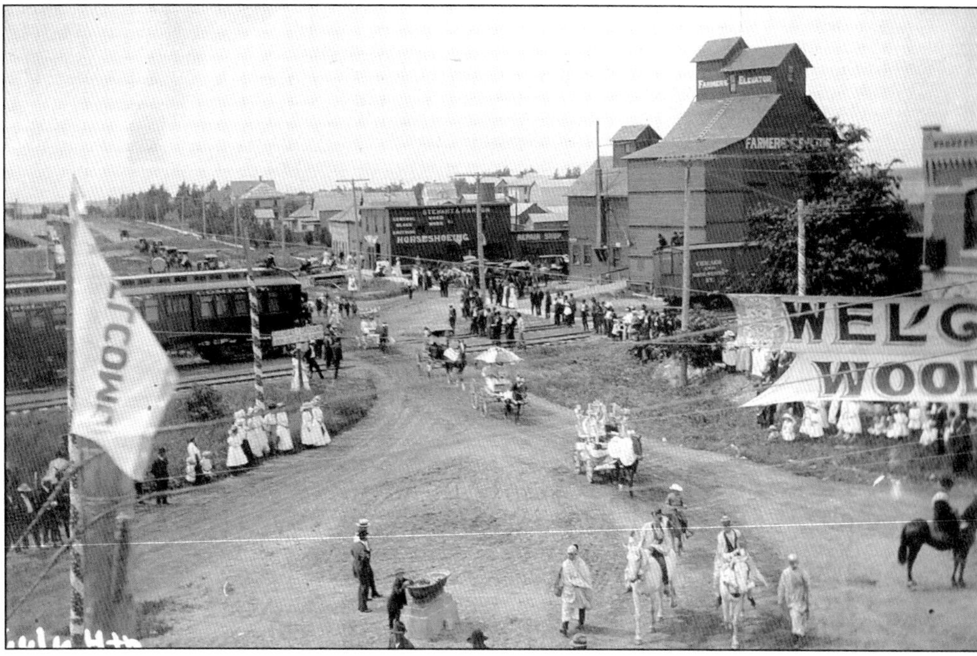

"Welcome Woodman" is what the banner hanging over the intersection of First Street (Highway 212) and Main Street (Commercial Street) says. This very early Fourth of July parade (around 1909) started on South Commercial Street near the Stewart Horseshoeing business and then came north and turned to the east. What a grand day! In the postcard below, the writer of the card states, "Here comes the Clark Band, the Garden City Band is coming further back and then the Clown Band." Where was the Clown Band from?

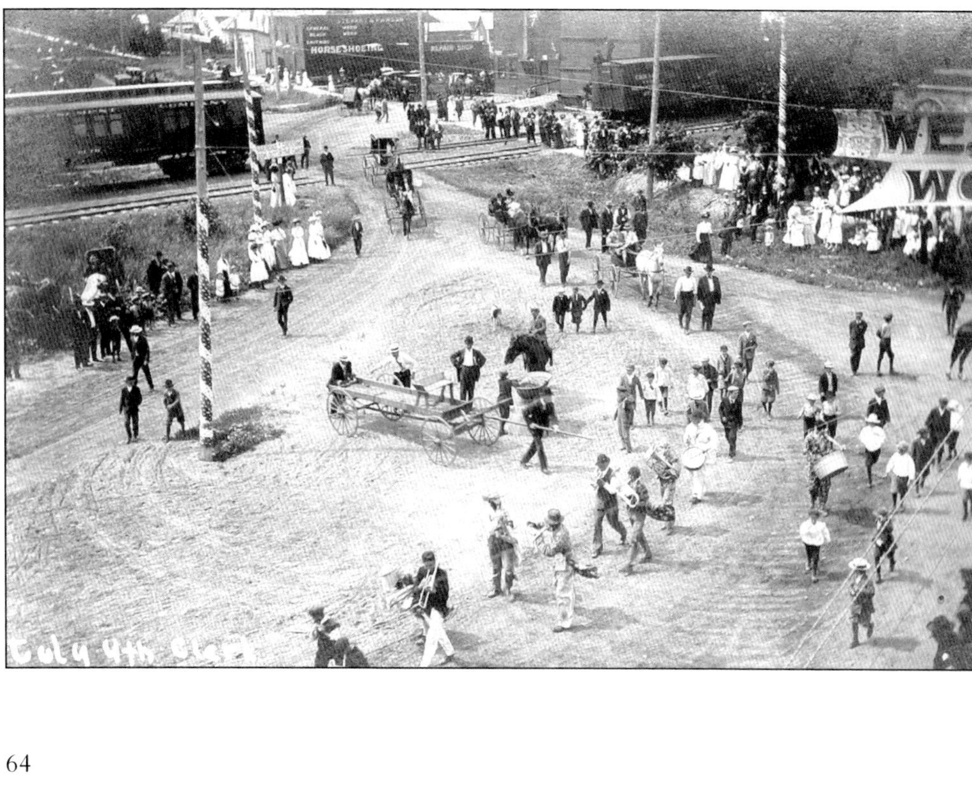

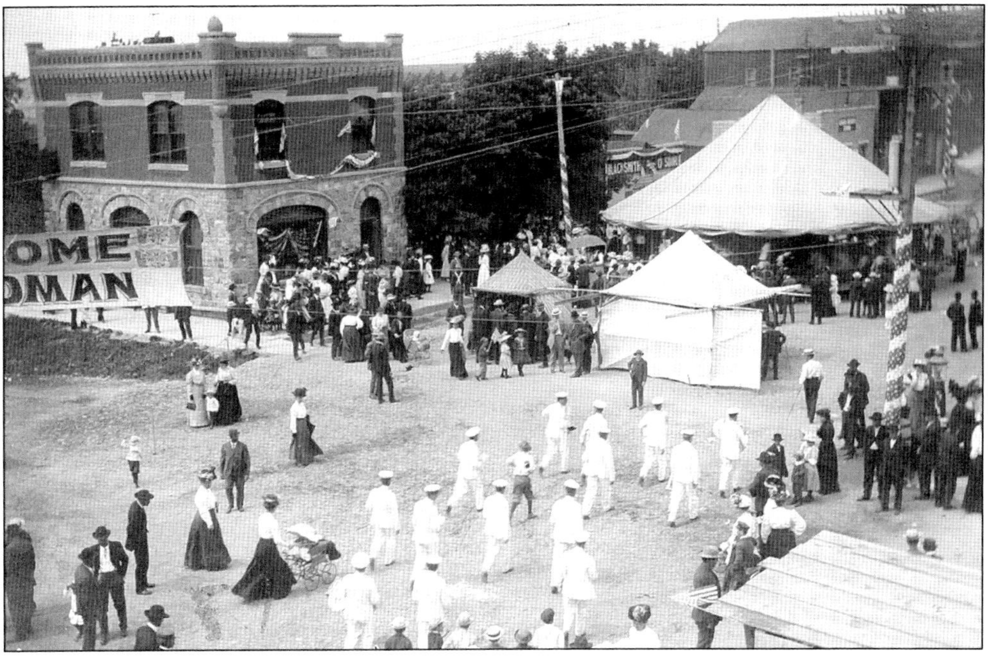

Here is the celebration in another view looking to the west from the corner of First and Main Streets. It looks like the Garden City Band was finished and they were going to the section where all the street events were taking place. Notice the merry-go-round, wow what a gala! Below is still another view in this four-card set; this view is looking east from a block west of the First and Main Streets intersection. A large crowd is gathered to hear a speech. The wagon in the middle appears to be advertising ice cream and is giving rides around the festival. C. H. Miller took all of these photographs.

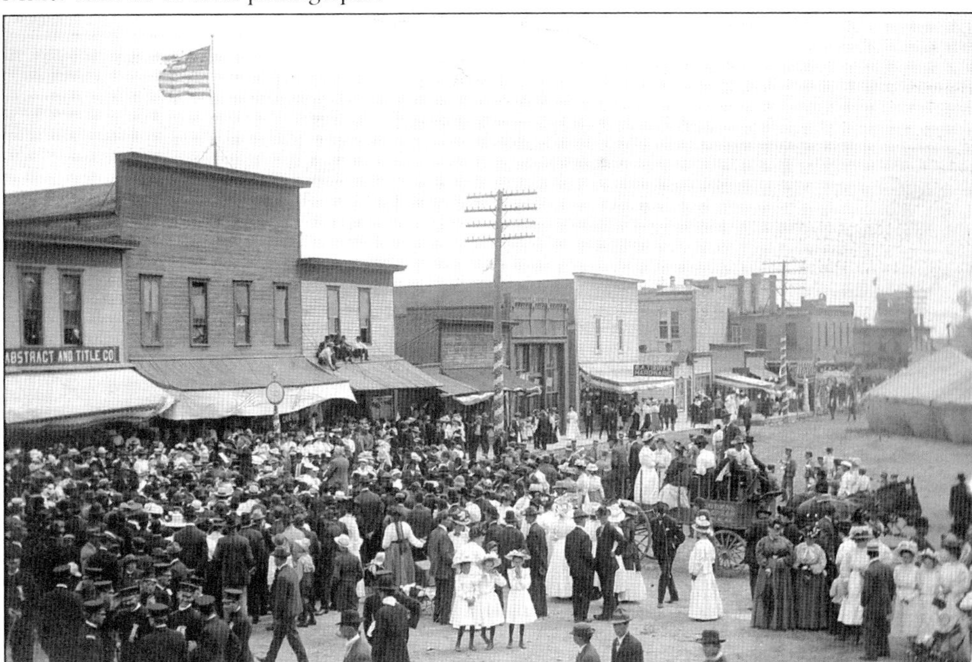

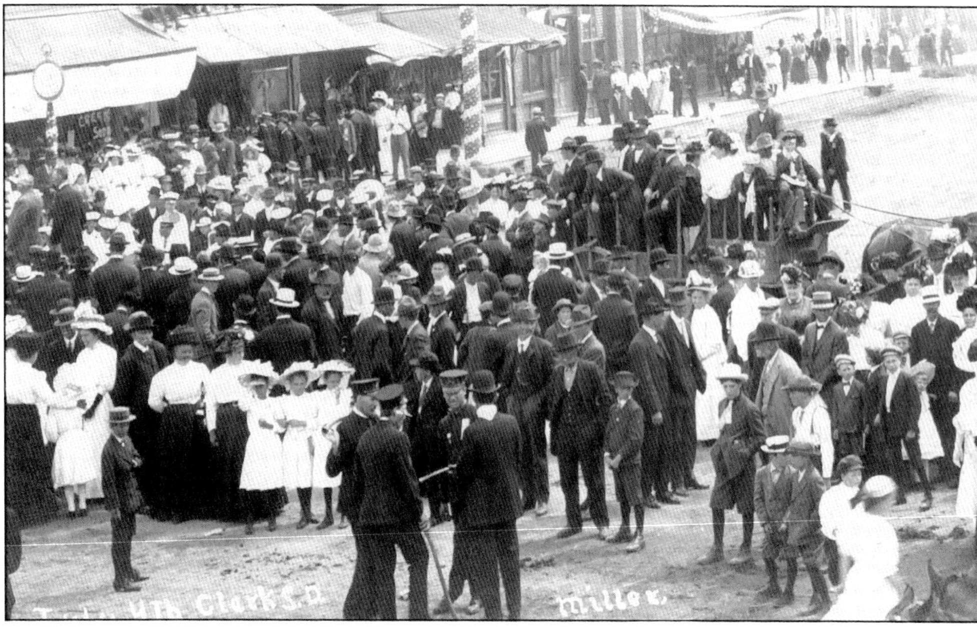

This is another great close-up view of the same Fourth of July/Modern Woodmen celebration taken by C. H. Miller of Clark. The author absolutely loves how everyone is dressed in their Sunday best! This was taken on First Street (Highway 212) in front of the Gales Confectionery building.

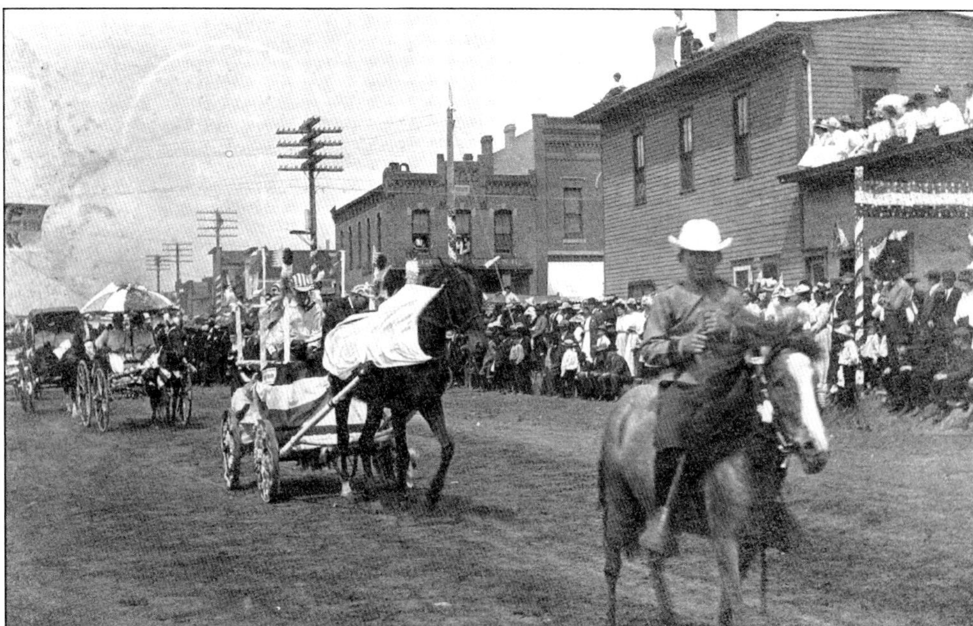

This view is just east of the intersection of First and Commercial Streets as the parade is approaching, with a huge lineup of people on the north side of the street, even on top of the old post office building. This is the corner where Hidden Springs Java, Clark Tae Kwon Do, and Hair-n-Stuff are currently located. This postcard was postmarked in Clark on August 4, 1909, and was sent to Hawarden, Iowa.

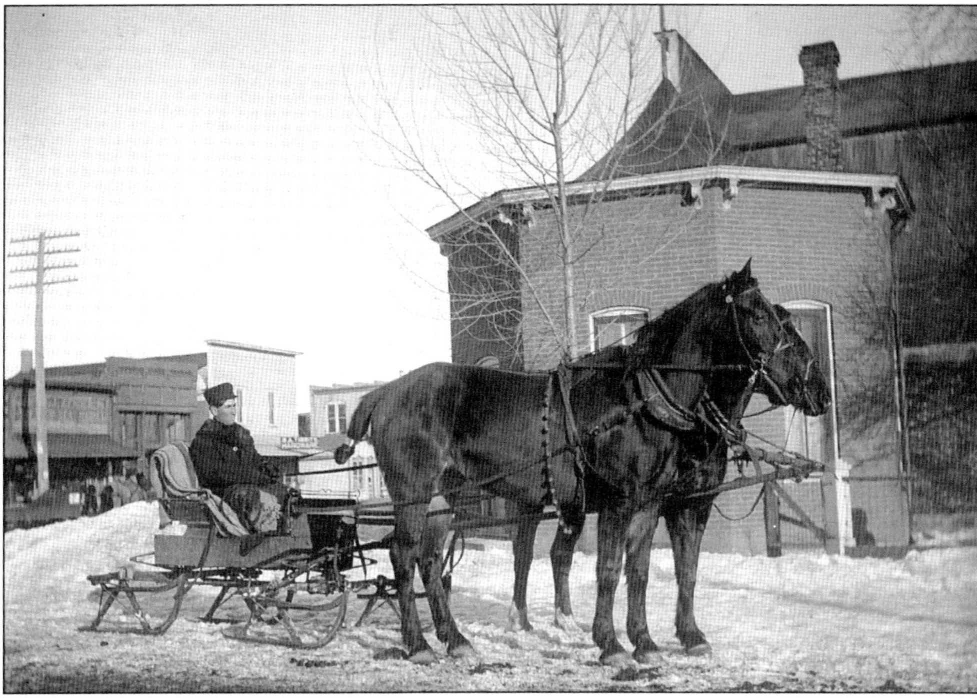

This real photo postcard was taken just to the west side of C. H. Miller's Studio. Miller was a prominent pioneer photographer in Clark for more than a quarter of a century. The brick building was located on the southeast corner of First Street (Highway 212) and Iowa Street (Smith Street). What a beautiful team and sleigh. Below is a full-color front view of the Miller building. The card was sent from Naples, South Dakota, (DPO) in 1909 to Chicago. It was printed in Germany. The building was purchased by Fred Hallberg in the 1930s and moved one and a half blocks west and became their private residence. It still stands today in that location.

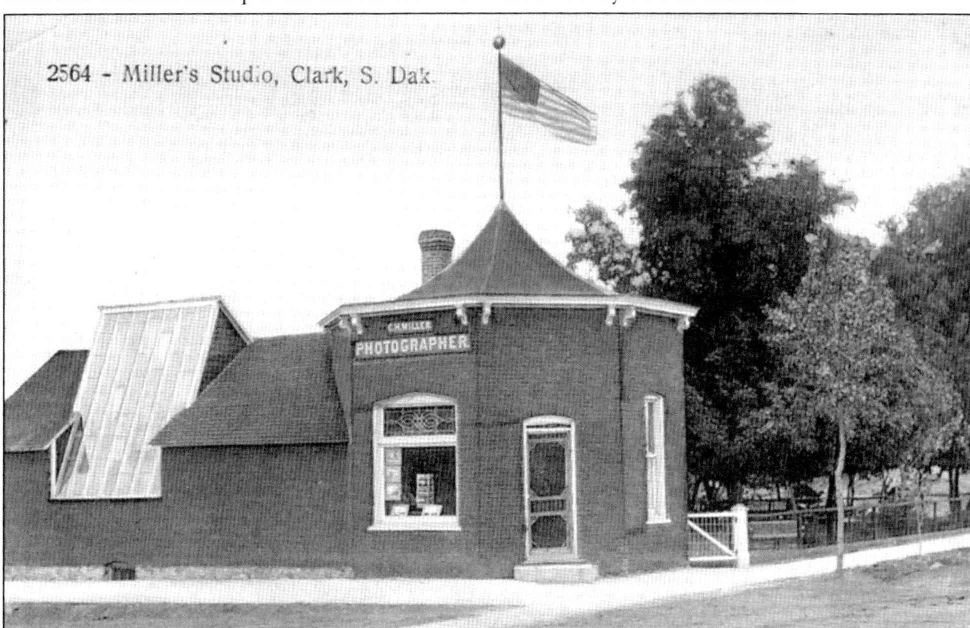

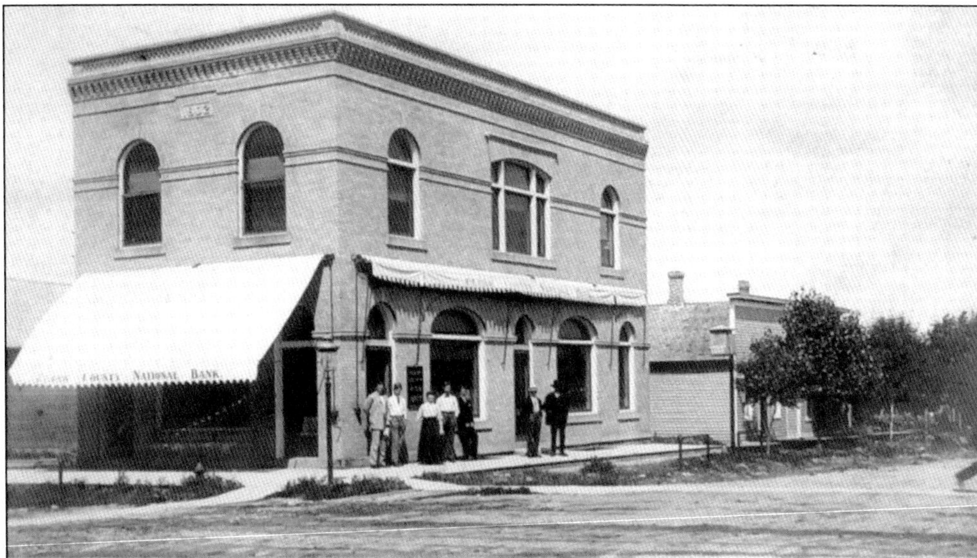

Clark County National Bank, Clark, South Dakota

These views show two early bank buildings in Clark. The Clark County National Bank (above), located at the northeast corner of Second and Commercial Streets, was built in 1902. Charles Carpenter was a cashier, and R. J. Mann was the president. Lyman Mann, son of R. J., later became president. Owned by Clark County, the building still stands and is the present Interlakes Community Action Program office and food pantry. Below is the Ware and Griffin Bank building. It still stands proudly at the southwest corner of First Street (Highway 212) and Main Street (Commercial Street). It was built in 1900. The bank closed in the financial panic of 1929–1930. Recently, the building was purchased by Clay Yeoman, DDS, and is in the process of being restored.

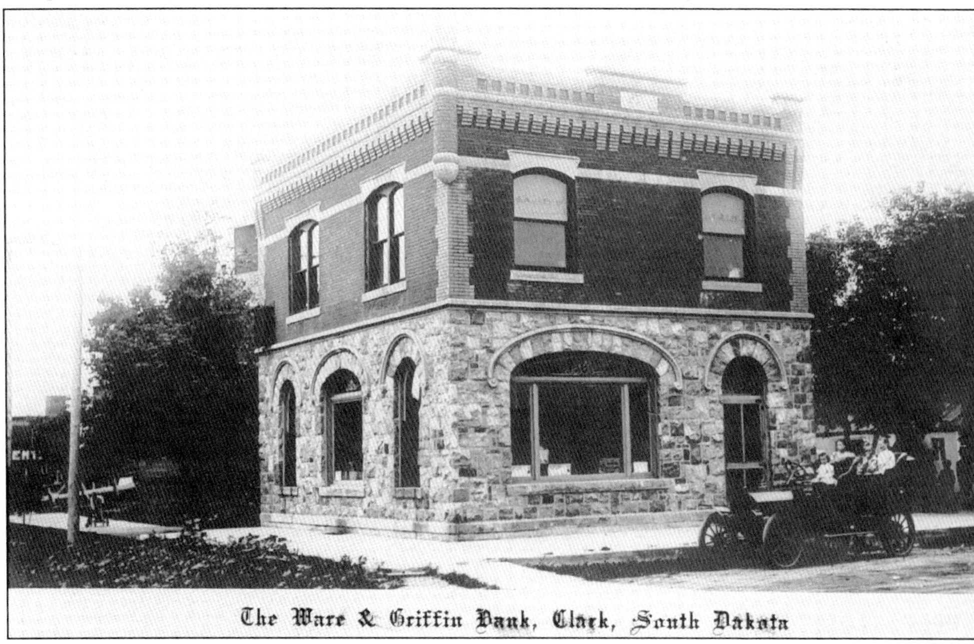

The Ware & Griffin Bank, Clark, South Dakota

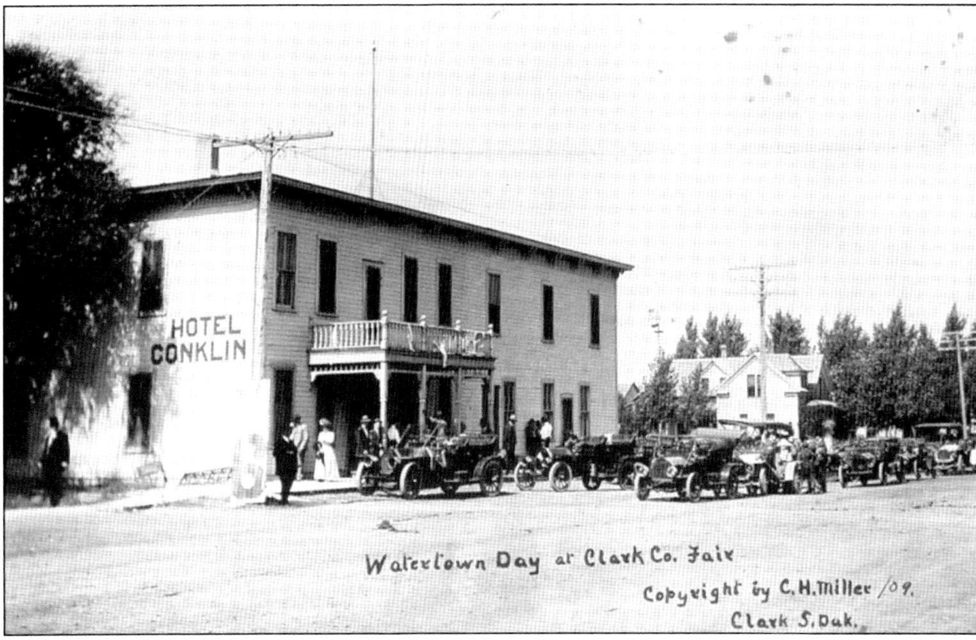

What a festive day "Watertown Day at Clark County Fair" was to be! C. H. Miller took this real photo postcard in 1909. The Hotel Conklin was built in 1881 by S. J. Conklin, who was one of the first five men who staked claim in Clark County. He was a Civil War veteran. The hotel, which was razed in 1935, stood where the Clark County Courthouse is now located.

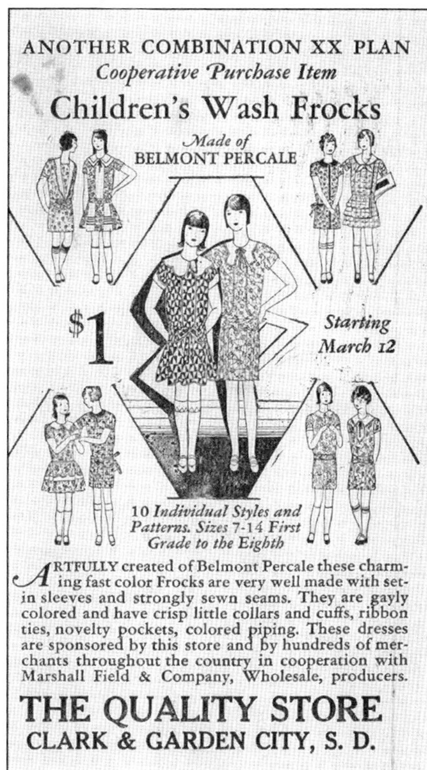

The Quality Store sent out this advertising postcard on March 8, 1928. In Clark, the store was located where the Clark Flower and Gift Shop is now located. It operated with Otto Baarsch as the proprietor. Groceries were on the first floor, with ladies ready to wear and children's clothes on the second. It was sold in the 1930s. No one recalls a Garden City store.

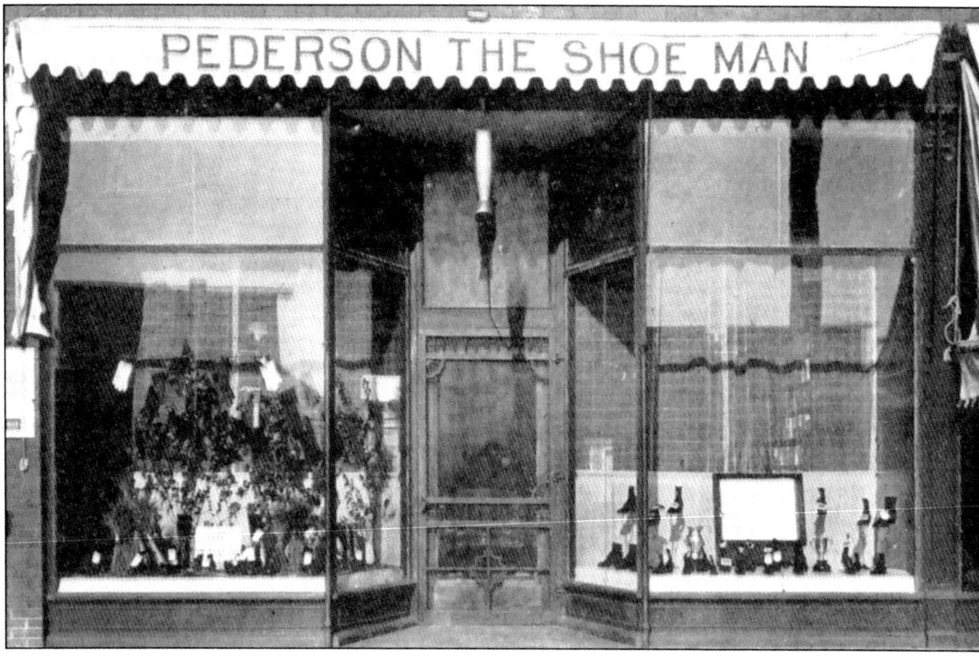

Knud Pederson owned Pederson the Shoe Man in Clark, which was located just south (where the produce section in Ken's Fairway is located) of the old Desnoyers building (currently where Florey Plumbing, J and J Heating and Air Conditioning, and the South Dakota Department of Fish and Game offices are). As evidenced by the inside view of the store, Pederson operated a neat, well-stocked store. Ladders on tracks on each side of the store made it much easier to get to the shoes on the top shelves. Old timers in town say he was known to always look at people's shoes when they walked into his store, before he looked at who they were! (Bottom card courtesy of Vance Neuberger.)

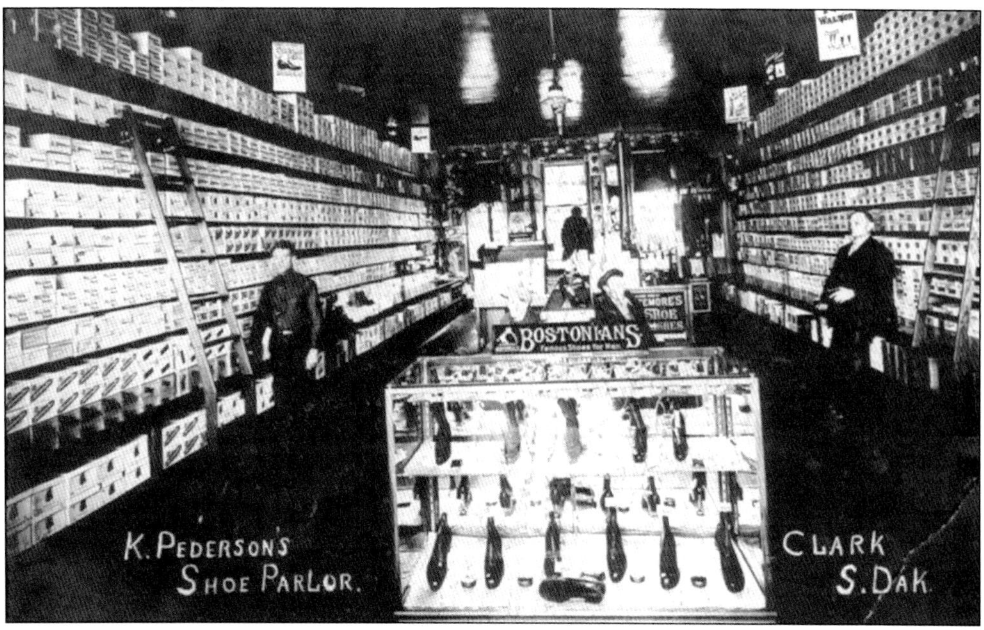

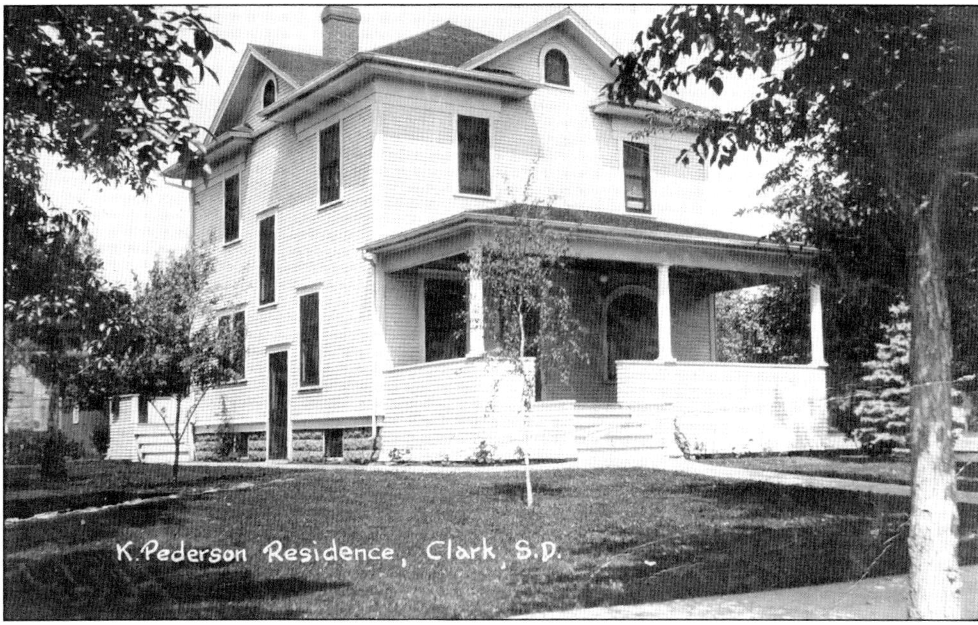

This was the residence of Knud Pederson, the shoe man of Clark. It sits at the southwest corner of Third and North Cloud Streets. In more recent years, it was known as the Kyle home.

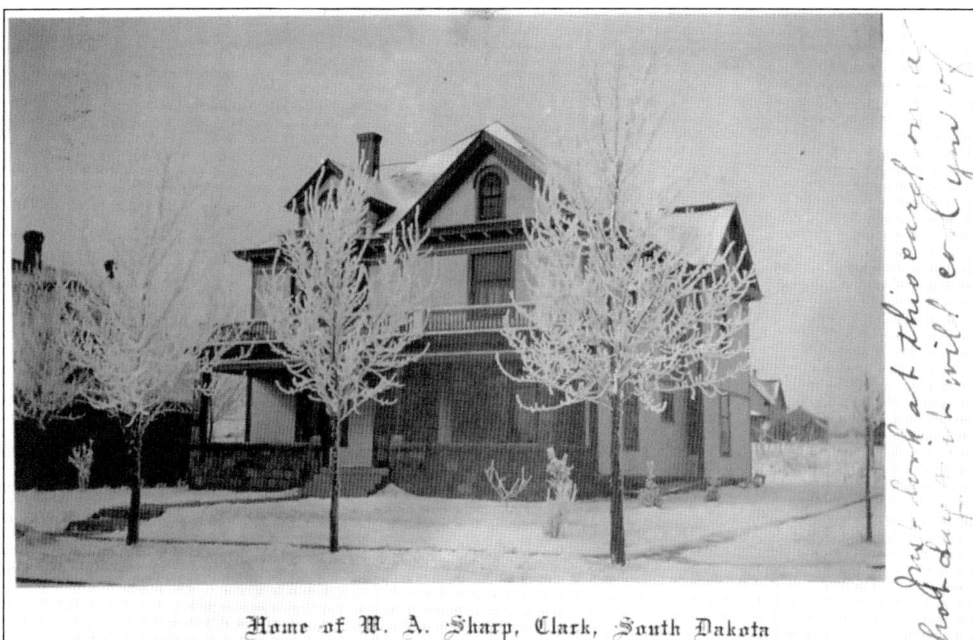

This home of William A. Sharp, local furniture man and undertaker, is located at the southwest corner of North Smith Street and Fourth Avenue. The home, built in 1906, has quite a story. According to family, Sharp had attended the world's fair in St. Louis in 1904/1905, and in the South Dakota Exhibit was a model home. He purchased the home at the fair, had it dismantled and shipped it to Clark, and reassembled it. (Information courtesy of Val Fleischacker.)

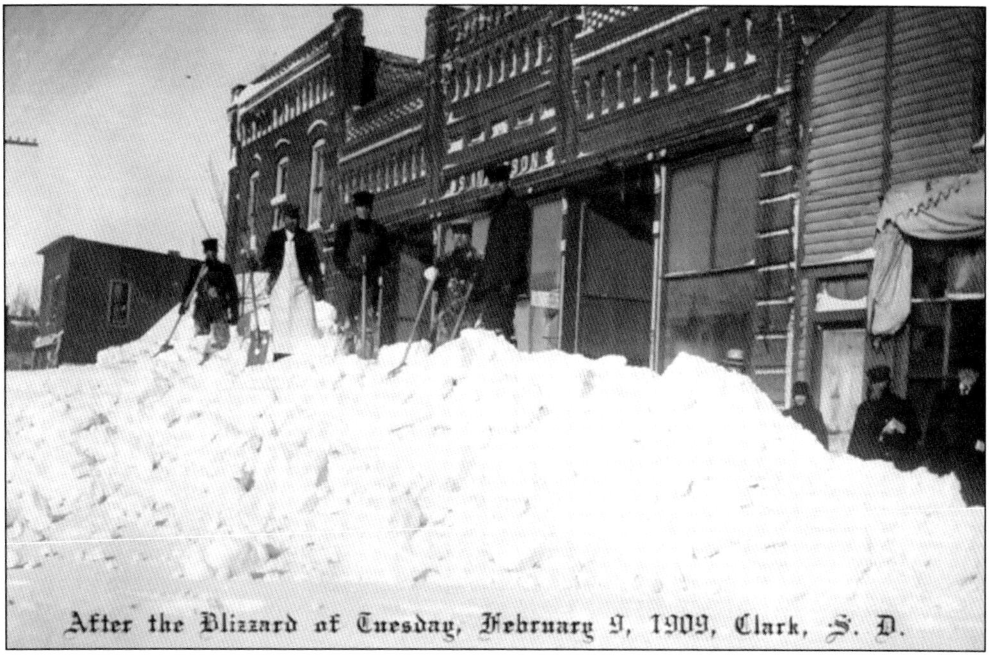

What a snowfall it must have been on Tuesday, February 9, 1909, in Clark. Both of these views were taken in front of the Sever Anderson building that was built in 1899. The building housed Anderson's General Store until 1898, at which time the Eric Foss family took over and operated the Foss Store. To the left side is the building that housed the Henry Lien grocery on first floor and apartments upstairs. Both of these buildings are now Olson's Motor Company. The photograph below is looking due west from in front of the Anderson building. The Northwest Hotel, which later became the Adams Hotel, sits across the street. That hotel has been a setting for murder mystery books by Harold Adams, great grandson of former owner C. F. Adams. It was razed in the late 1960s when the Hegdahl family owned it.

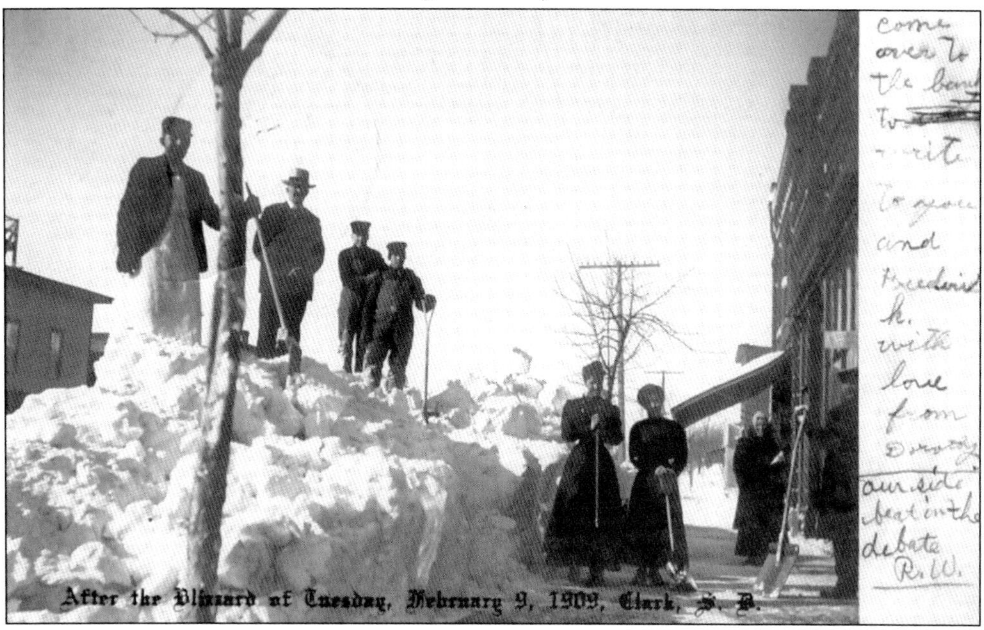

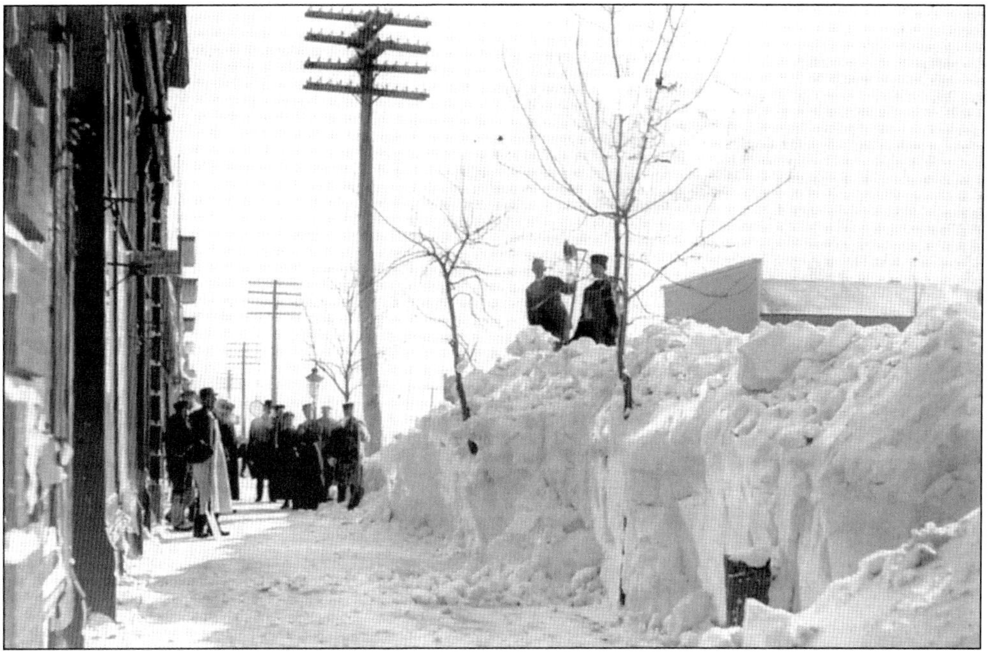

A view of the blizzard looking due east from the front of the Anderson and Lien building shows the McClelland Hall (just the roof top) sitting across the street. C. H. Miller, whose home is pictured below, took all four of these pictures of the blizzard of February 9, 1909. Miller took both of these real photo postcards after the blizzard. The home sits at the corner of First Street (Highway 212) and North Idaho Street.

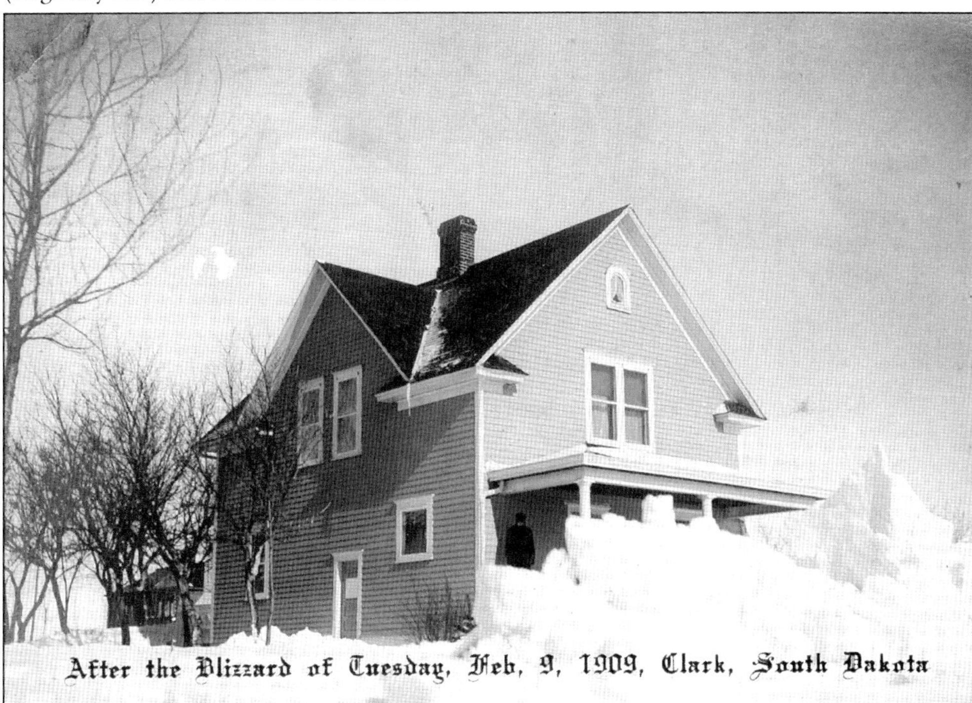

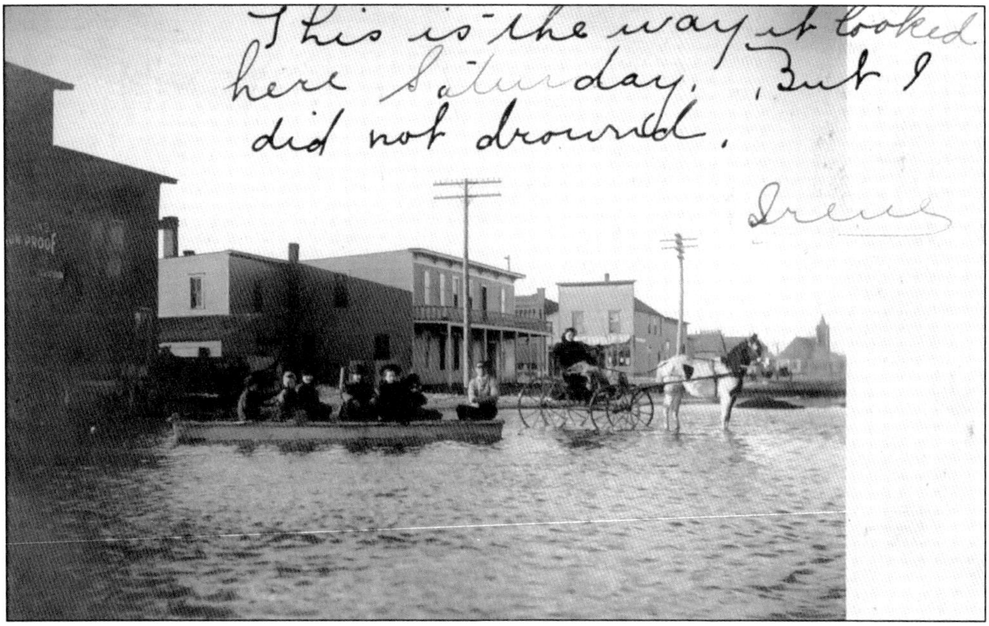

After all the snow melted, this is what happened next. This view was taken on South Smith Street, in front of what is now the Roetell Senior Housing. The Northwestern/Adams Hotel is on the corner. "This is the way it looked Saturday, but I did not drowned." Irene (possibly Irene Rasmussen, as it was sent to L. Pillsbury at Crocker) on March 10, 1909, states she had been practicing basketball. (Irene Rasmussen was a member of the 1909 girls team.)

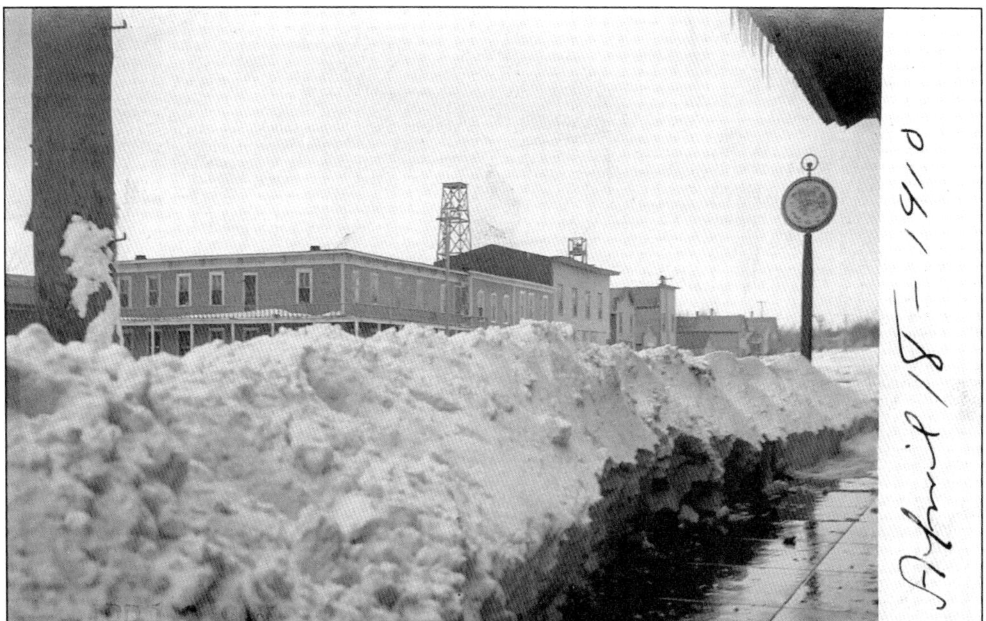

Here is more snow, another year later, on April 8, 1910. This photograph was taken in front of Gale's Confectionery and Candy Store looking southwest. The Northwestern/Adams Hotel is across the street. Not much is known about the building next to the hotel. The old city hall building was not yet constructed, as it was not built until 1914.

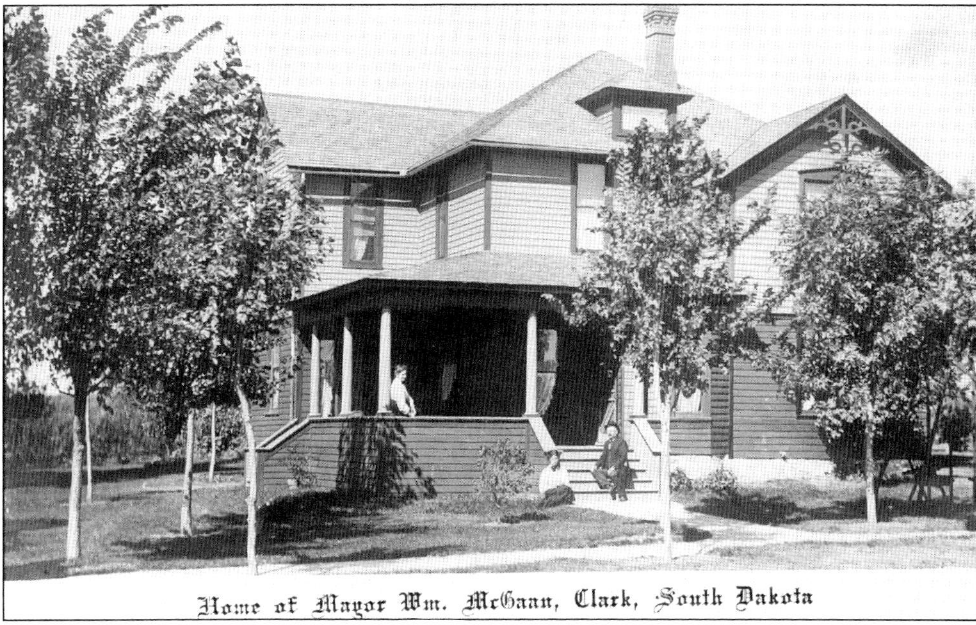

William McGann, a young lawyer from Illinois, came to Raymond, South Dakota, in the late 1880s. McGann married Emma Dice in 1889 and moved to this home in Clark. They rented for a short period until buying it in 1899 and remodeling it in 1904. The house is located at 110 North Utah Street. William later became mayor of Clark in May 1906, and served until 1912. He also served as a judge in the area.

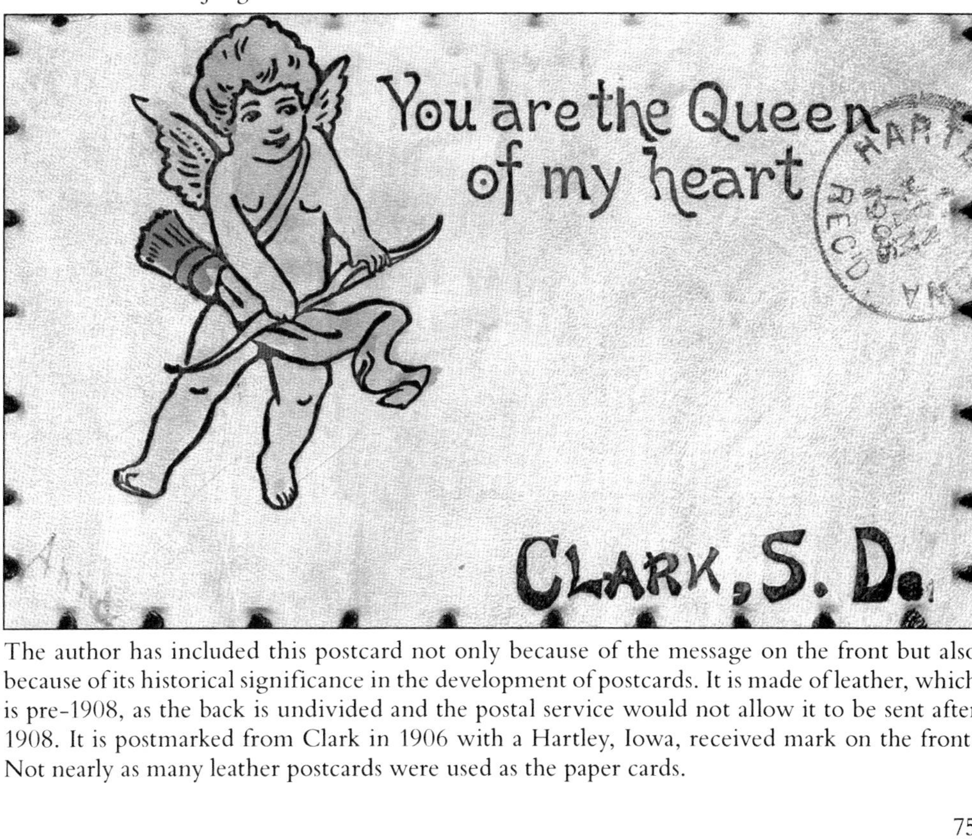

The author has included this postcard not only because of the message on the front but also because of its historical significance in the development of postcards. It is made of leather, which is pre-1908, as the back is undivided and the postal service would not allow it to be sent after 1908. It is postmarked from Clark in 1906 with a Hartley, Iowa, received mark on the front. Not nearly as many leather postcards were used as the paper cards.

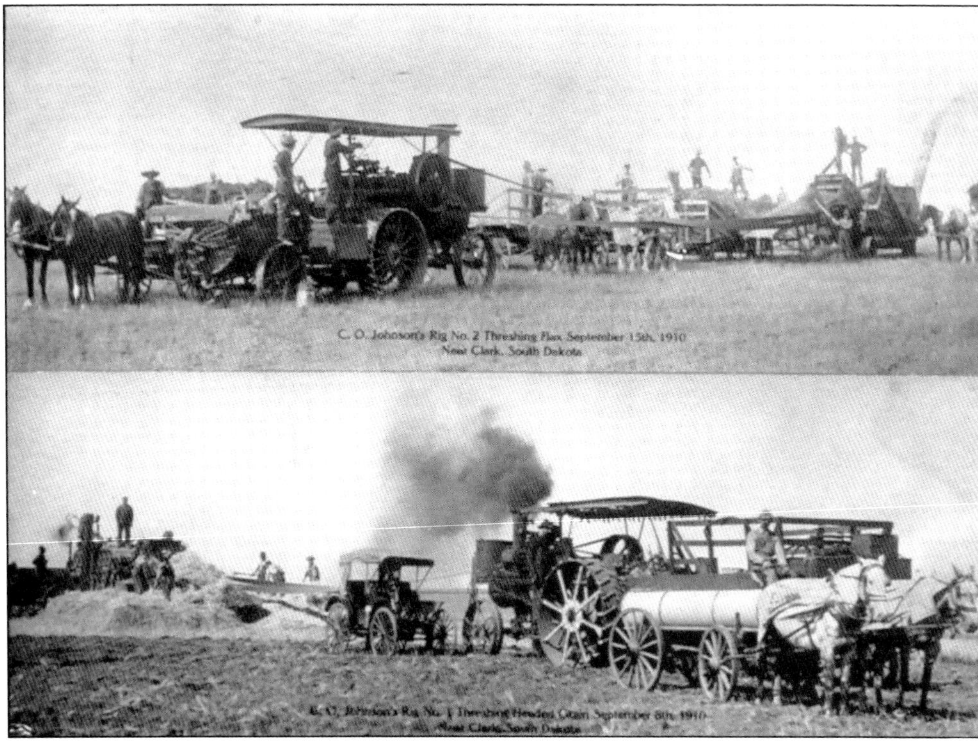

These fabulous threshing scenes were taken near Clark in 1910. The top part of this card was taken on September 15, while harvesting flax with Rig No. 2, and below on September 8, while taking in headed grain with Rig No. 1. Both rigs were operated and owned by C. O. Johnson.

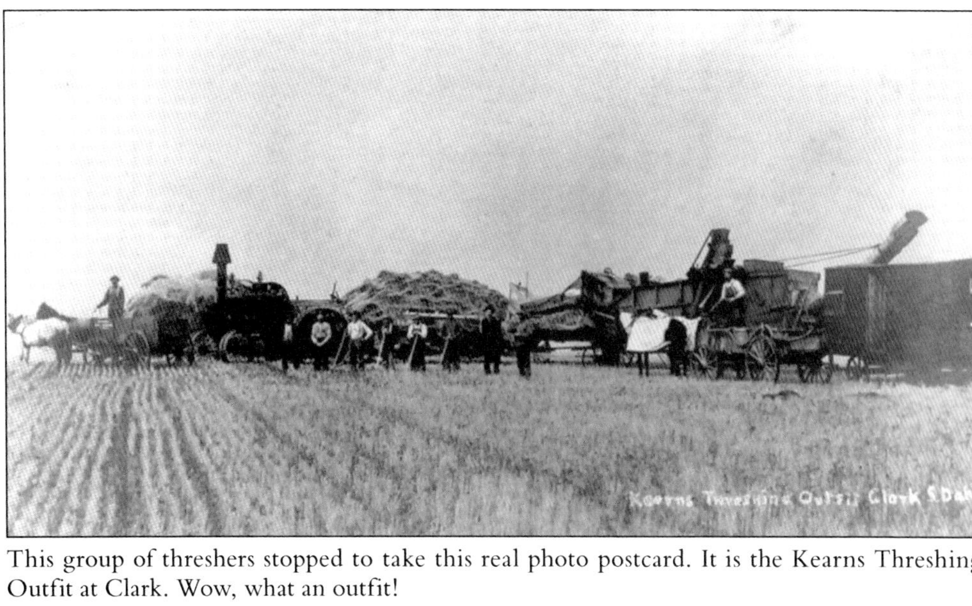

This group of threshers stopped to take this real photo postcard. It is the Kearns Threshing Outfit at Clark. Wow, what an outfit!

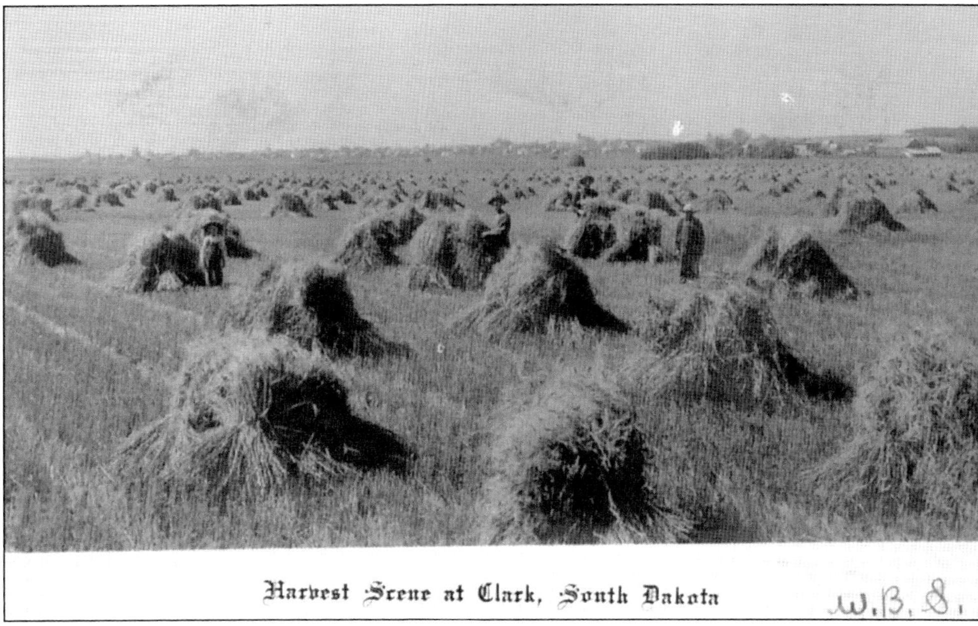

Taken just northeast of Clark, this is John George Rohrback in Mount Pleasant Township standing in his recently bundled field. The farm in the background is the current farm site of Bob and Marlys Benson. The city of Clark is in the far background. There are three people standing by the bundles.

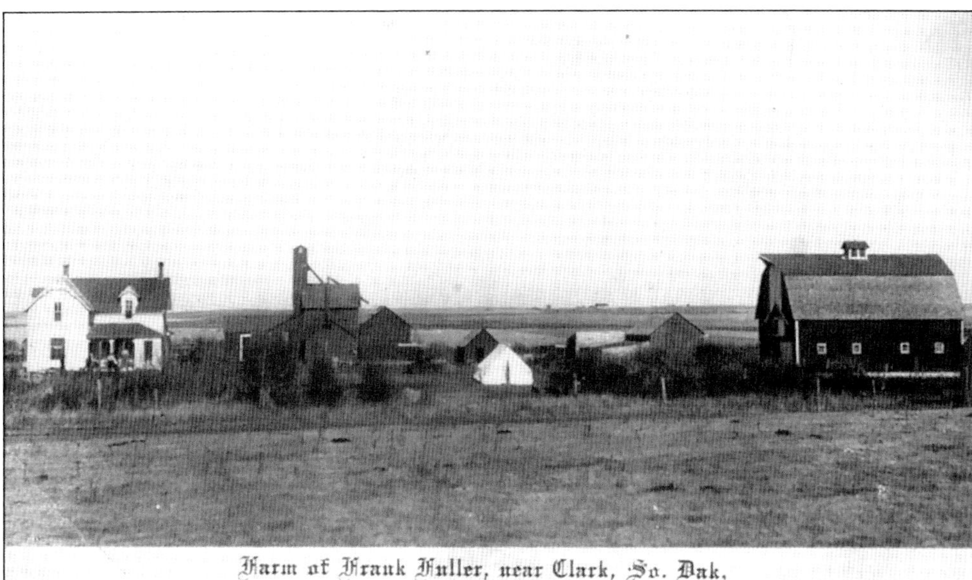

Located in Foxton Township, southeast of Clark, was the farm of Frank Fuller. Fuller came to Clark County in 1890, at the age of 19, to Elrod Township. He married Ollie Fox, and they had seven sons and one daughter. This farm has been in the Fox/Fuller family for over six generations.

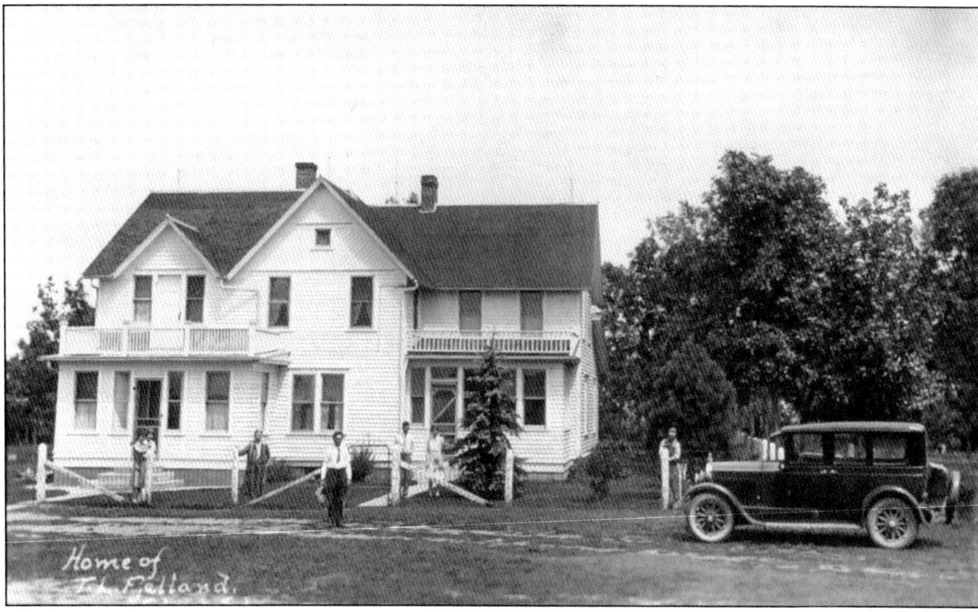

This is the residence of Tom L. Fjelland in Garfield Township. On the back, it states, "A Gledelig, Jull 1931, Mr. & Mrs. TLF." (Courtesy of the Merlyn Schubloom family.)

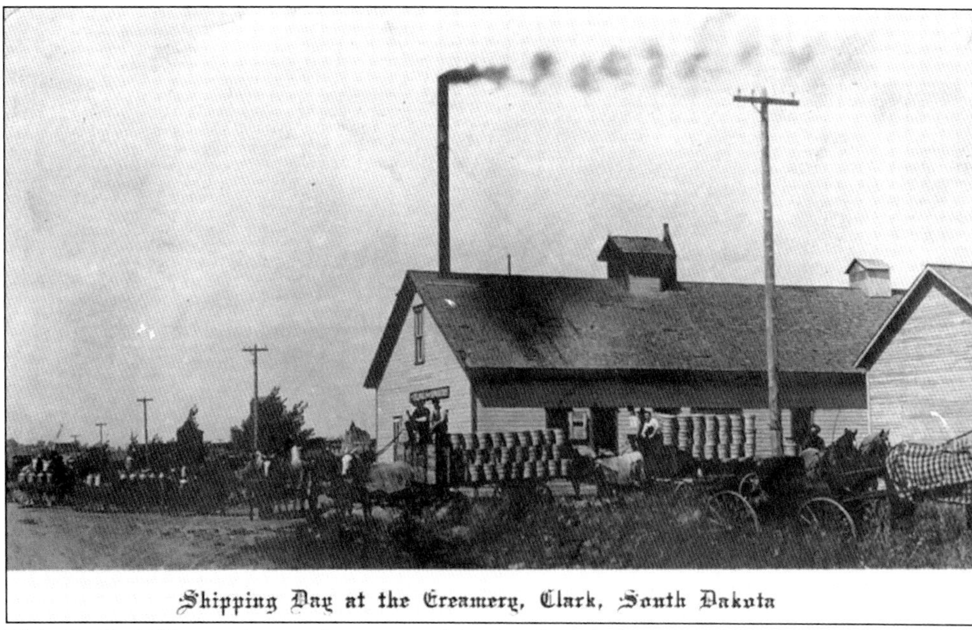

This C. H. Miller card was taken around 1908. The Clark Farmer's Cooperative Creamery was located on the east edge of Clark, across from the Geise home. George Baldwin began his interest in the creamery business while riding along in a one-horse delivery wagon with Levi Eckerson, father of Earl Eckerson. In 1921, when the above creamery burned, Baldwin started a cream station in downtown Clark.

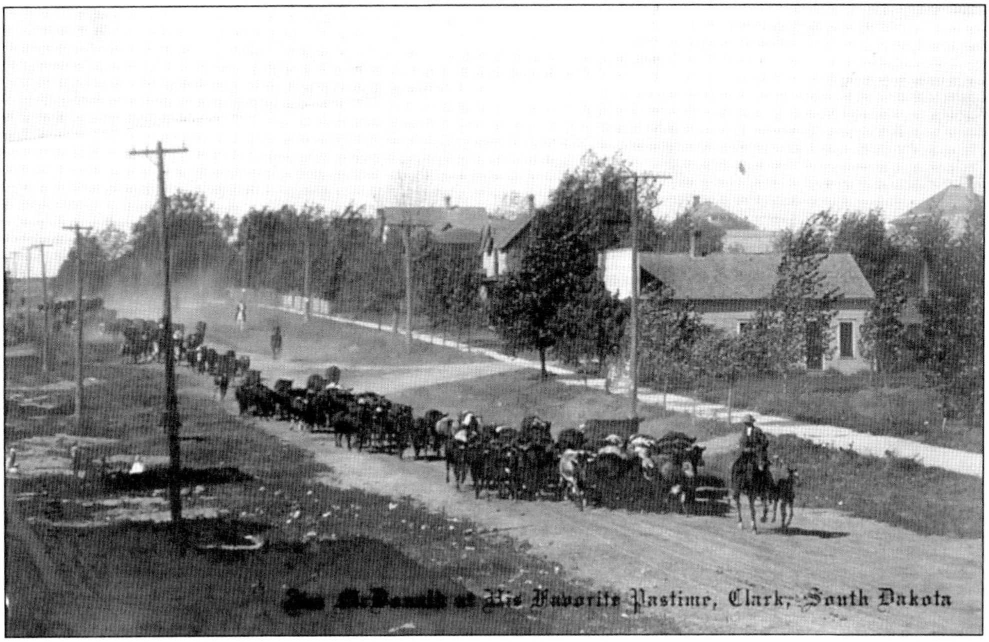

Most postcards have some type of story of how they were acquired. This one was sent to the post office in Clark, around 2001, in an envelope addressed to postmaster. It states on the back "Postmaster- found this card in some old papers, thought maybe some one in Clark might like to have it." Marcella Arthur of Long Beach, California, sent it.

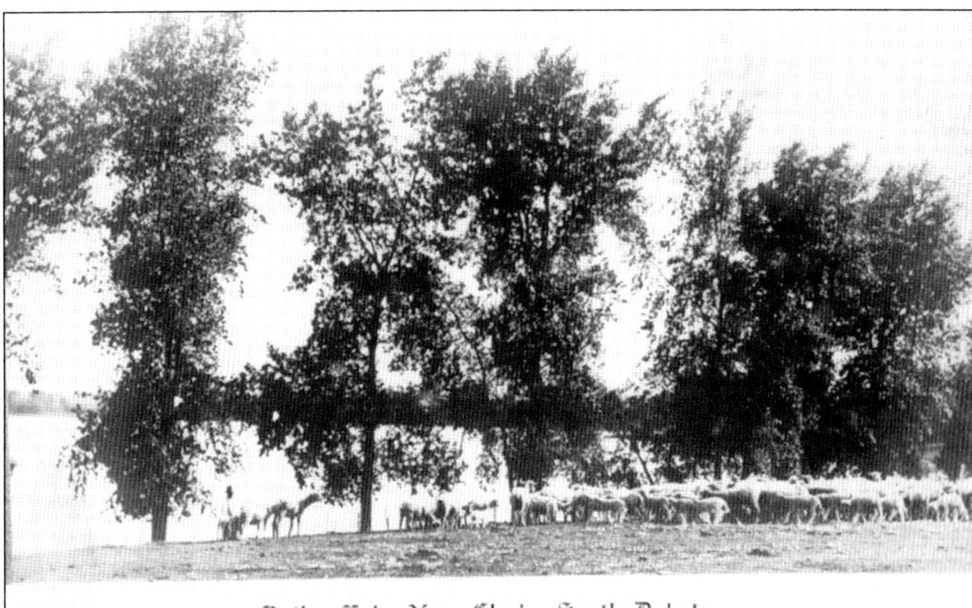

Bailey's Lake was named for John Bailey, who settled in Clark County on June 29, 1878. He, his wife, and adopted son, along with Joseph Woodland and his son, came to Dakota Territory. They were among the first white settlers in Clark County. The first post office was in the Woodland house on April 28, 1879. It was named Julian, after John's wife, Julia.

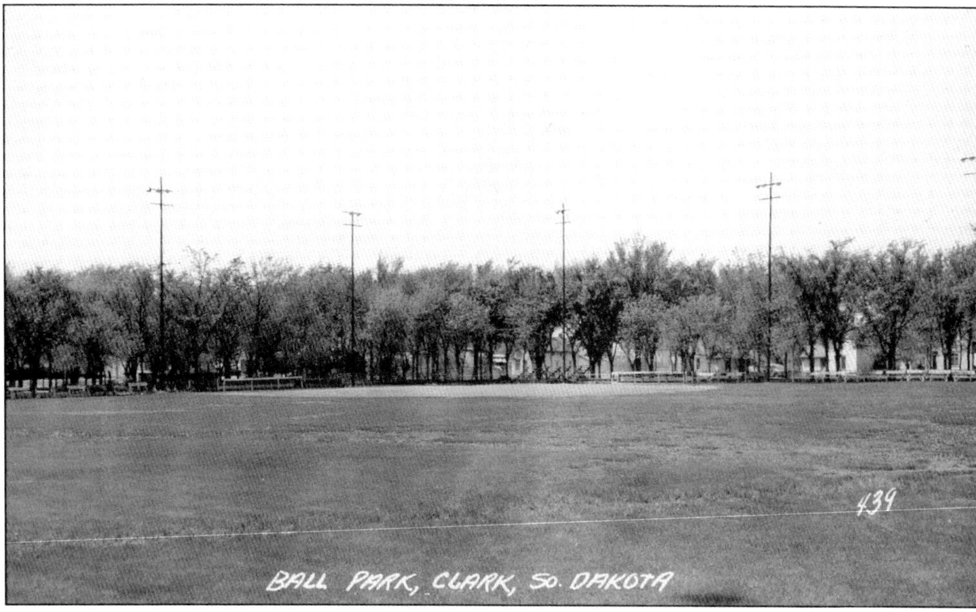

Another recreation area in Clark is the ballpark. Samuel H. Elrod acquired the land, with the help of the local depot agent, for $1 from the Chicago and North-Western Railroad and deeded it to the City of Clark. They bought and planted trees, one tree for every man in the armed forces, in honor of H. E. Dickenson. Dickenson had been the local depot agent who helped secure the land, thus, Dickenson Park.

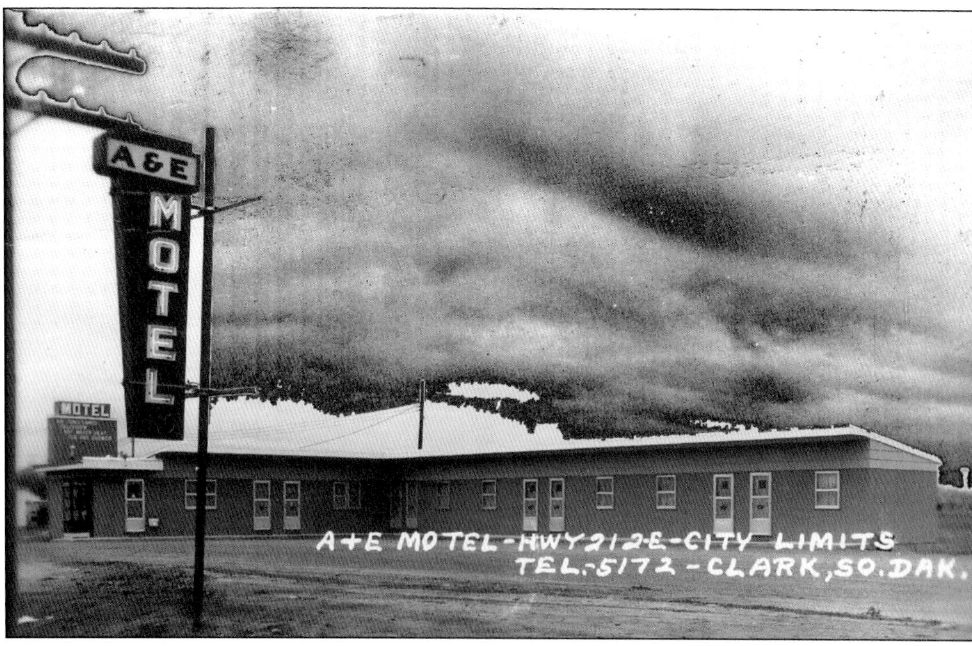

Air Conditioning, telephone, hot water heat, tub, and shower were all modern conveniences when the A and E Motel was built on the east edge of Clark in the early 1960s. Abe and Edith Hegdahl, former owners of the Adams Hotel, which had been raised just prior to them building this facility, owned the building. Today, it is called the Pheasant Motel, with many updates, and is owned by Terry and LaVonne Binger.

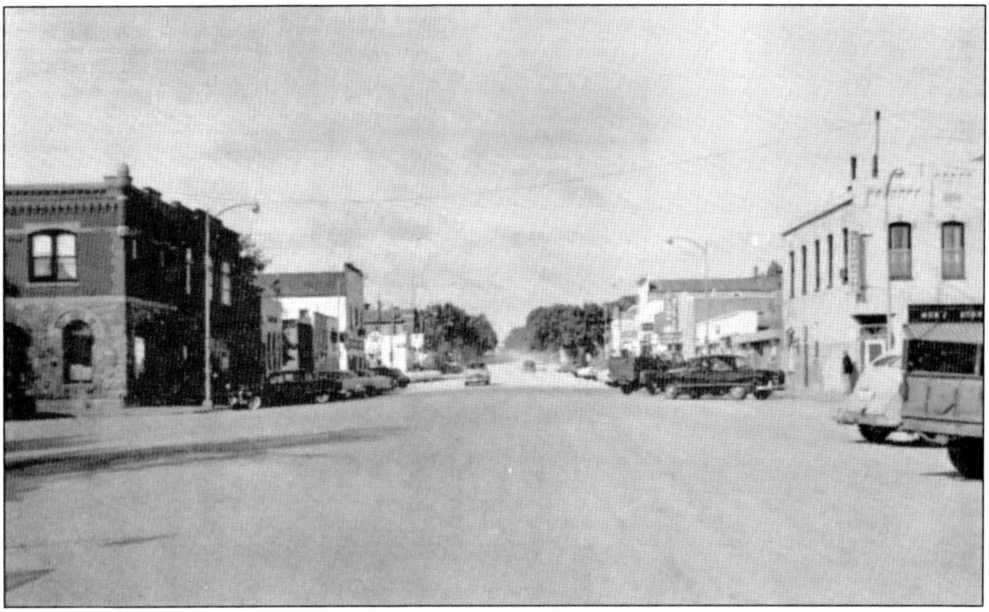

This Buelow Studio photograph was taken in the early 1950s, and the Lockharts Men's Store was in the Security Bank Building from 1950 to 1956. This is a nice view of Highway 212 looking west with the Clark Theatre marquee and the Texaco sign—two memorable landmarks. Al Buelow had a photography studio in Clark for many years, located two doors south of the current post office building.

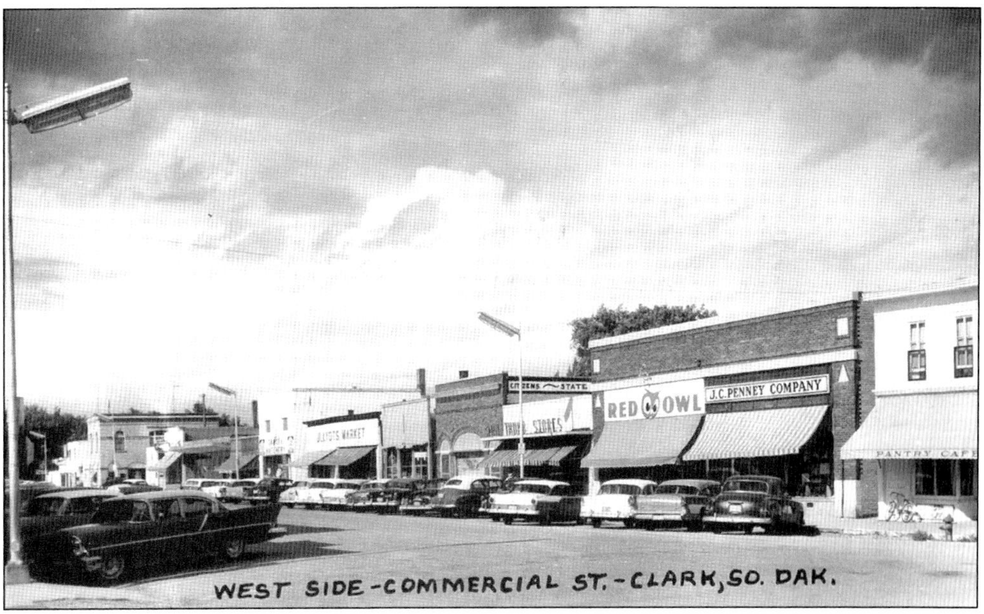

Taken in the late 1950s, this view of the east side of Commercial Street shows the Pantry Café on the corner. North is the J. C. Penney Company. (Remember the cash tubes to the office from the cashier station?) Continuing north is the Red Owl Store, Tom Thumb Store, Citizens State Bank, Bennie Ullyot Market, Dakota Hatchery, Eckerson Barber Shop, Edna's Dress Shop, Kyle Hardware, and Baldwin Creamery. (The author cannot help but think about the Saturday night ice cream cones.)

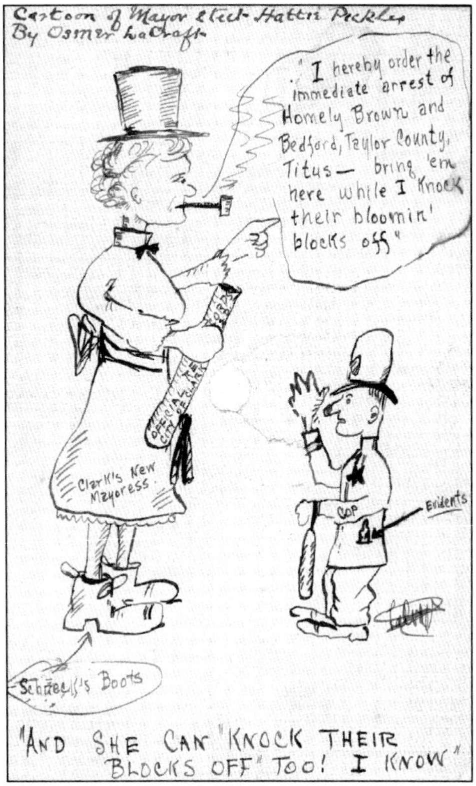

Most likely this card is the only one of its kind in existence. This is a hand-drawn cartoon card by Osmer LaCraft of Mayor Elect Hattie Pickles holding the official records of the city of Clark. Pickles was elected as Clark's "New Mayoress" in 1922. She served as an educator in Clark County and also as the county superintendent of schools from 1904 to 1908, and 1912 to 1916. It is signed by LaCraft next to the cops' boots.

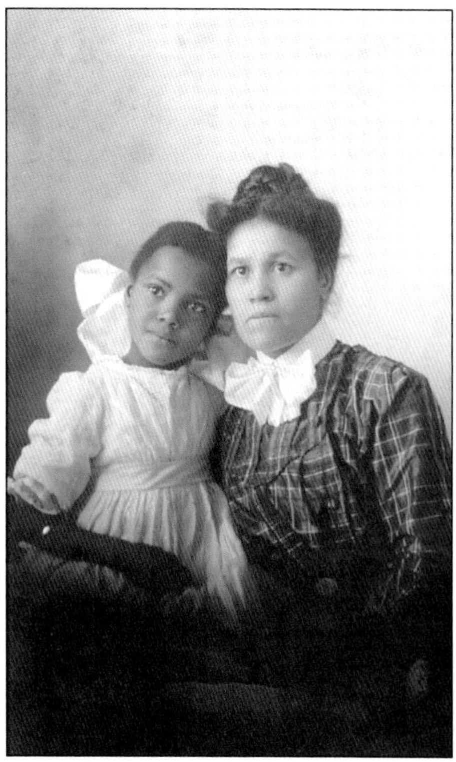

This photograph is of Rosa and Grace Simmons. Rosa's husband, Cal, was a personal servant (slave freed) of Captain McSpadden who had served under General Sherman in the Civil War. The Simmons came to Clark County in 1881, with the McSpaddens, and homesteaded two miles west of the Clark Center Lutheran Church. They had four children. Rosa and the children left the area sometime between 1912 and 1914 and their whereabouts is unknown. Cal died in Clark in 1915.

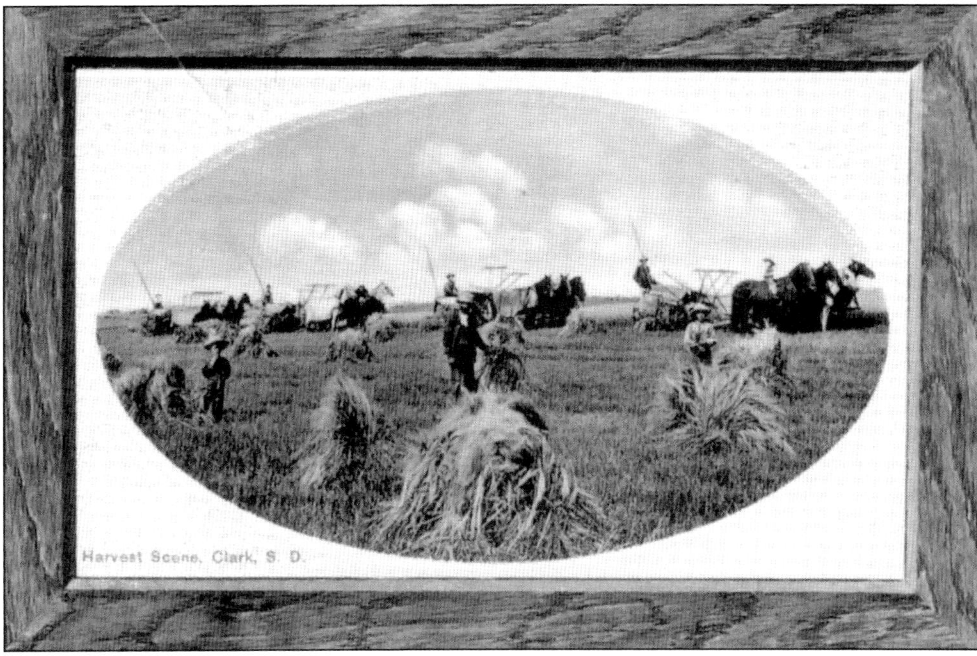

This printed series of postcards was published by Bloom Brothers in Minneapolis and is copyrighted by C. H. Miller. They were printed in Germany. There are eight postcards in the series, the author has seven and is still looking for the eighth. They all have a series number printed on the reverse side. This one is number 2,726—Harvest Scene, Clark, South Dakota.

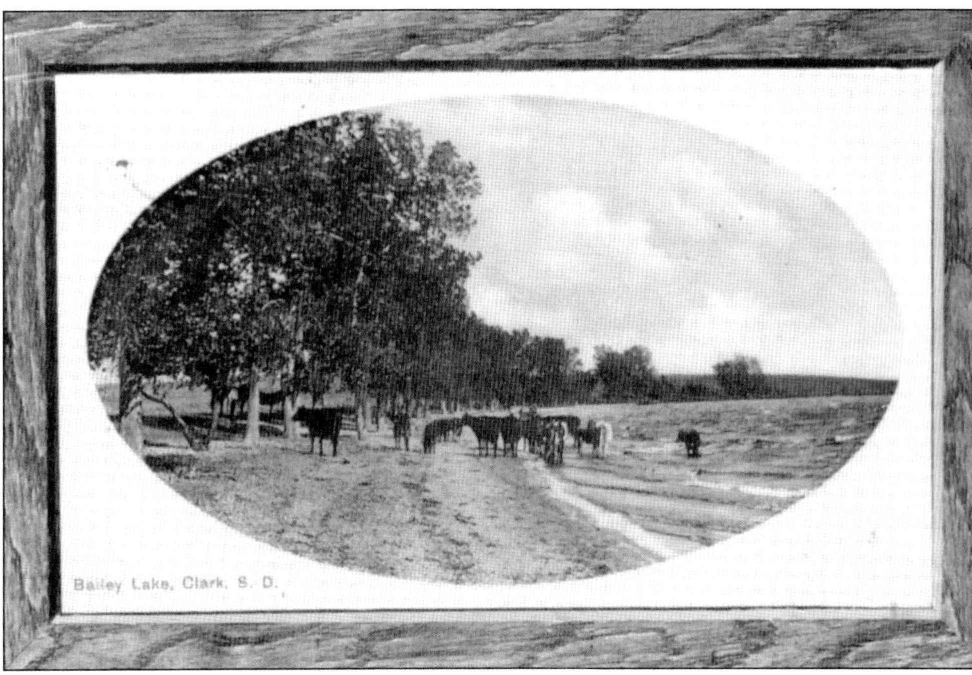

This is the second card in the series from Clark that was published by Bloom Brothers. It is of Bailey Lake, a local recreation spot named for John Bailey, one of the first white settlers in Clark County. It also must have been a favorite spot of the local cattle!

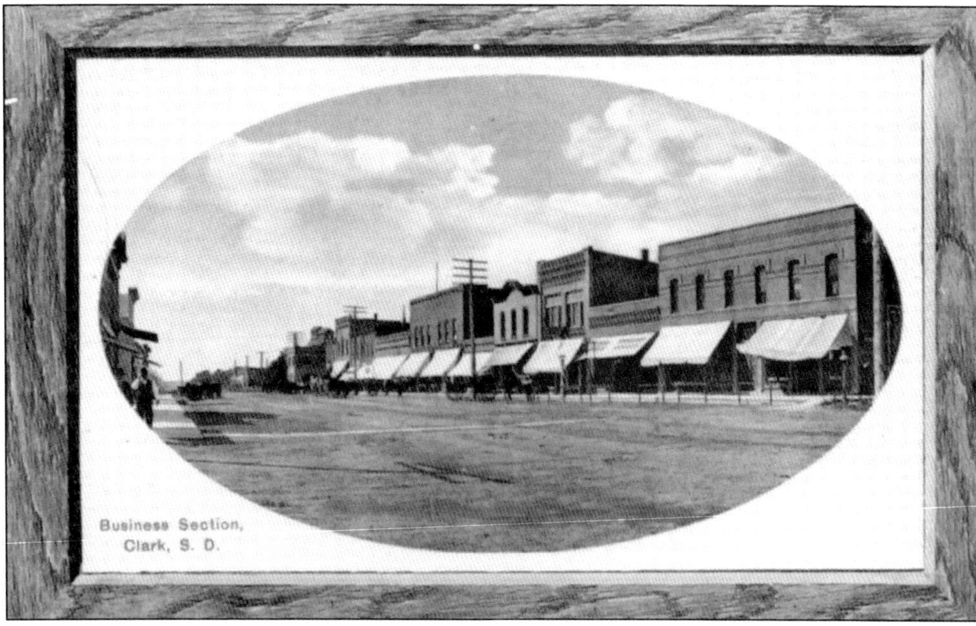

This is the business section on the west side of Commercial Street in downtown Clark in a view looking from the northwest to the southwest. It is an early view from the C. H. Miller Studio and was published by Bloom Brothers of Minneapolis. It is number 2,728, number three in the series of Clark postcards.

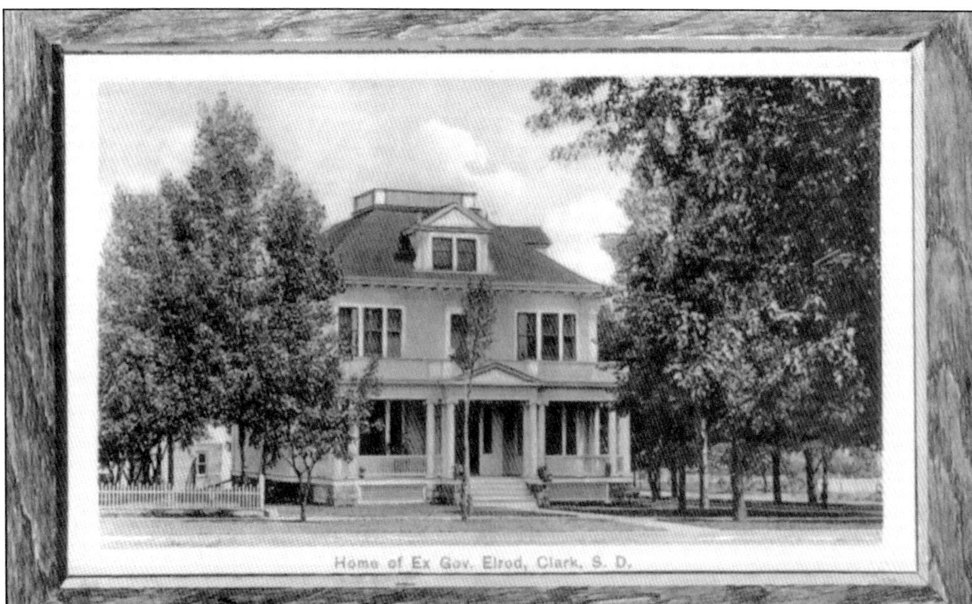

Number four in the series published by Bloom Brothers is numbered 2,729 and is the home of ex-governor Samuel Elrod. This home was built between 1907 and 1908 and stands today in Clark as a private residence.

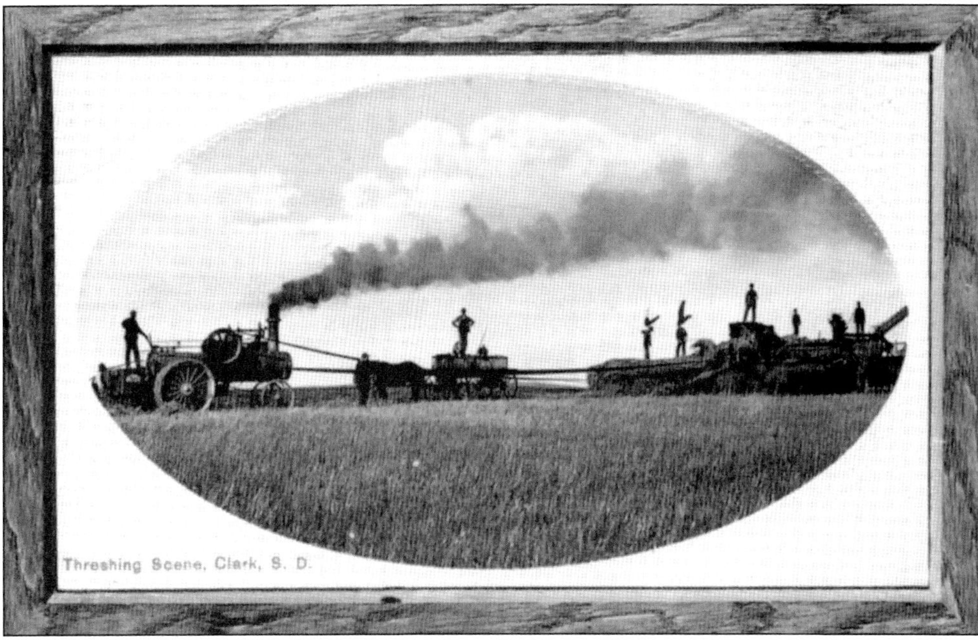

This threshing scene taken near Clark is the fifth in this series of C. H. Miller postcards published by Bloom Brothers. Agriculture has always been a very important part of the economy in this area. The postcard is numbered 2,730. The author has been unable to locate the card numbered 2,731, although he knows it is entitled "Lover's Lane." Maybe no one wants to admit Clark had a lover's lane and they have done away with all of the cards. The author has only seen a copy of it.

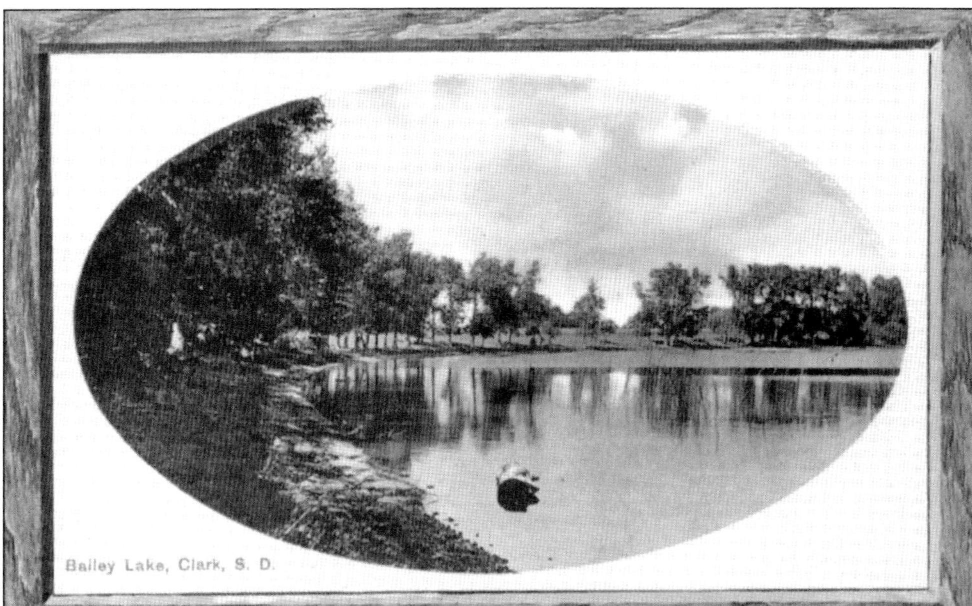

This is yet another view of the recreation area northwest of Clark named Bailey Lake. For years, it has been referred to as Bailey's Lake and has been used for recreation, including fishing. A Saturday night prom party has been known to happen there also. This is card number 2,732.

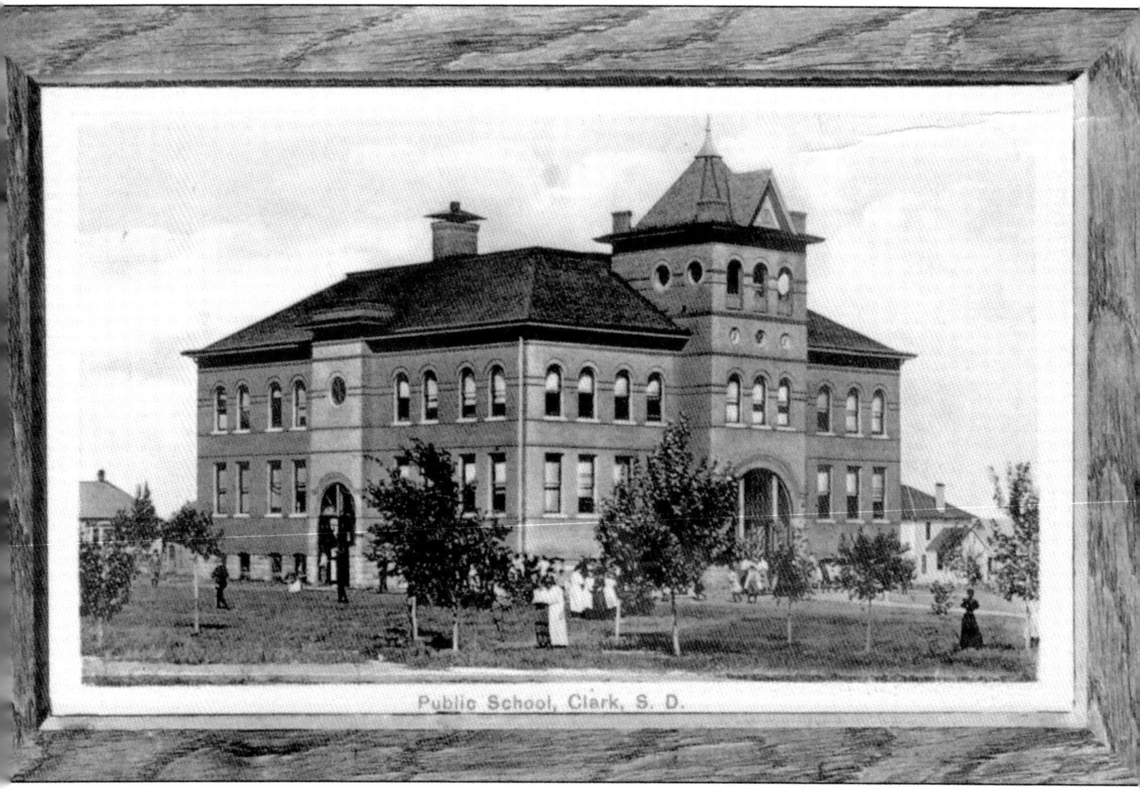

The author thought he would end the Clark section with this landmark building, the public school. This view was taken a few years after the construction in 1906, as the trees have a bit of growth to them. This is card number 2,733 and was also published by Bloom Brothers in Minneapolis.

Four

Naples and Vienna

Naples was established in 1888 and was named for Naples, Italy, by an Italian railroad worker. Some accounts also say that the Milwaukee Railroad officials may have named it for Naples, Italy, because of the Italian rail workers in the area. It was a very thriving town, although it never really had a large population. Only 175 to 200 people ever lived in Naples. Today, there are less than 25 residents, and there is no post office—it closed in 1971. The Naples Lutheran Church, Evangelical Lutheran Church in America (ELCA), just closed its doors in the last three years, after nearly 100 years of worship

The town of Vienna was started during the later part of 1887. Austrian immigrants whose hometown was Vienna, Austria, named the town Vienna. It is located in the northeast corner of Pleasant Township in Clark County. The Milwaukee Railroad was then in operation, the Great Northern Railway began operation during the year 1888. A town that was started on the Milwaukee Railroad, named Kent, about one mile south of the present location of Vienna, was then moved to Vienna. The town site was laid out on the H. D. Butler property. Two people of much interest inhabited Vienna, both were blind, Charles E. Keller and Chauncey Long. Keller wrote and published music in addition to being a piano tuner, and Long, who came from England, wrote poetry and lyrics to Keller's music. The author owns an original score of the song, "If the Kaiser Had His Way," published in Vienna, South Dakota, in 1918, by Keller and Long.

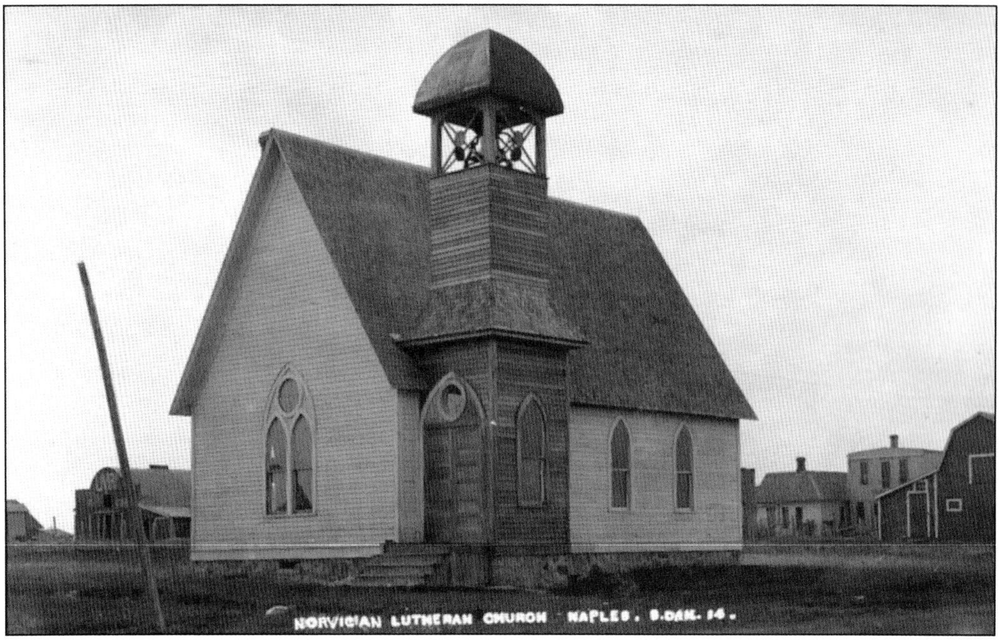

This card of the Norvigian (Norweigan) Lutheran Church in Naples, South Dakota, was sent from Naples, in 1909, to Maud Croker at Henry, South Dakota. The church still stands, now called the Naples Lutheran Church, although services are no longer held. It was built in 1906.

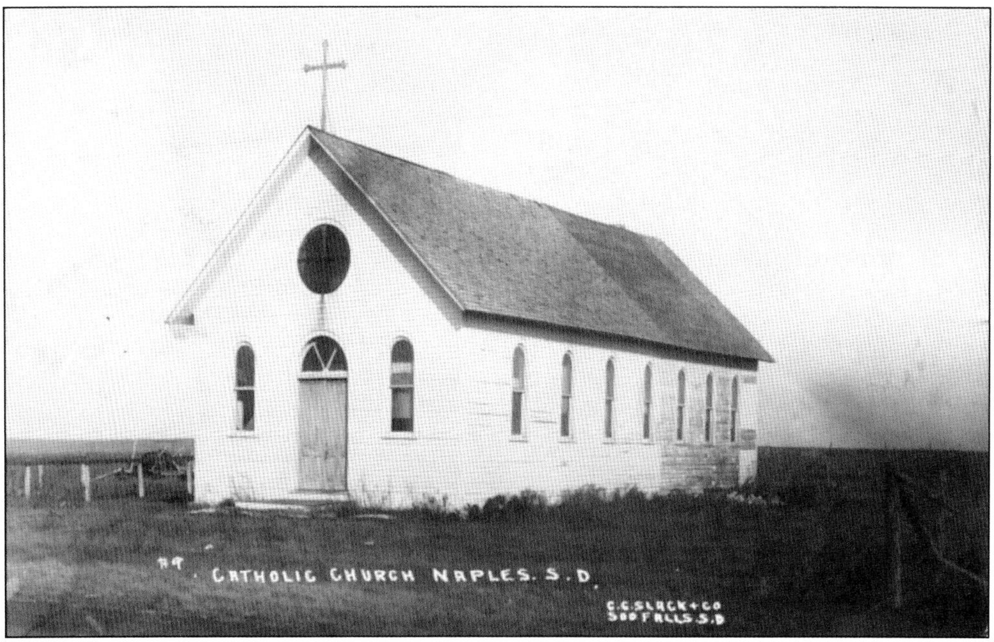

This postcard showing the Catholic church was mailed from Naples in 1919. The church was built in 1890 and was called St. Patrick's Catholic Church. It was added on to in 1904. The church was dismantled in 1930 by Joe Holida, even though it had closed in 1912. The cemetery, which is a quarter of a mile east of the original church location, still remains and is in the process of being refurbished.

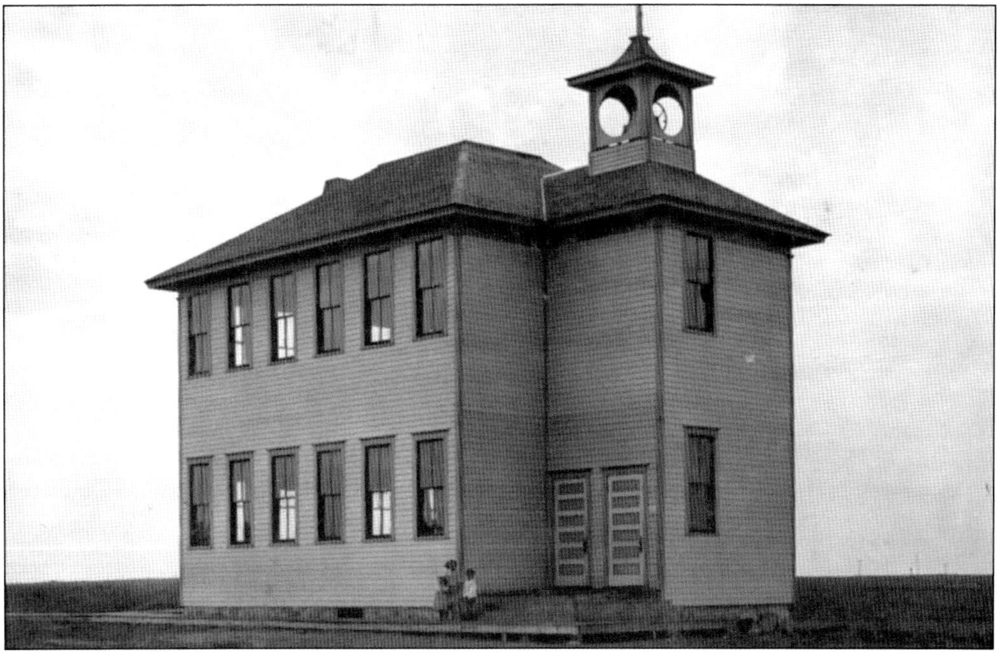

This view of the Naples School was taken shortly after the school was moved into town in 1907. It had been located a mile north of town, where it was built in 1884. This card has a Vienna postal cancellation from 1909.

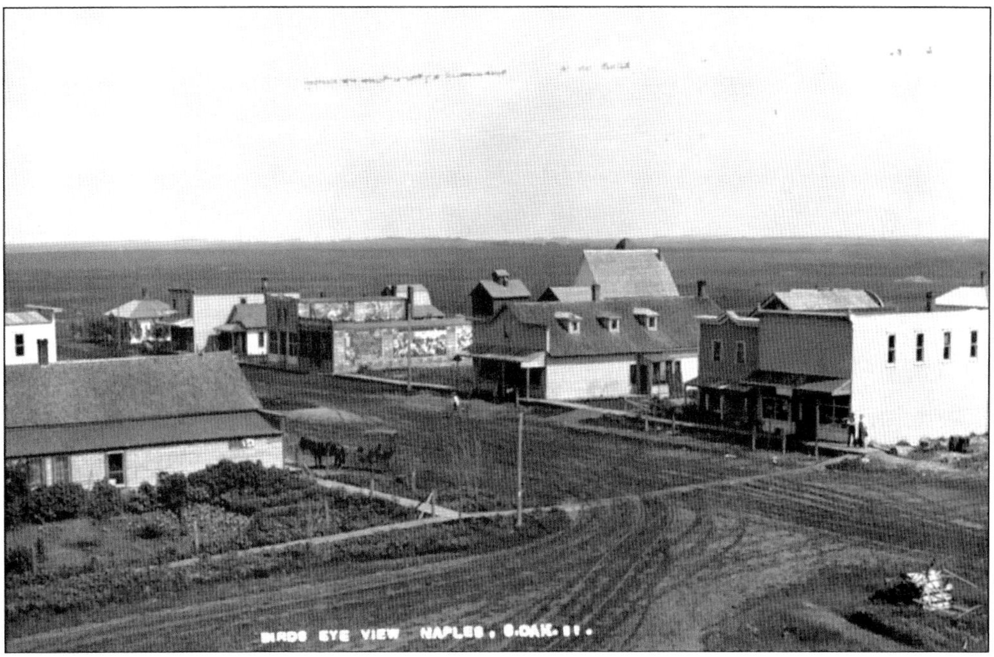

A bird's-eye view of Naples, taken about 1909, shows the post office building on the right corner. Also on Main Street was a hotel and café operated by Emery Blanchette, a barbershop, a lumberyard, and the Clark County Bank, built in 1905. Notice the circus advertisement on the side of the building in the middle of the card.

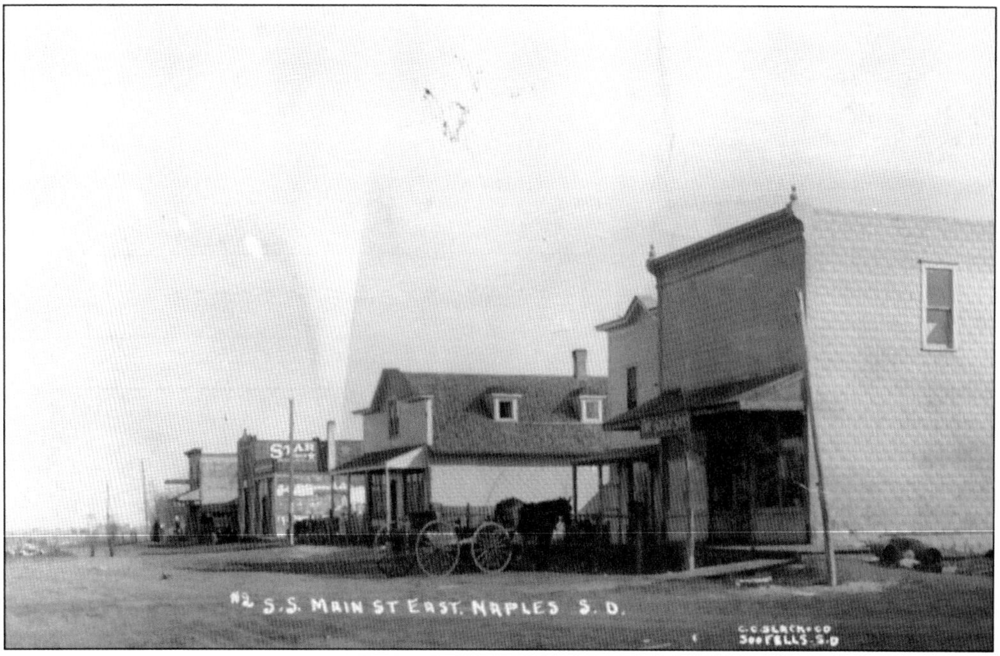

Here is another great view of downtown Naples, although this view is most likely prior to 1909, as evidenced by fewer buildings than the previous card. The horse and buggy are tied up outside the Foot-Schulze Shoes Store.

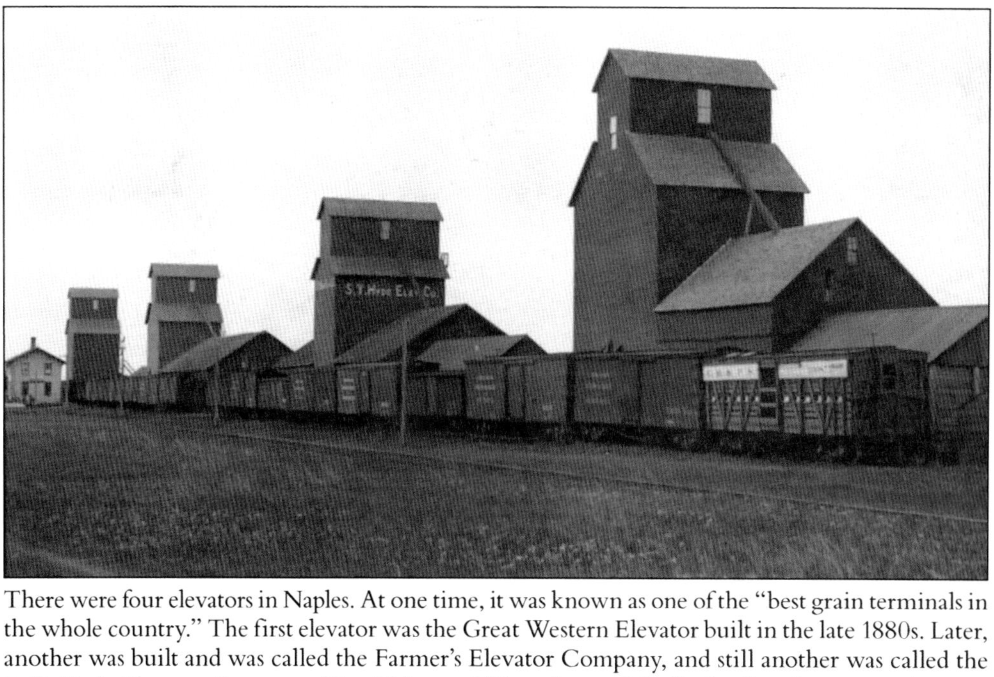

There were four elevators in Naples. At one time, it was known as one of the "best grain terminals in the whole country." The first elevator was the Great Western Elevator built in the late 1880s. Later, another was built and was called the Farmer's Elevator Company, and still another was called the S. Y. Hyde Elevator Company. The Chicago, Milwaukee and St. Paul railroad was prominent.

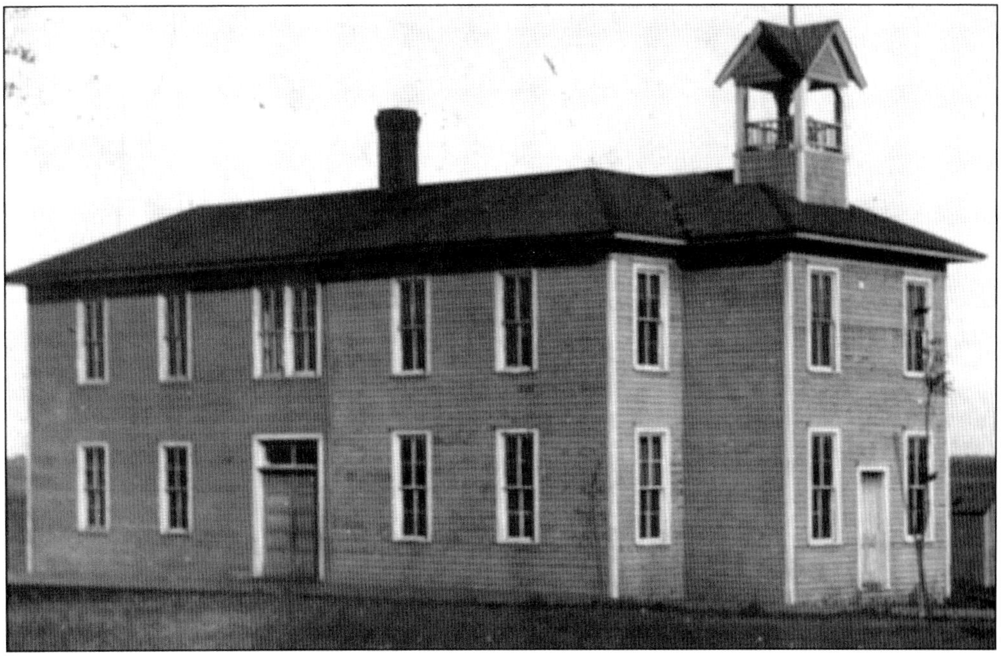

The Vienna school district was organized in 1893. In September 1893, the above building began construction; it was a two-story frame structure with the upper story being used for the Modern Woodman Lodge for a year or two. After that, the upper rooms were furnished for school. This facility served well for over 20 years.

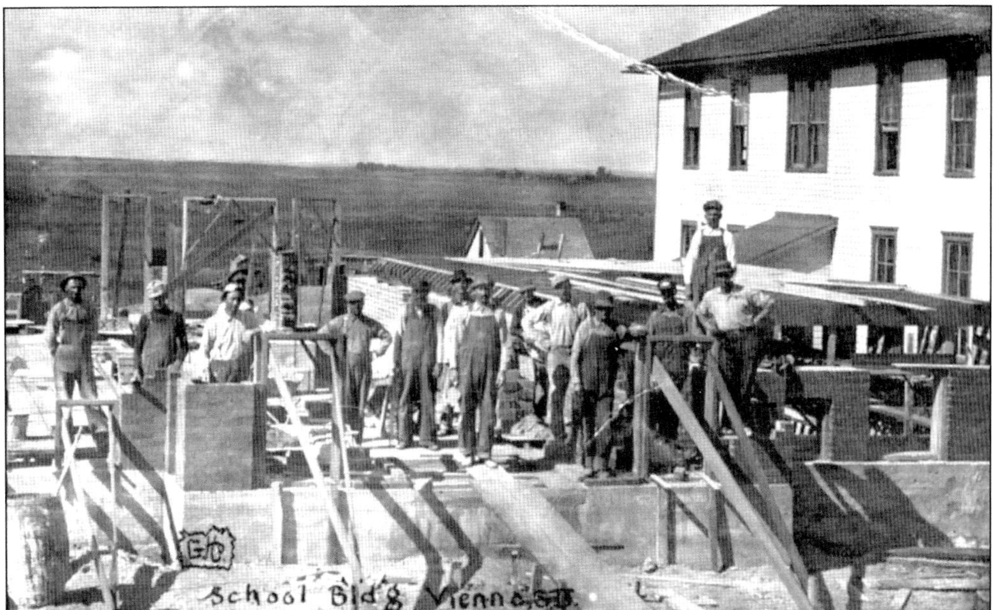

In 1914, a new brick building was constructed next to the first school building and this card clearly depicts that construction. It was postmarked from Vienna on September 30, 1914, and was sent to Mrs. S. Bertilson in Watertown, South Dakota, and is signed, "SB."

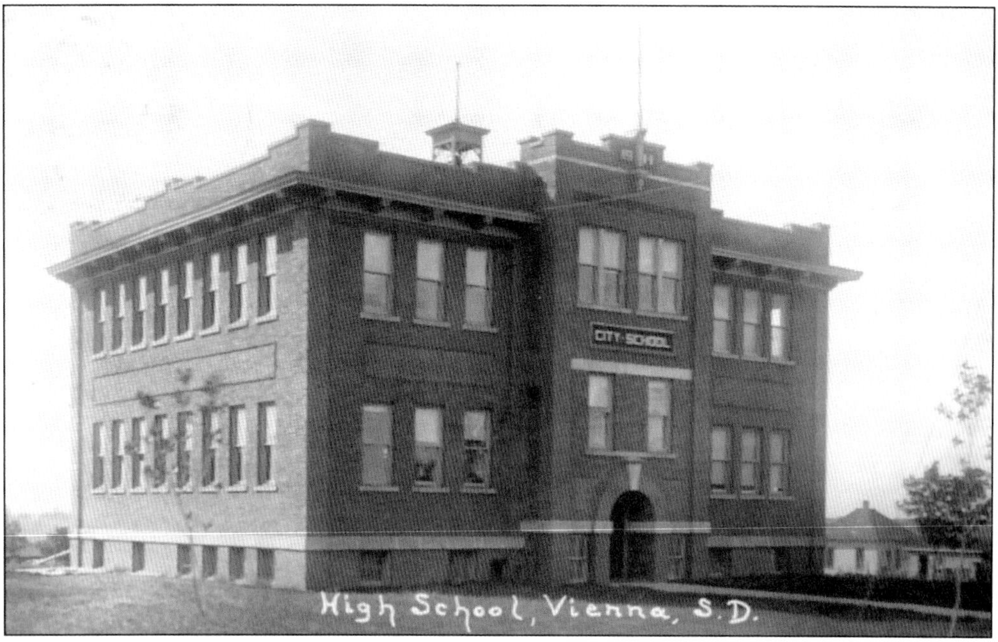

Here is a nice view of the finished school, a modern structure equipped with hot-water heat. Melvin Froke was the caretaker of the school building and prior building for 40 years. His children, Margaret (Froke) Hallberg and Lester "Sonny" Froke, often helped on Fridays after school, scrubbing blackboards and cleaning erasers. (Margaret told the author this story in 2005, at her 95th birthday coffee party.)

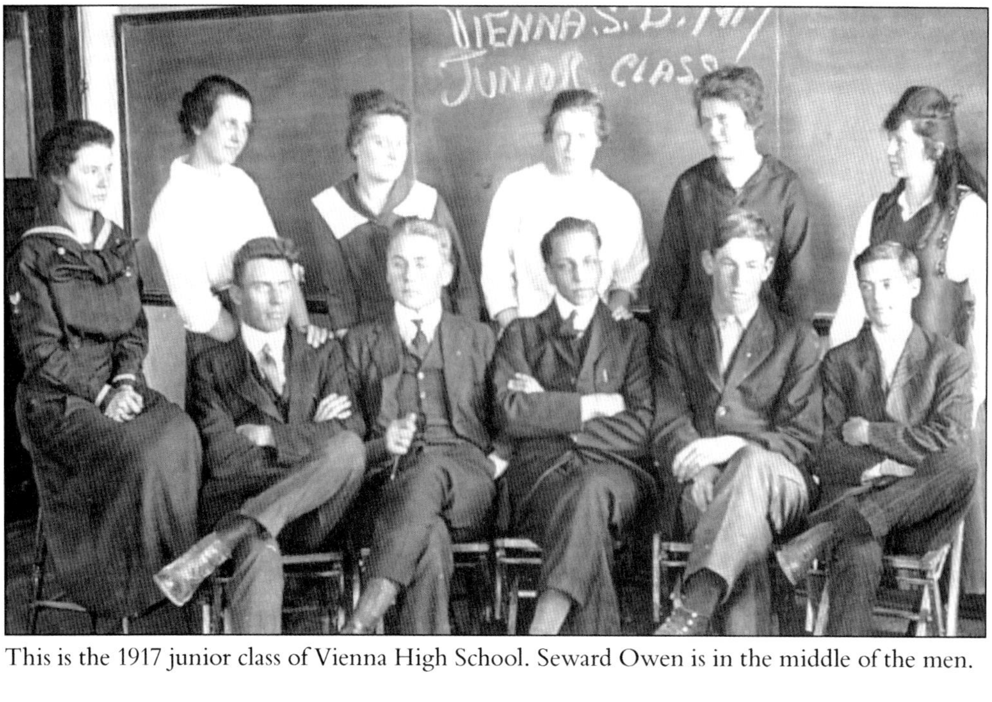

This is the 1917 junior class of Vienna High School. Seward Owen is in the middle of the men.

The Methodist Episcopal Church was the first church built in Vienna. It was built during the 1890s and stood near the northeast end of Main Street. The church later became the Congregational church.

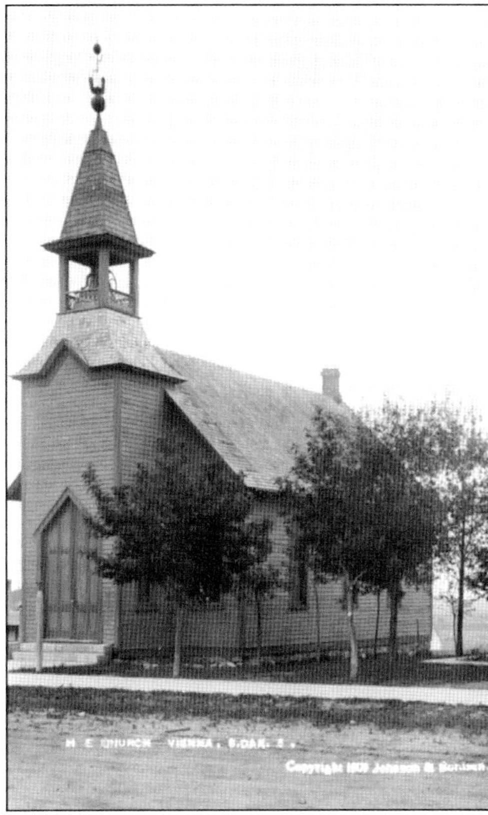

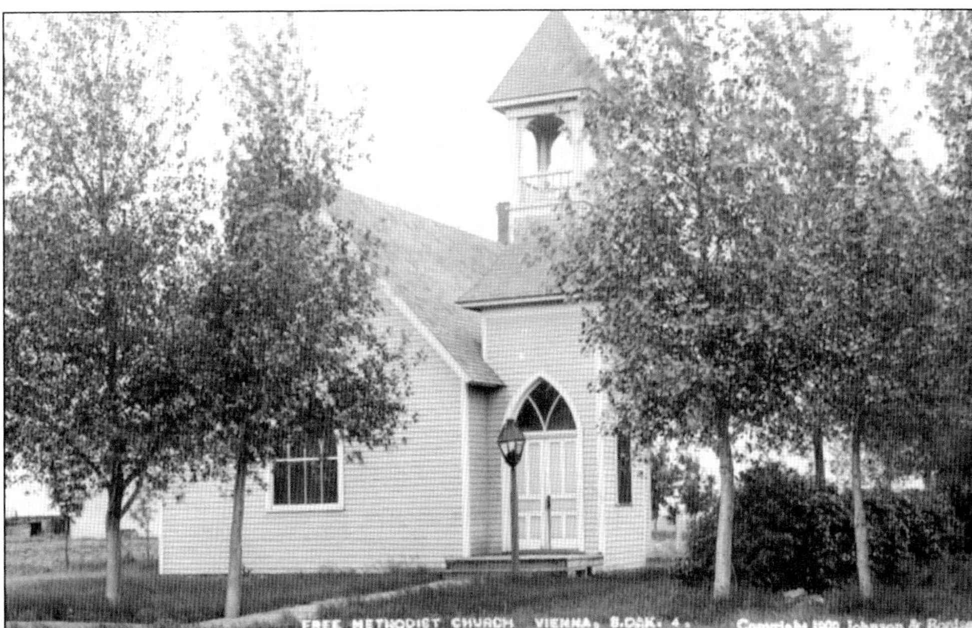

The Free Methodist Church was built in 1906 and was located on Milwaukee Avenue in the eastern part of Vienna.

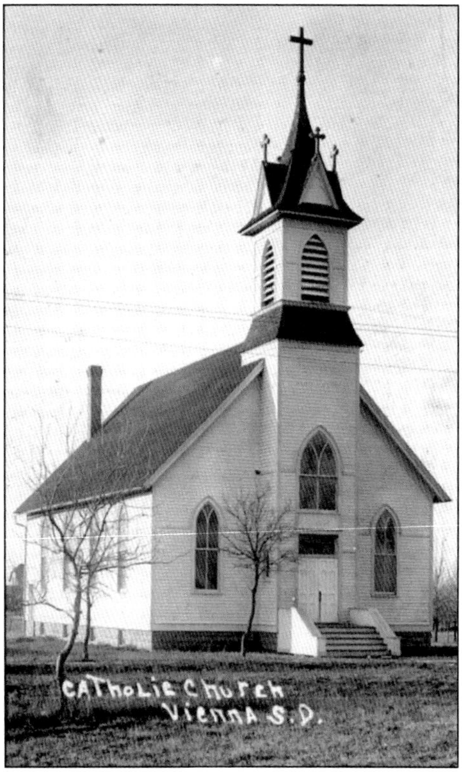

Built in 1911, the Catholic church was located in west Vienna. In the mid 1950s, the church discontinued services and was moved to Bryant. It sat west of the present Lutheran church on the lot where Carl Gebhart built a home, which is also gone.

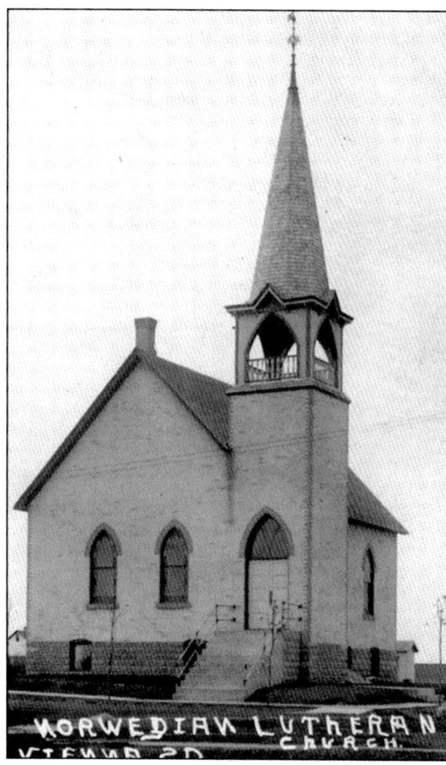

"This is the Norwegian church and it is the nicest church we have" is what is written on the backside of this real photo postcard. It was built in 1912 in the western part of Vienna and is a brick structure. Over the years, the building has had extensive remodeling and is still in use today, with services being held every Sunday.

What a beautiful card of the landmark building, the First National Bank of Vienna. The penmanship is even more remarkable. The postmark is from Vienna on July 30, 1908. Grace Johnson sent this card to a Bretzke's Studio in Brownsville, Wisconsin.

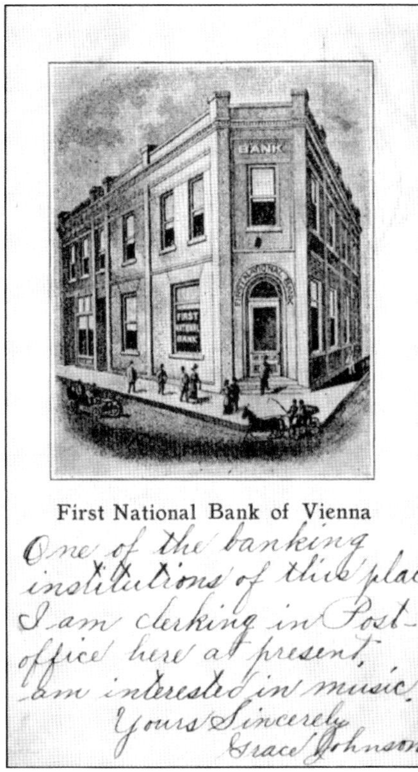

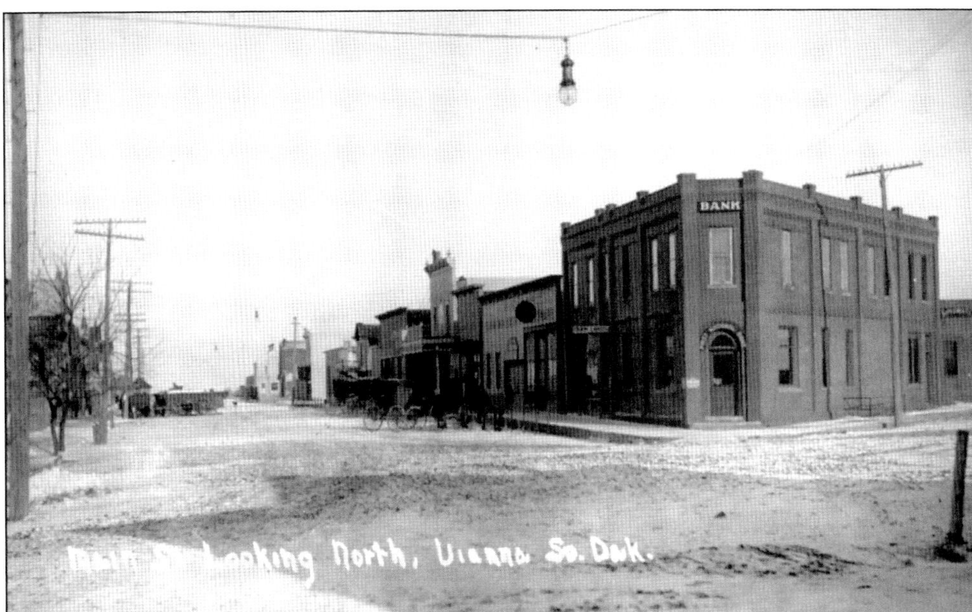

Notice the light bulb hanging in the intersection. This early view shows once again the triangular-shaped bank building on the corner; next to it is the J. M. Heher Hardware and Implement building. This must have been taken in early winter as evidenced by the lack of leaves on the trees and snow under them, yet people are in town with horses and buggies, not sleighs.

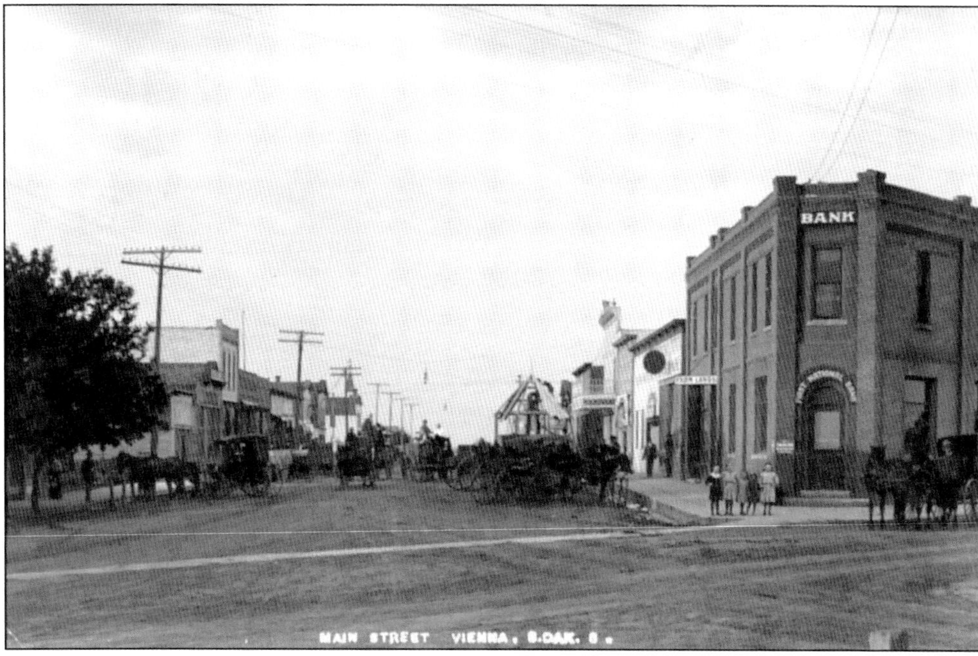

Shown here is a busy day in downtown Vienna around 1911, which was the most progressive and prosperous period for the town. Overhead streetlights lined Main Street and Drs. Staley and McNamara both had offices in the upstairs of the bank building.

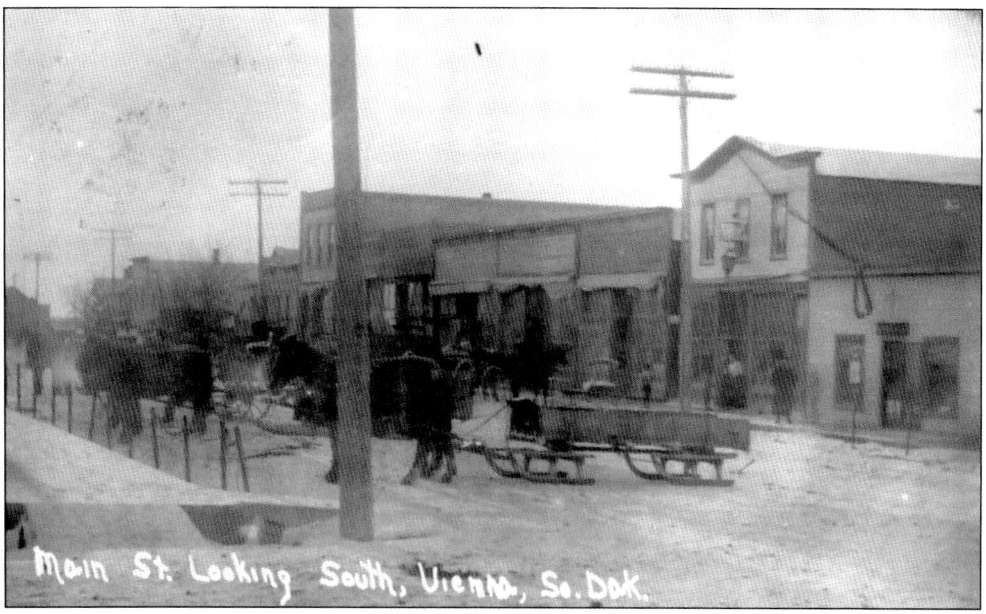

The west side of Main Street included the following businesses: a lumberyard at the far north end, the Rierson home, the Foss rooming house, a printing office, Eggen Hardware, Oaks and Rosegren Land Office, Hoffman Hall, a saloon and pool hall, G. M. Eggen Meat Market, Engen Store, and Jens Eggen Real Estate. The first six businesses (from the right to the left) were destroyed in a fire in December 1913. (Identification courtesy of 1976 Clark County Courier Bernice Elisa Kirkeby.)

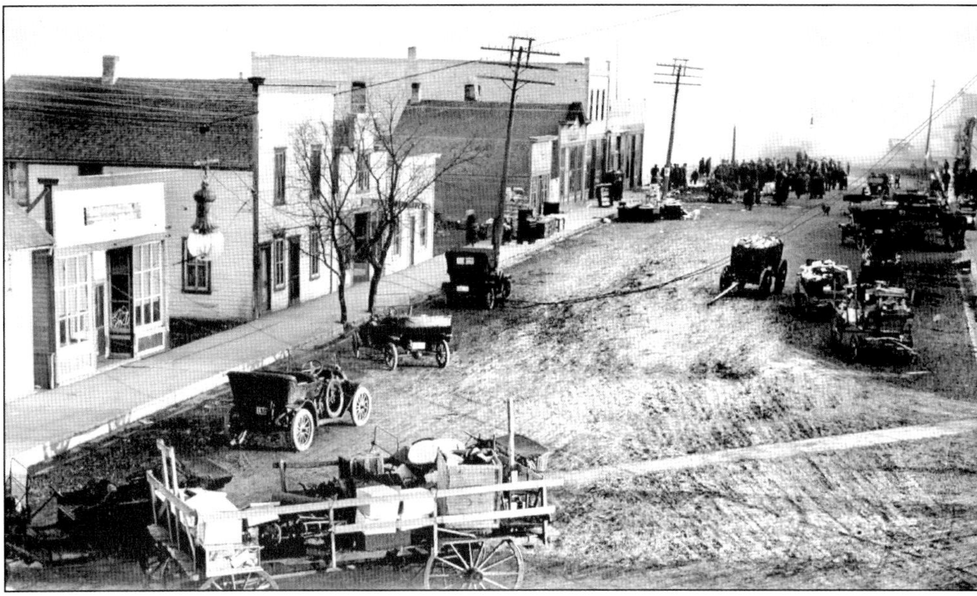

The fire on the northwest end of Main Street on December 13, 1913, destroyed six business buildings. It certainly was a distinct setback to Vienna. Sarah Seim wrote this card in Norwegian, and it was sent to Iowa in 1914.

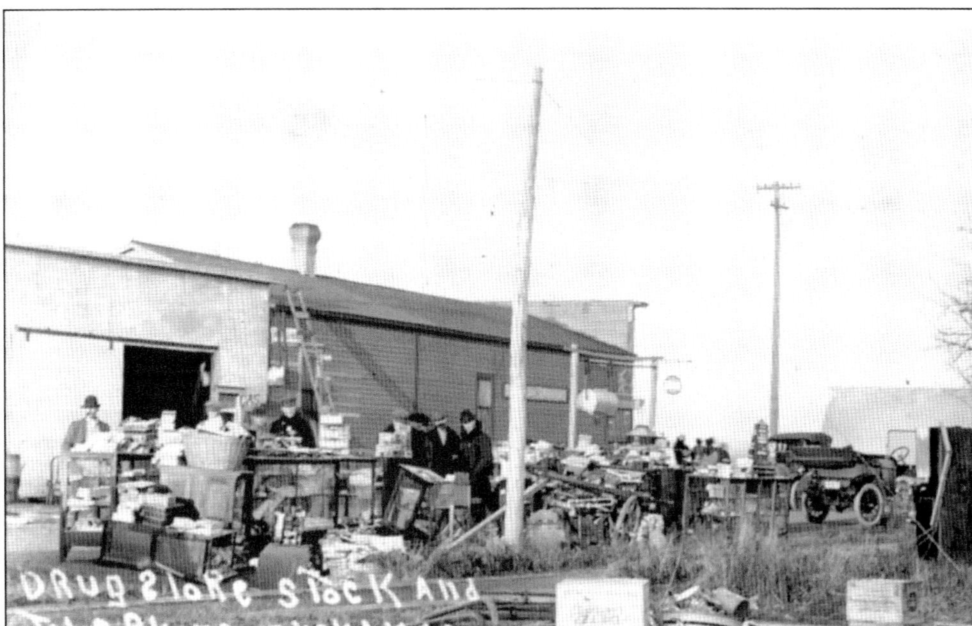

The Drug Store stock and Telephone Exchange items were set aside after a 1913 fire. The author owns an eight-foot oak display case that could be the one in the picture, as it did come from Vienna. Oh the history in these postcards! The author wishes he had the case of Dietz lanterns sitting on the ground.

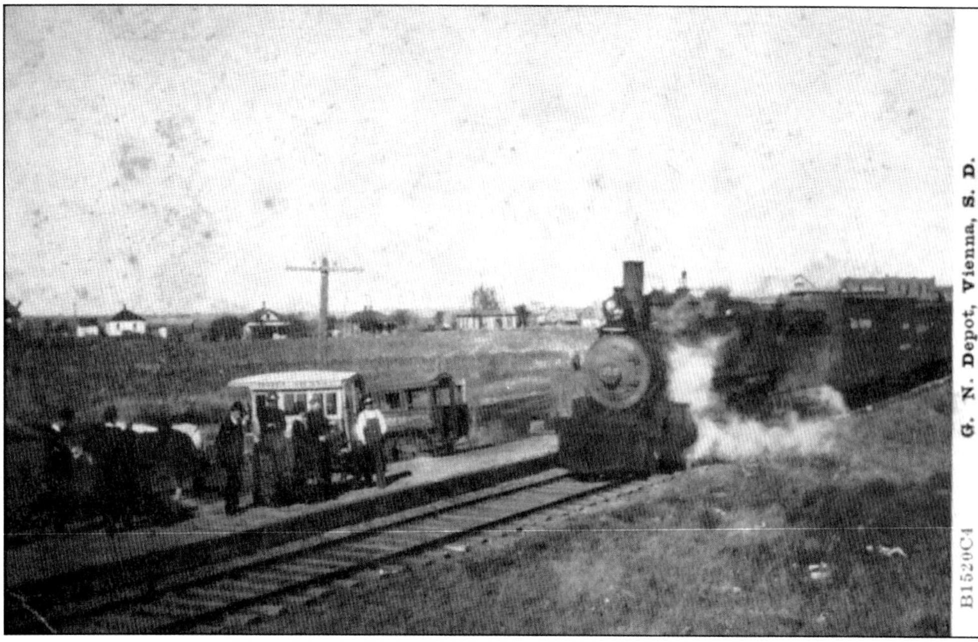

The Great Northern Depot was completed, and trains started running through Vienna in 1888. This is a postcard published by Zimmerman and Company in Chicago and shows the hotel taxis waiting for the arrival of the passenger train. The wagon says Hotel Vienna with the team of horses ready to go.

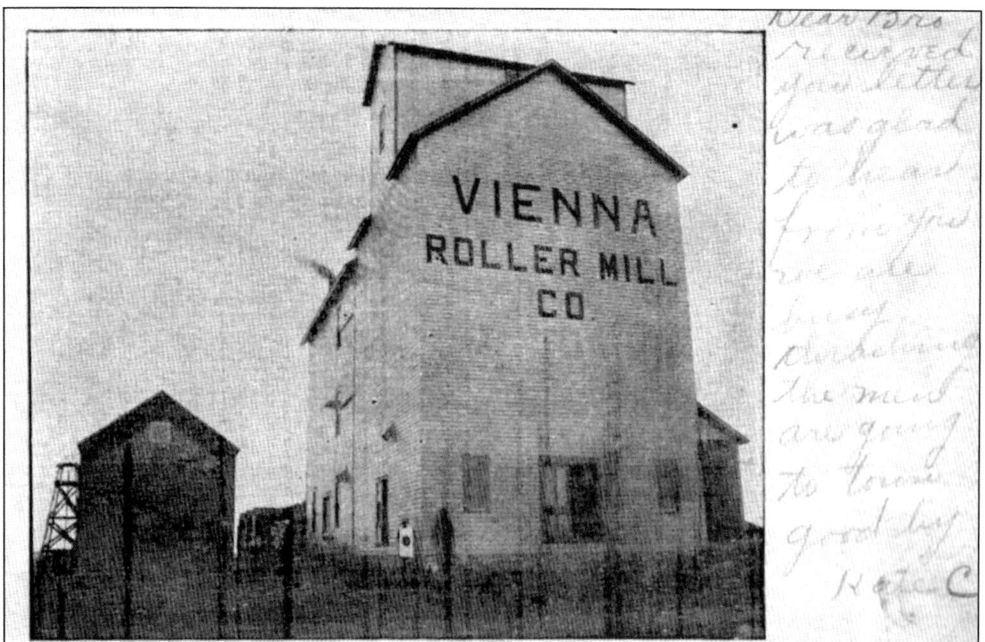

This undivided back card, sent from Vienna on September 5, 1907, shows the Roller Mill Company. It was a large flour mill built in 1901 in Vienna.

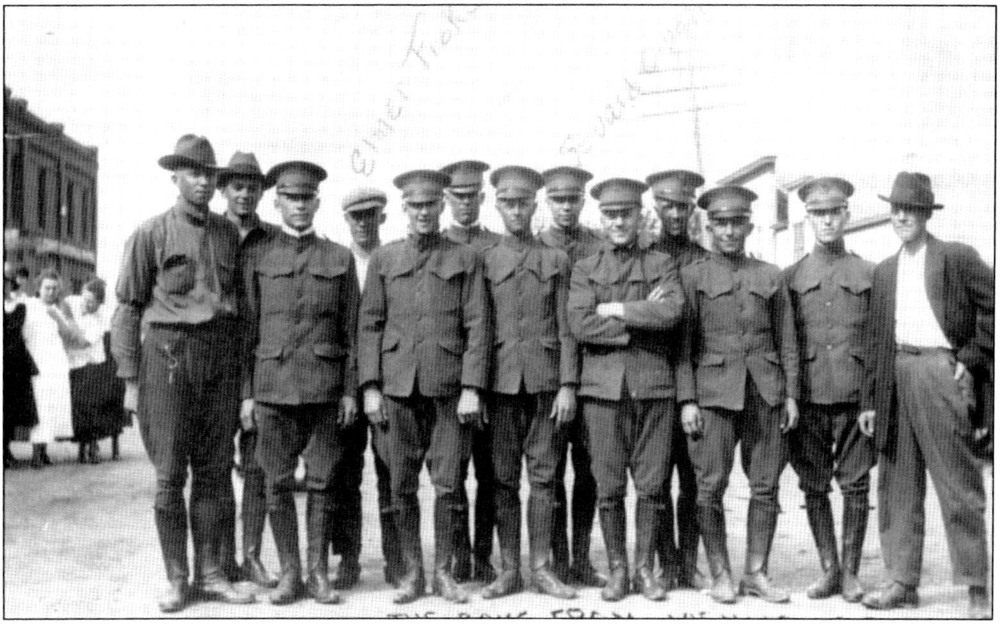

Shown here are "The Boys from Vienna, SD." This Cook-Montgomery postcard, published in Minneapolis, shows the young men that were enlisted in the 1st South Dakota Calvary, except for Elmer Froke. Seward Owen was in high school at the time. After war was declared in 1917, he had to finish school when he returned from the service. (Courtesy of Margaret Hallberg.)

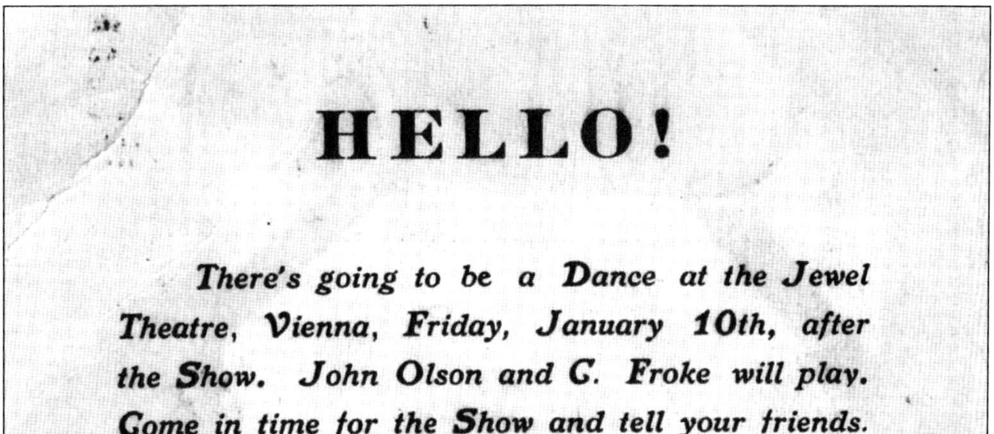

The "Dance at the Jewel Theatre" in Vienna was on January 10, 1913. This card was mailed from Vienna on January 9, 1913, and was sent to Gust Vorseth in Vienna.

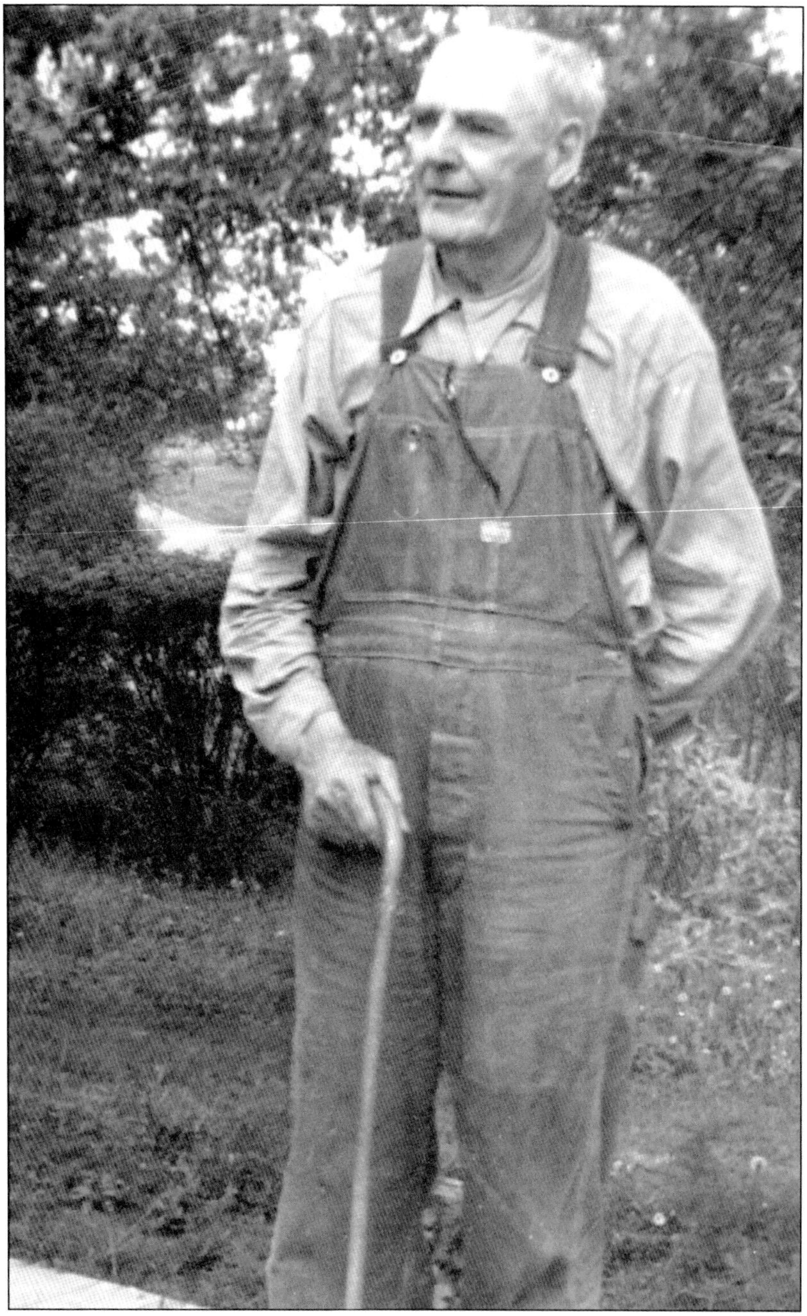

Chauncey Long of Vienna was known for many things around town, although most did not know that he was poet. The author has visited with Mel Hamre and Margaret Hallberg, both now living in Clark. They remember Long well from when they lived in Vienna back in the 1930s. He was a private man that came to the Vienna area by train between 1910 and 1911 from the east coast. He had immigrated to the United States from England and was blind. The dust from years of sandblasting may have caused his blindness. He died in 1951. At least one of his poems was published in *Pasque Petals*, a booklet featuring South Dakota poetry authors. (Information courtesy of Margaret Hallberg.)

Five

Willow Lake, Melham, and Carpenter

The town of Willow Lake was platted on the northeast side of the lake in 1884, and for 10 years or so, was known by the plural form, Willow Lakes, although the post office name was officially Willow Lake. The town gradually conformed to that of the post office, although there are still old timers of the area that refer to the town as Willow Lakes. In the fall of 1887, the town was moved to the north half section of Collins Township. The Dexter Creek flows through the town. It is said that the creek was named in 1882 by J. C. Berry for a horse that he owned who was named Dexter. A tremendous cyclone hit on August 20, 1904, and it took 15 years to rebuild. Willow Lake was ready for the Roaring Twenties.

Melham was founded in 1910 and was named after John Melham of Watertown. Before the post office was granted the present name, the town had been named Collinsburg, Gallargerville, Bareville, Midway, Phelps, and Tango. The post office closed in 1932. Today, only a partial building stands where the town once stood, and remnants of the jail still exist.

Carpenter was founded in 1899 and was named for T. W. Carpenter, an agent in the land office in Watertown at the time the town was founded. He was a close friend of John C. Opsahl, the first postmaster of Carpenter. T. W. died while the residents were searching for a name for the newly settled town. Opsahl submitted the name of Carpenter to the post office department, and it was accepted.

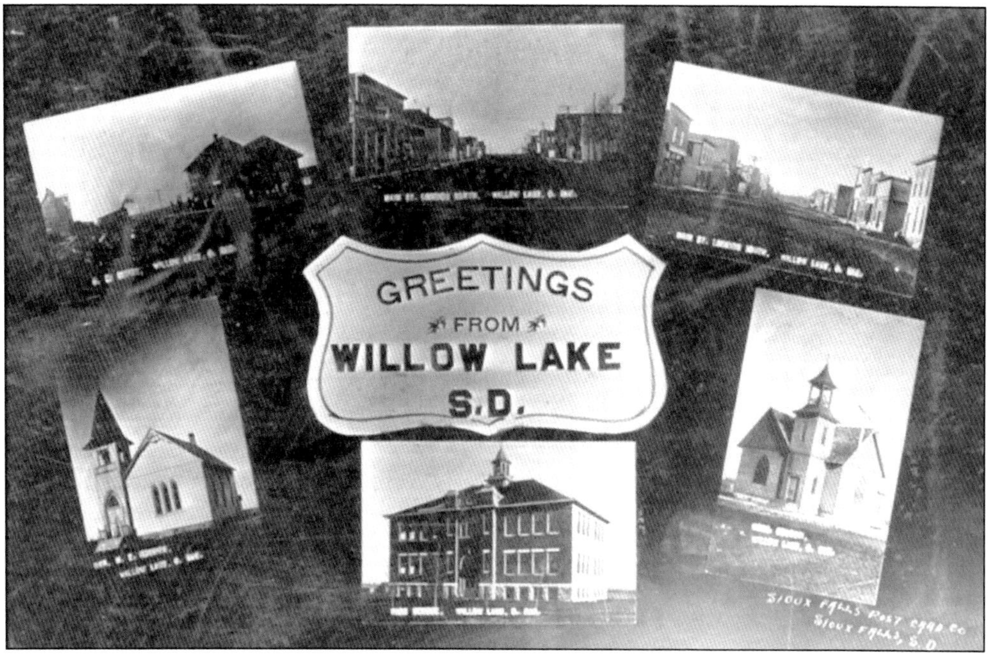

This six-scene "Greetings from Willow Lake" card shows the Great Northern Depot, Main Street in a view looking north, Main Street in a view looking south, the M. E. Church, the high school, and the Congregational church. It is dated on the back May 12, 1912.

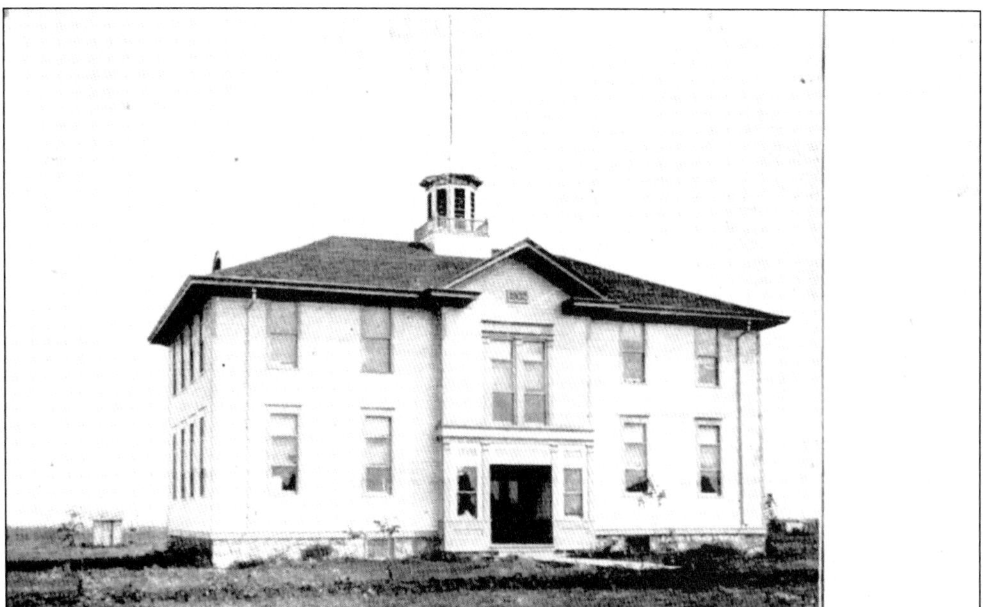

This undivided-back printed card is postmarked Willow Lake in 1908. It shows the schoolhouse in Willow Lake built between 1902 and 1903. It was destroyed by the cyclone in August 1904.

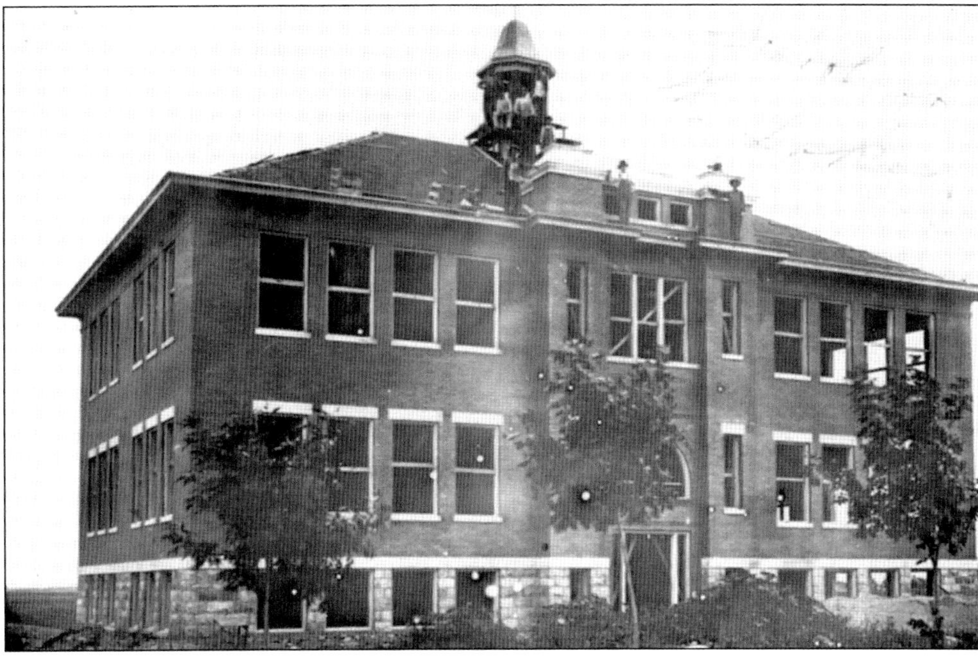

Bids were let in March 1909 on the brick schoolhouse built in Willow Lake by Gray Construction of Watertown. It opened in November 1909. This card shows a view during the construction and is postmarked from Willow Lake in August 1909.

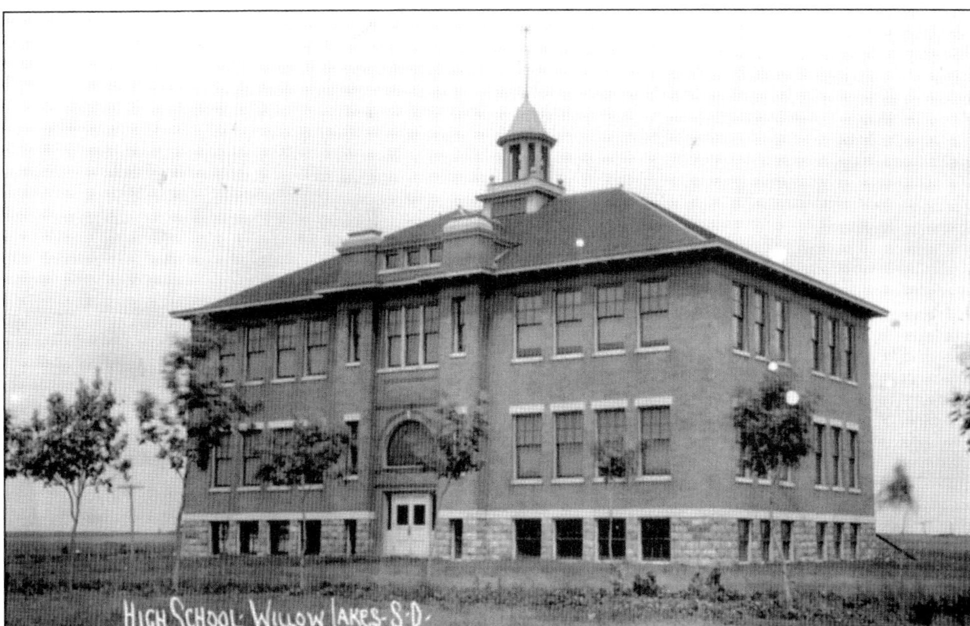

The high school in Willow Lake was a beautiful building after its completion in 1909. This view was taken after 100 trees were planted on the grounds in 1915.

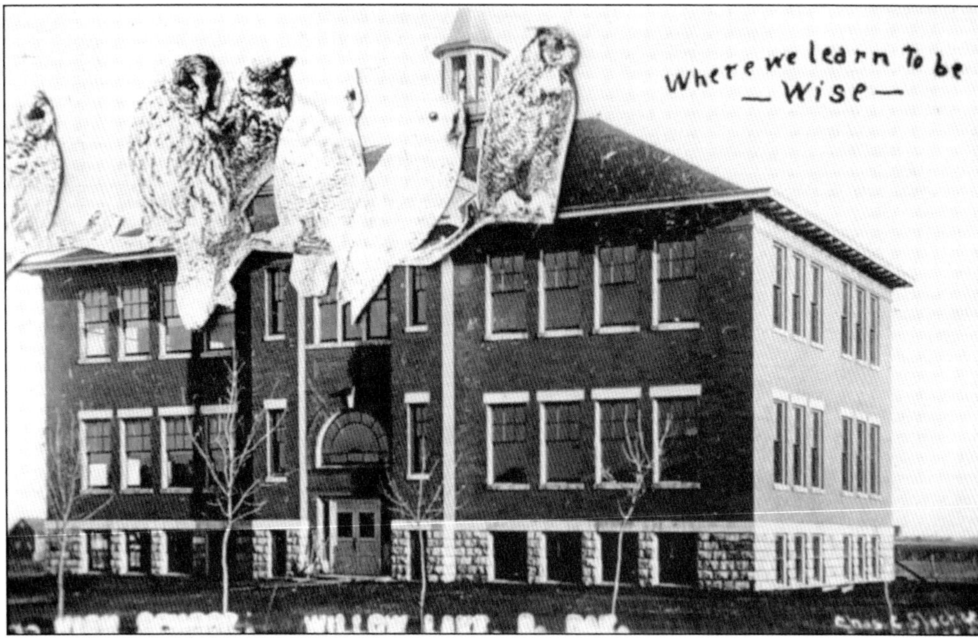

The author had to include this clever card with the superimposed owls. Postmarked in 1919 from Willow Lake, "Where we learn to be – wise –," it was sent to Winnie Reints in Forsten, Illinois.

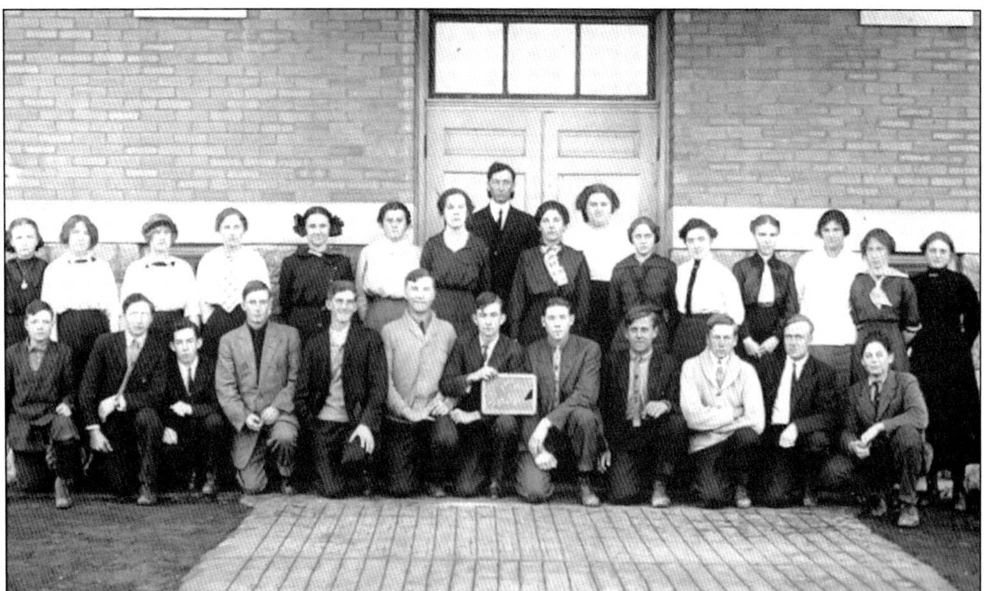

Willow Lake High School is shown here in 1914. Pictured from left to right are (first row) Horace Crawn, Paul Underwood, Robert Schmidt, Clarence Downs, Fred Downs, Wendell Johnson, Paul Millington, Lloyd Olson, Sidney Borgeson, Otto Disrud, Don Peck, and George Lord; (second row) Elsie Kuhnert, Beulah Forbes, Sylvia Borgeson, Odena Haug, Mary Johnson, Hazel Hanchett, Lavinia Olson, Minnie Meyer, Marjorie Peck, Mildred Howard, Alice Kuhnert, Cecil Pettit, Mary LaMont, and Emma Pautz; (third row) superintendent Charles Paul and principal Miss Huginin.

Bethlehem Lutheran Church in Hague Township was built in 1905. It was razed in the late 1990s. Some of the contents of the church are on display on the grounds at the Clark County Museum. The cemetery, which had been plotted in 1890, is maintained by the Willow Lake Evangelical Lutheran Church (WELS).

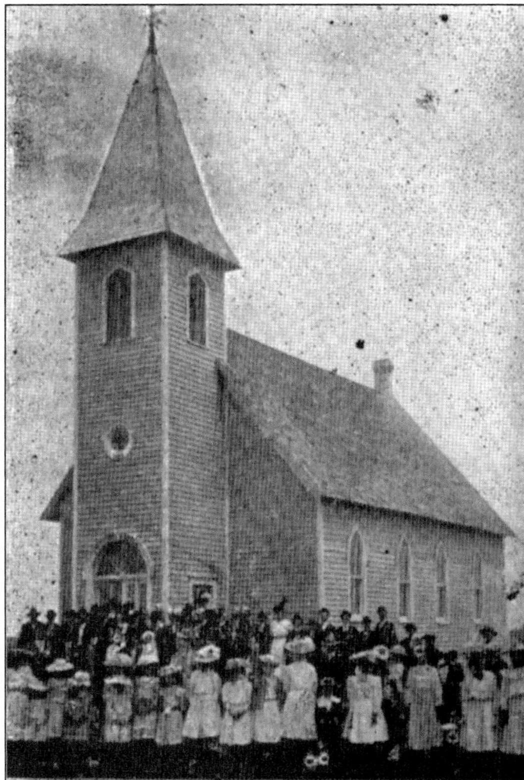

Bethlehems Kirche zu Hague,
Clark Co. S. Dakota.

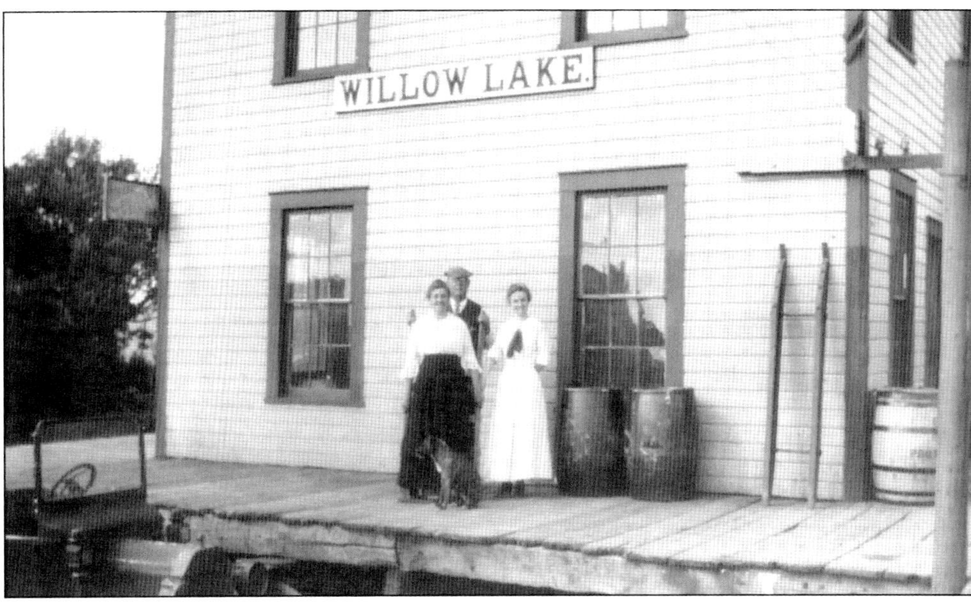

The Great Northern Railway Depot at Willow Lake is shown here.

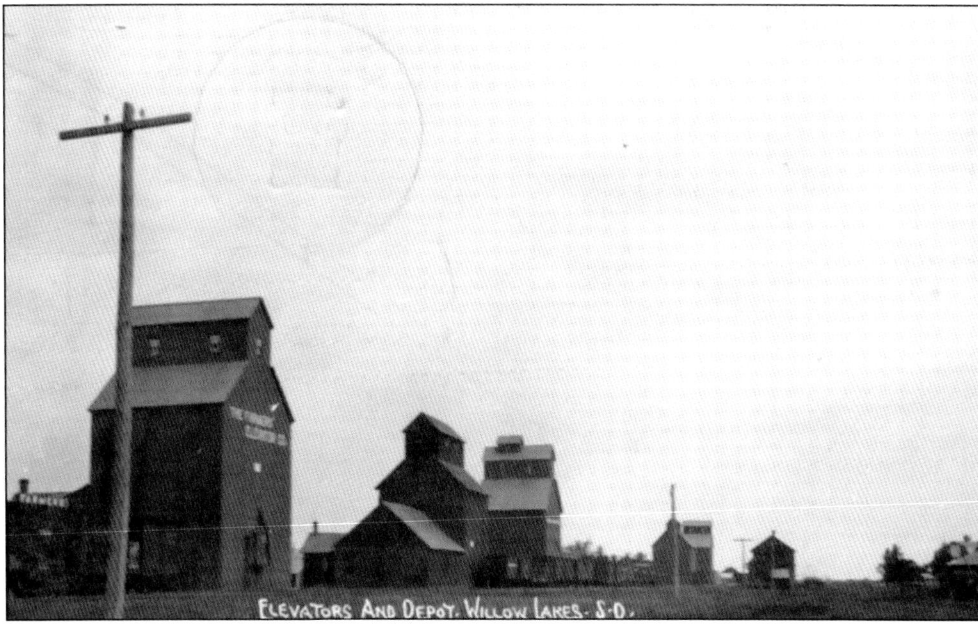

The grain elevators have always been a very important business in Willow Lake. This card shows five elevators and the depot. It is dated 1913, and is postmarked from Clark.

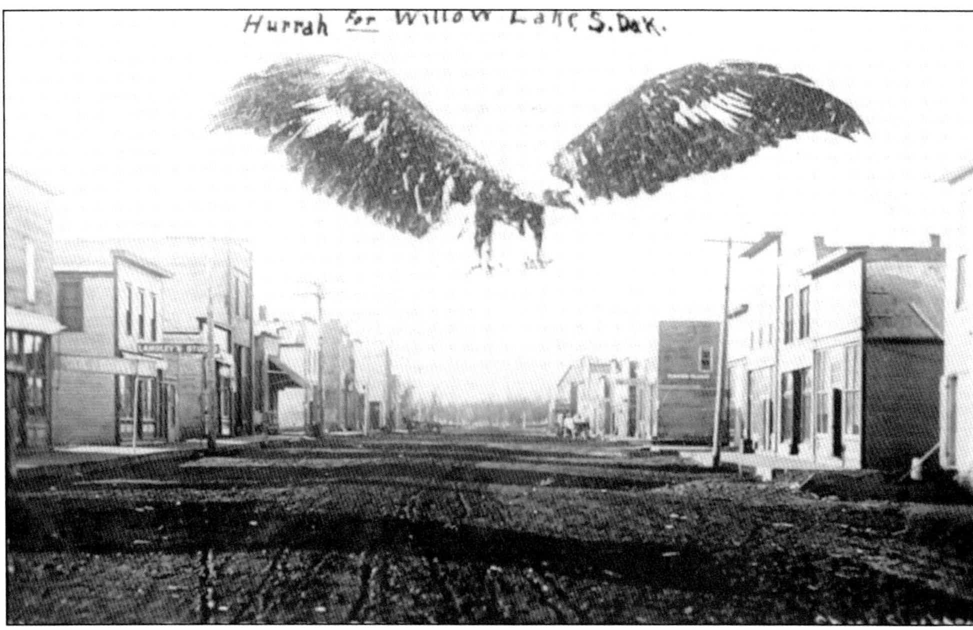

Another clever postcard from Willow Lake says "Hurrah for Willow Lake, SD." This view is looking south on Main Street with the eagle landing. Langley's Studio is on the left side. This card was sent by R. McPeek and states, "Perry has just left with a car of 20 cattle and 14 horses, thinks he will get their Saturday night."

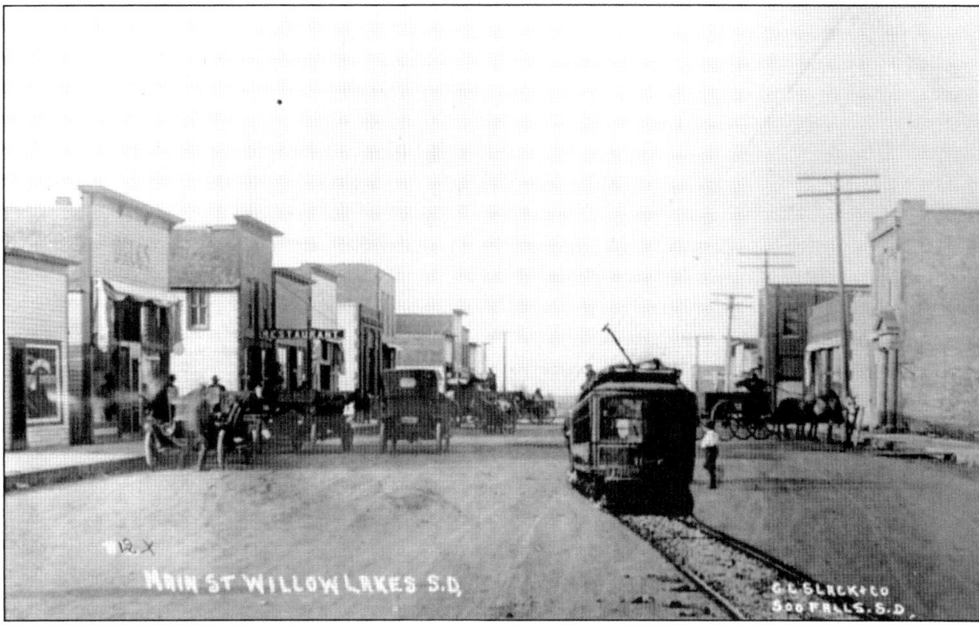

Gertrude wrote to Fred Weier in 1913, "I'll send a card to show how we travel in this town, Ha Ha! I can ride on a street car as well as you." Another superimposed image is by Slack and Company of Soo (Sioux) Falls, South Dakota.

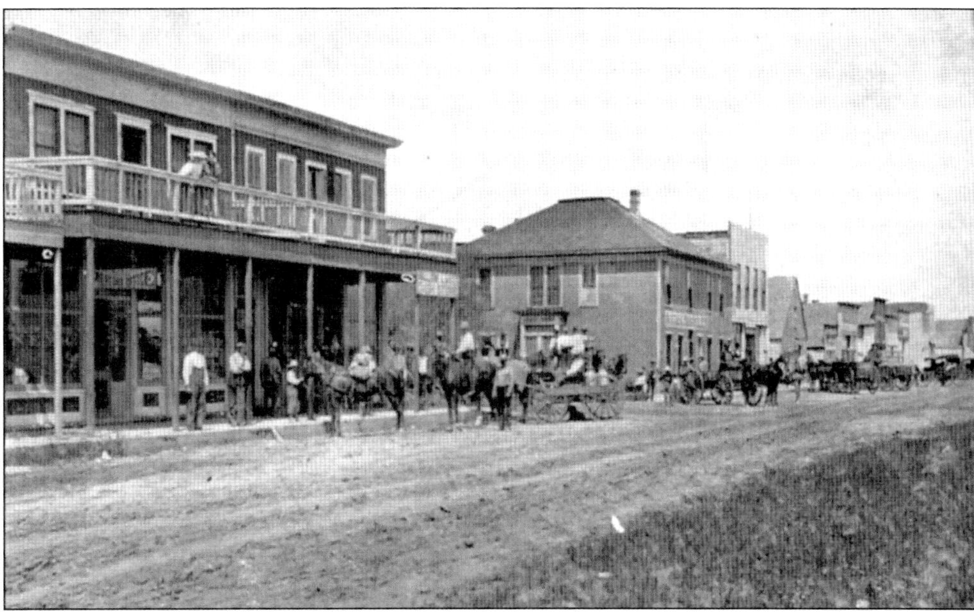

This unused, undivided-back postcard is from about 1907. The photograph was taken near the intersection of Garfield and Second Streets at the north end of the two-level building that housed the Willow Lakes Cash Store, and the Willow Lakes News and Printing Office. The next building on the west side of Garfield Street was the Hotel Nicollet; it burned in 1910.

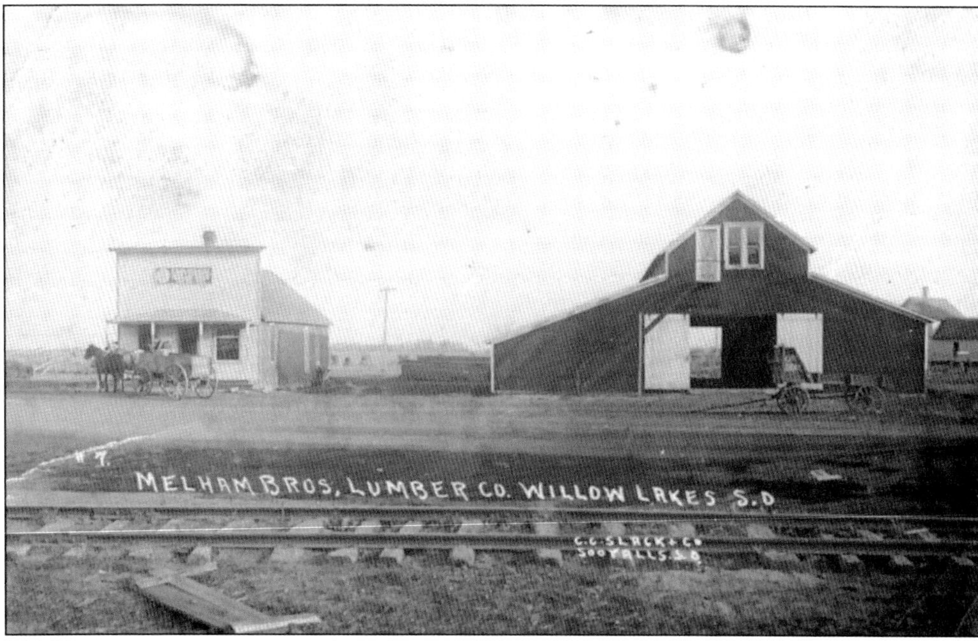

Melham Brothers Lumber Company at Willow Lakes must have sold Universal Portland Cement as stated on the sign in the middle of the building. The city dray line wagon must have already unloaded its freight. The lumberyard was located south of the tracks and next to Grant Street. This building still stands and is used by the elevator.

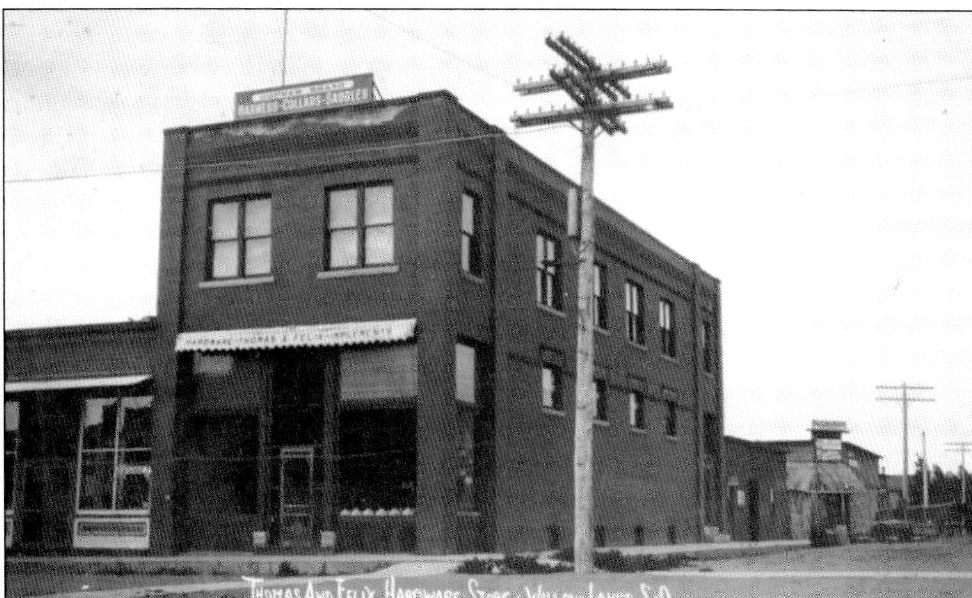

The Thomas and Felix Hardware Store was a prominent brick building, one of the first, built around 1909. It was home to the Gopher brand harnesses, collars, and saddles. It was known as a fine hardware store and implement dealer.

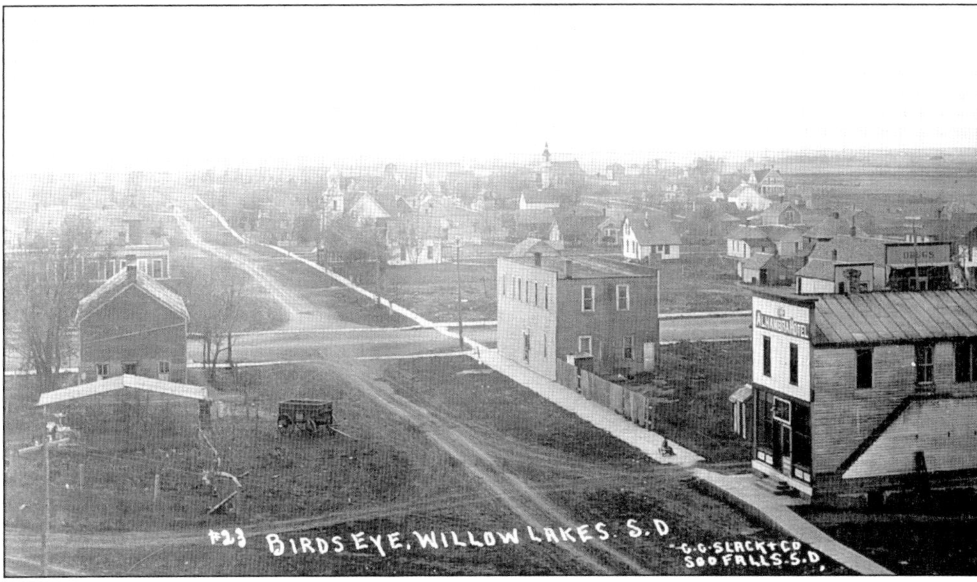

Willow Lake in 1912, in a view looking west on Second Street, shows the Alhambra Hotel in the foreground. The empty lot in the middle is where the Hotel Nicollet and Livery Barn stood; it burned in 1910.

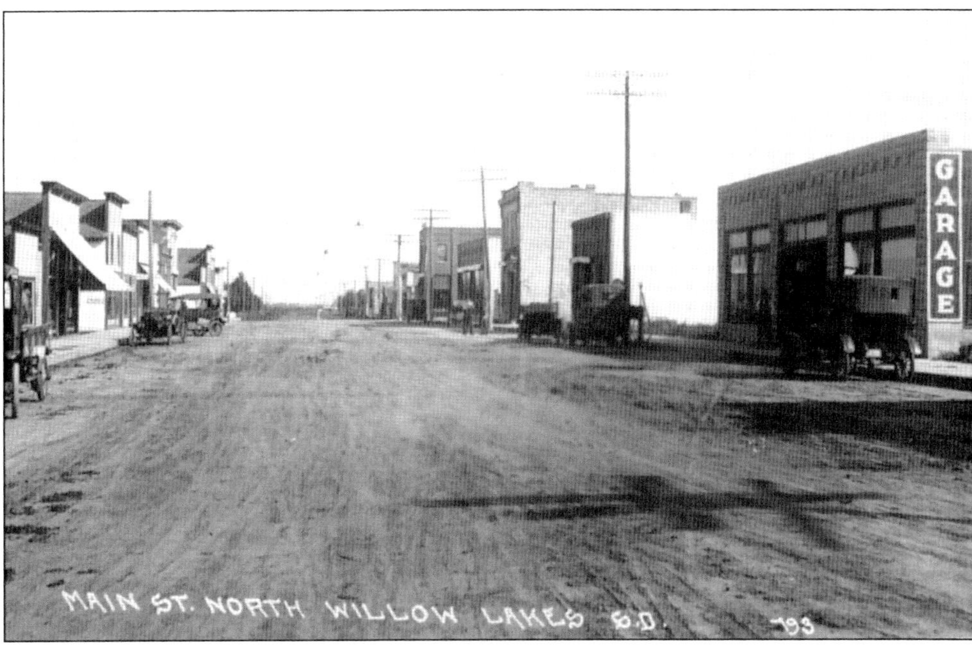

This postcard, published by Cook-Montgomery in Minneapolis, was taken after 1915, as evidenced by the electric poles. The lights went on in Willow Lake on November 9, 1915.

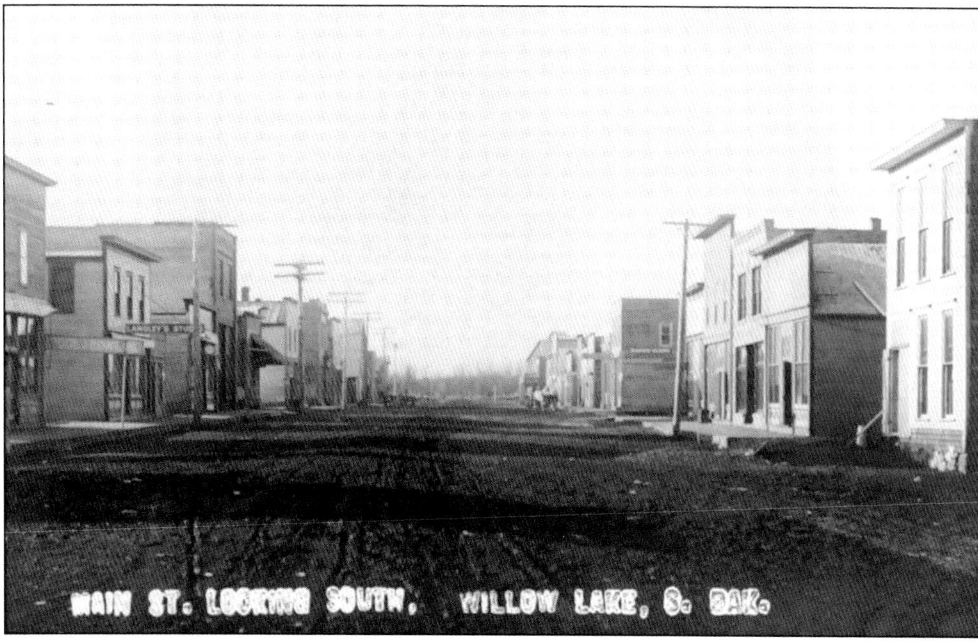

This is an earlier view of Main Street (Garfield) looking south. There are no lights hanging across the street, and it still appears to be a wooden sidewalk, but the hitching rails have been removed at the north end of town. There are still horses and buggies to the south. Langely's Studio is on the east side; note the sign for pool and bowl.

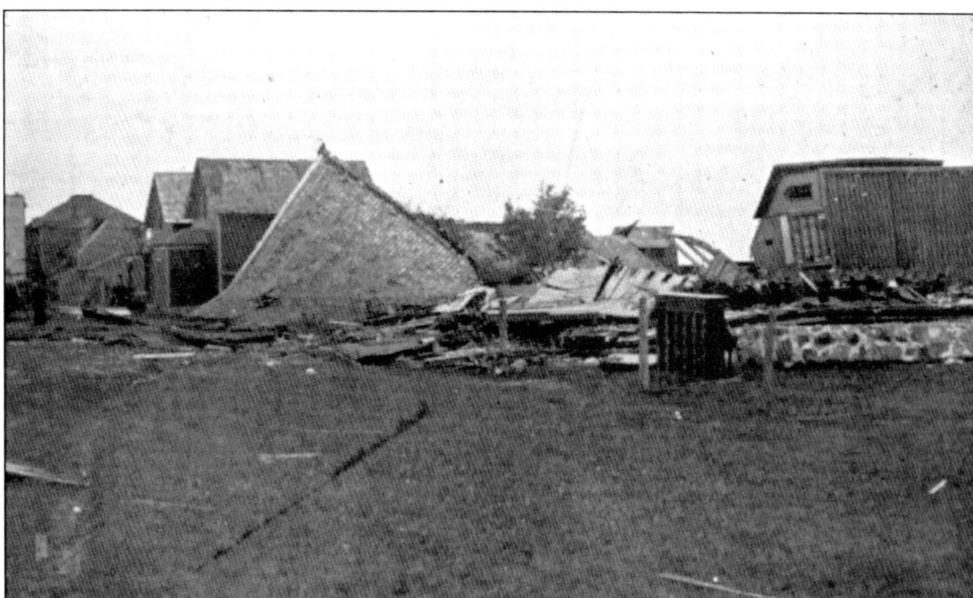

The Willow Lake section would be missing a huge part of its history if this postcard of the Willow Lakes cyclone, which happened on August 20, 1904, was not included. This natural disaster took three lives in the area, none were in the town of Willow Lake. The piano sits untouched in the foreground.

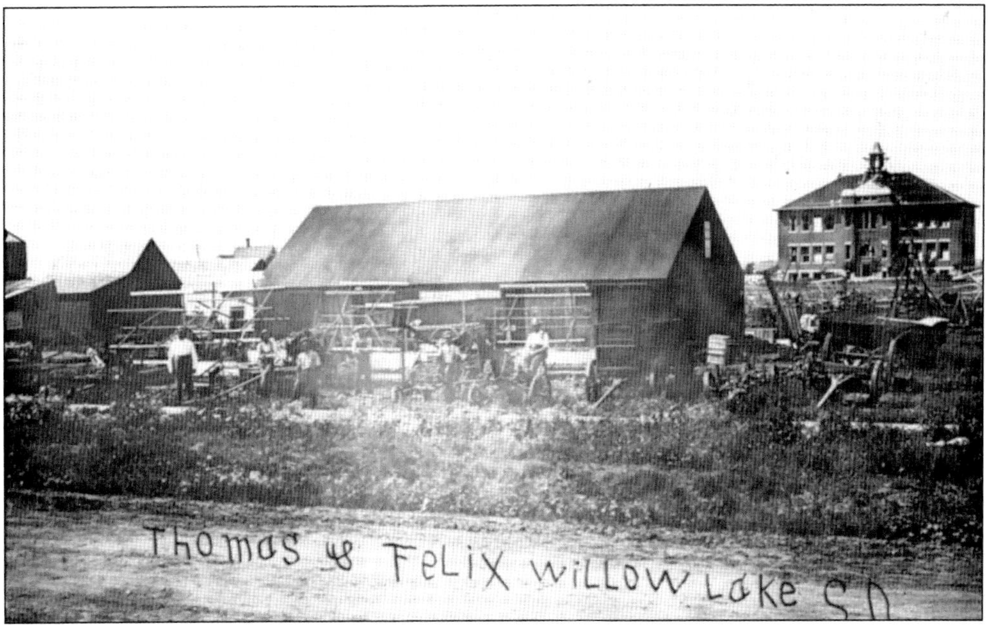

The Thomas and Felix Hardware Machinery lot is thought to have been behind Herman Meester's Implement Shop (to the north).

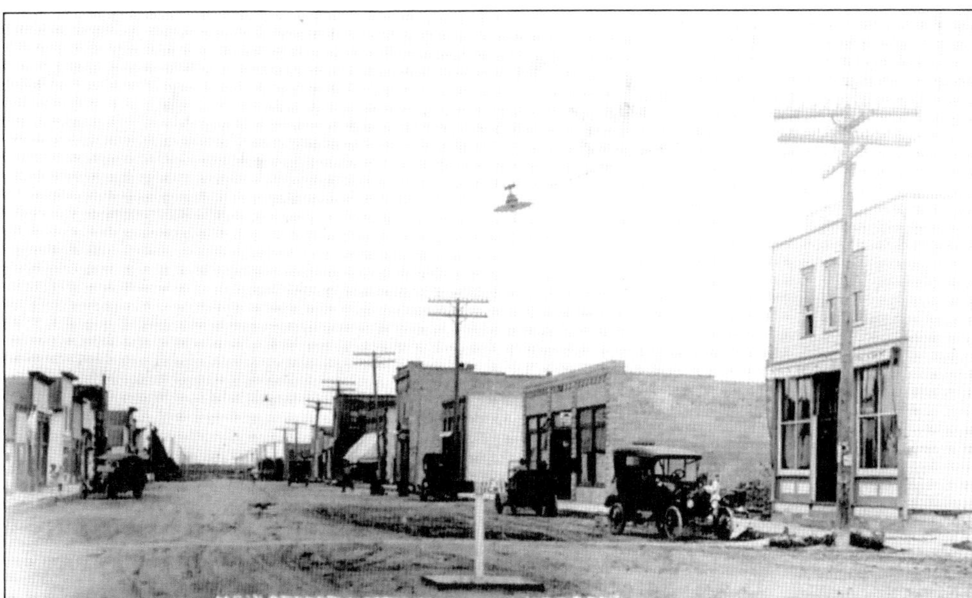

This printed card shows the Aaby Brothers Hardware building on the right side. It is postmarked from Willow Lake in 1917. (Courtesy of Mike Korbel.)

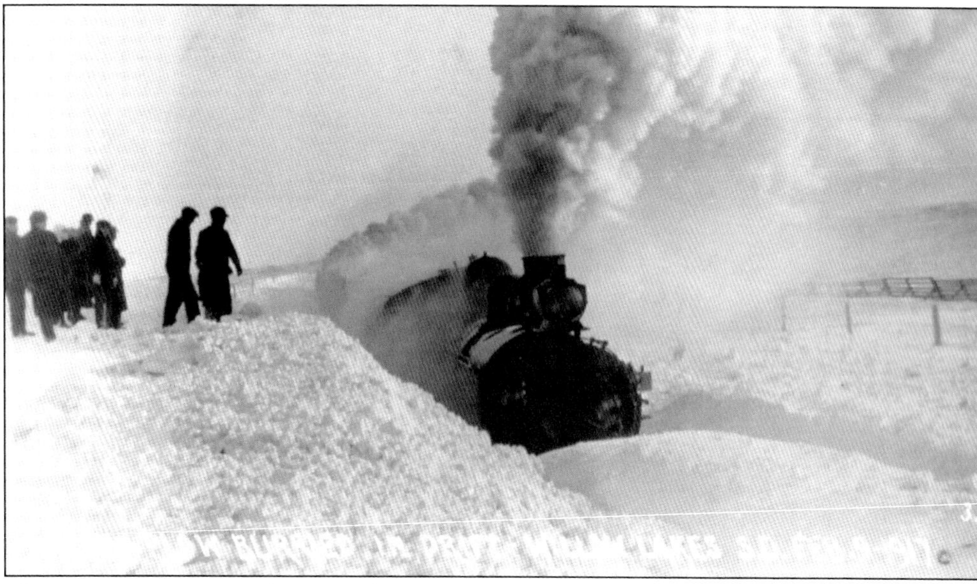

These two views were taken on February 9, 1917, east of Willow Lake, and shows the wedge plow buried in a drift and the crew that came to dig it out. Imagine the hours it took to get the train rolling again.

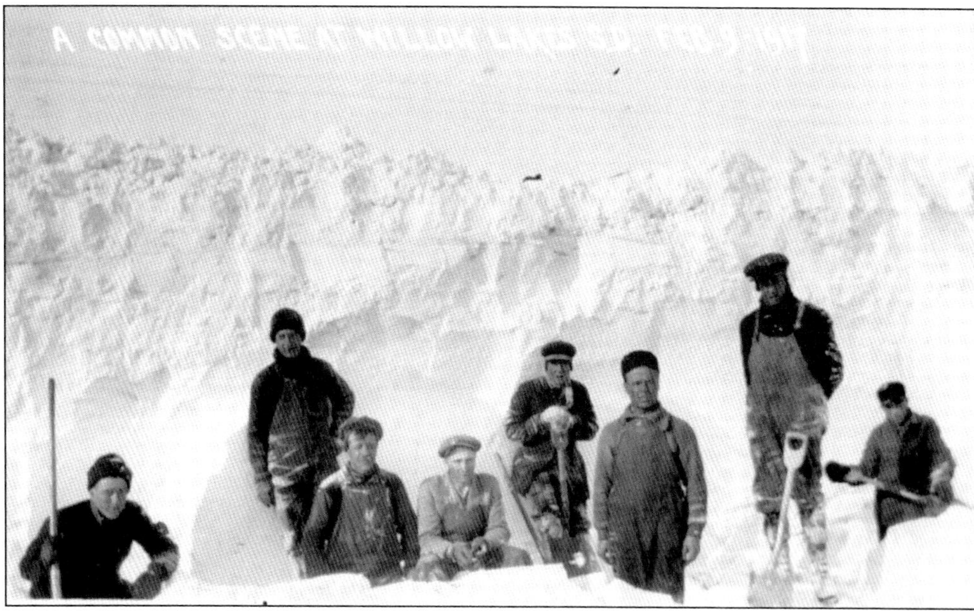

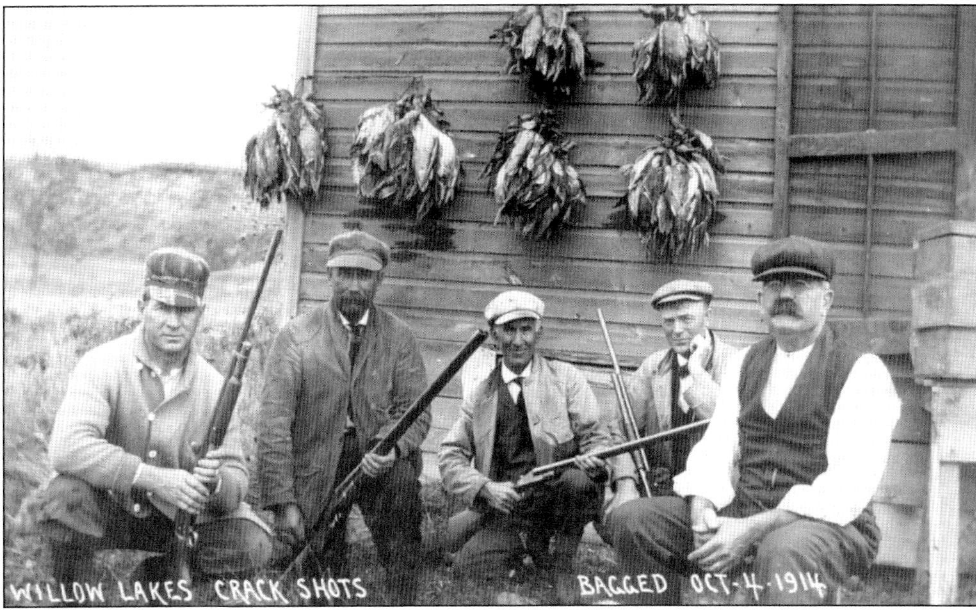

This group of hunters, "Willow Lakes Crack Shots," bagged (what was the limit?) on October 4, 1914, south of Willow Lake. The group consisted of, from left to right, William Michael, Jim Henry, Otto Schmidt, John Imlay, and Jake Bergstresser. (Courtesy of Mike Korbel.)

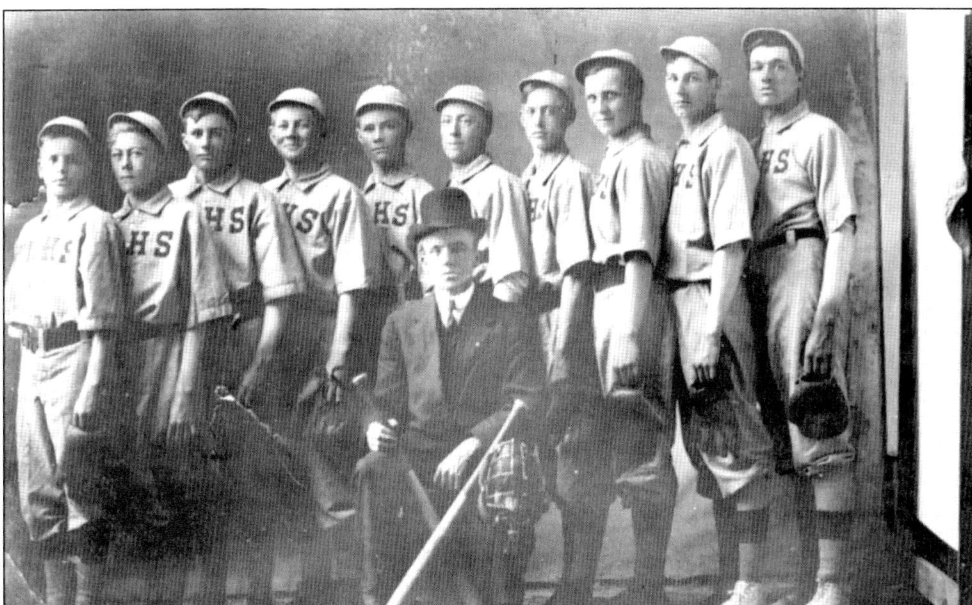

The 1910 Willow Lake baseball team is shown here. (Courtesy of Willow Lake Museum.)

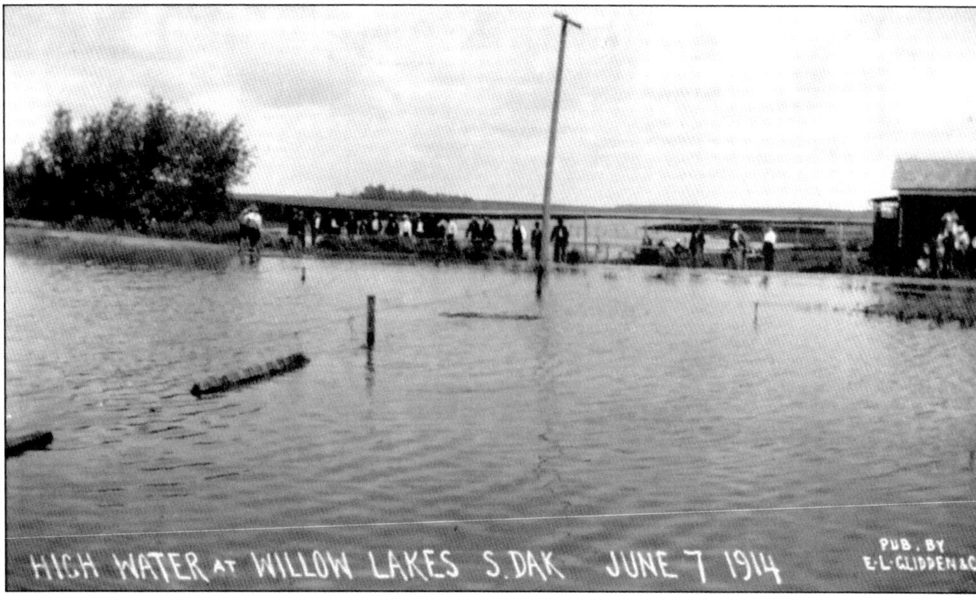

This real photo postcard was sent from Rockham, South Dakota, on June 18, 1914, to Mary Brown in Willow Lake. It shows the high water in Willow Lakes on June 7, 1914.

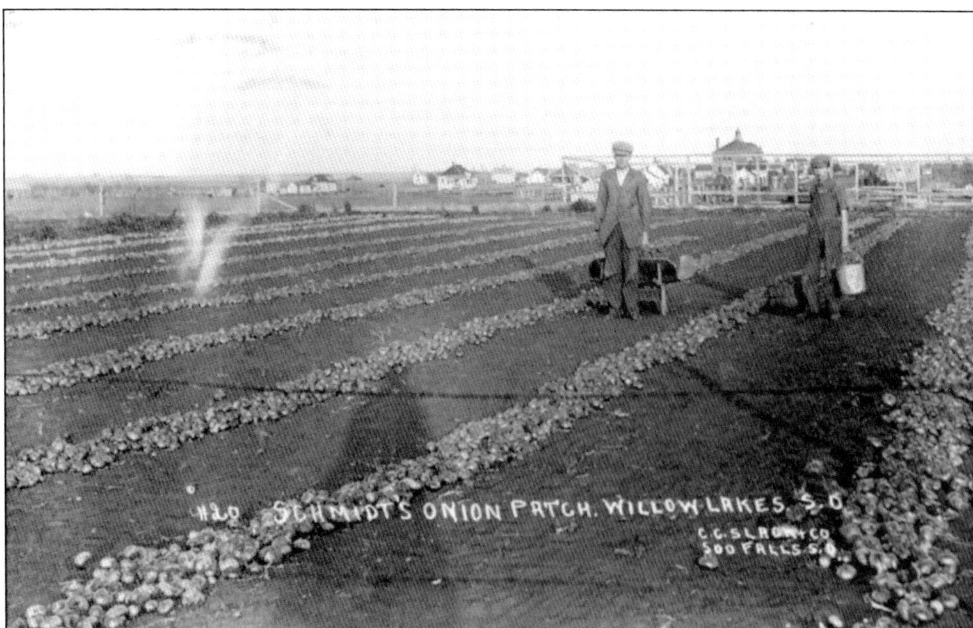

Otto Schmidt and his son Robert Schmidt are shown here in the famous "Schmidt's Onion Patch," located in the northwest part of town, just north of the present Janice Hovde home.

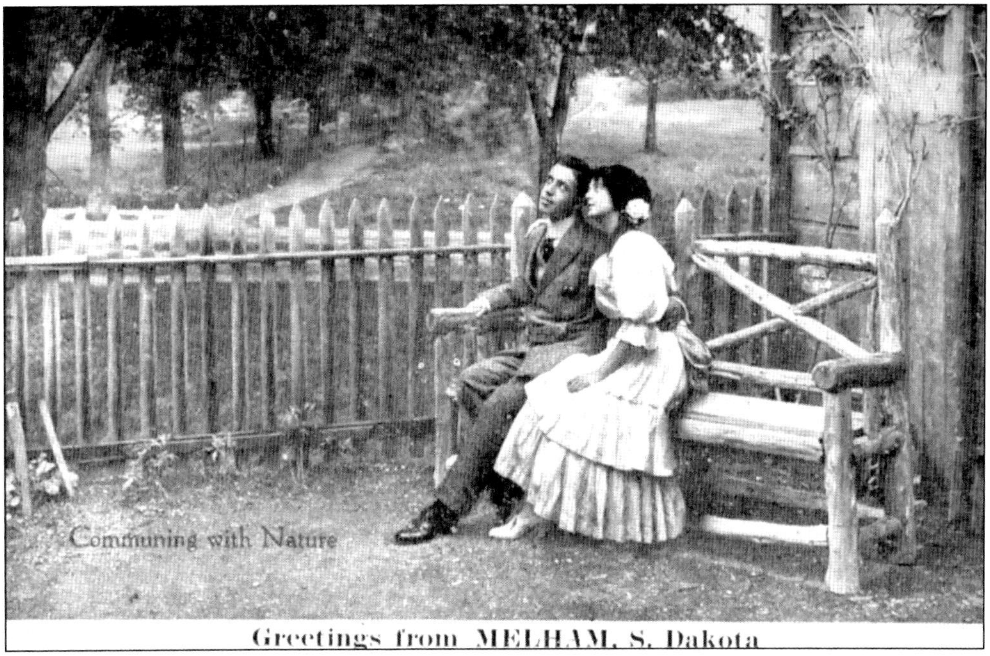

The author has not been able to locate any Melham postcards showing the town, only three like the one above. All are greetings from Melham. The author purchased them at a postcard show in Minneapolis. Collinsburg was the original name of the town.

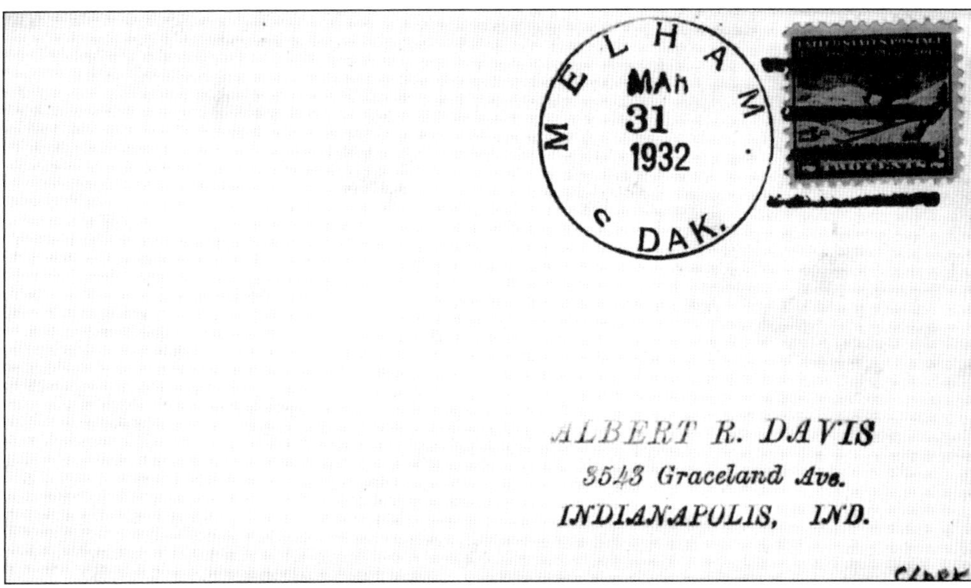

This envelope with the Melham cancellation is from the last day, according to the note on the back of the envelope, the post office was open, on March 31, 1932.

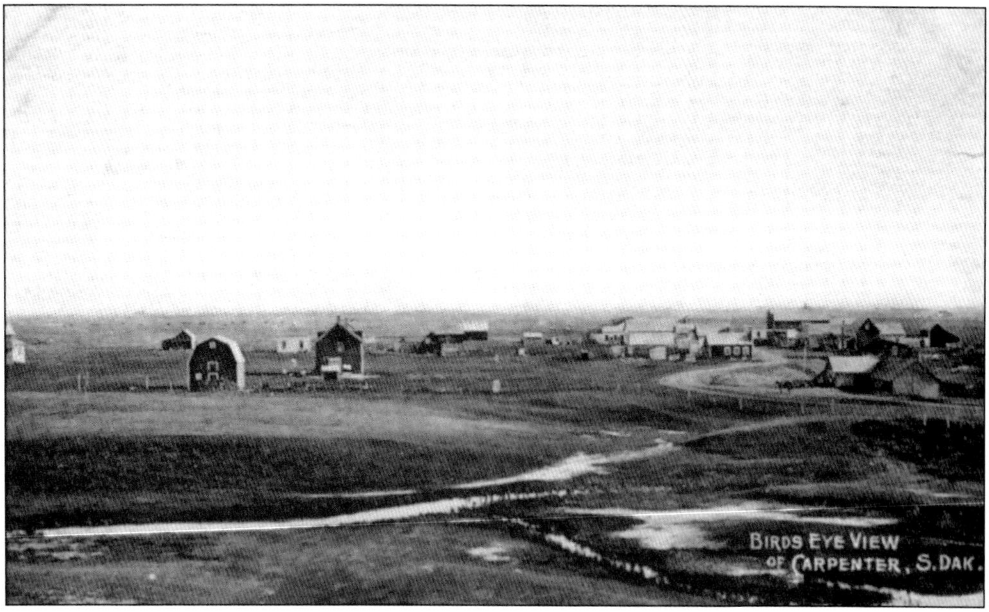

One surely does not have to worry about the view being obstructed due to trees in this "bird's Eye View of Carpenter." This card has not been used and is from between 1908 and 1910.

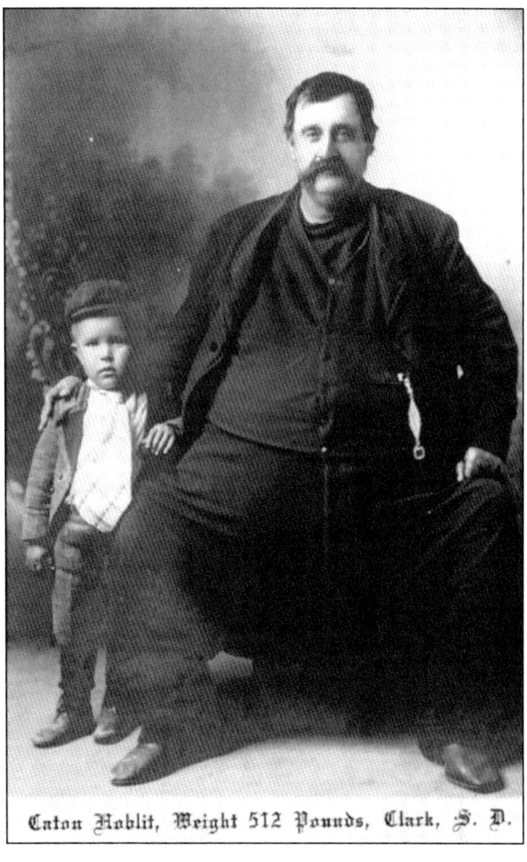

Caton Hoblit, Weight 512 Pounds, Clark, S. D.

Canton Hoblit weighed 512 pounds, and was from Carpenter. It was widely reported that he even had a board that would go from his buggy to the ground, just to slide off. The writer of this card, F. O. Brannon of Clark, states, "This is the kind of men living in South Dakota, It is fair week in Clark." The card was postmarked from Clark on September 24, 1908.

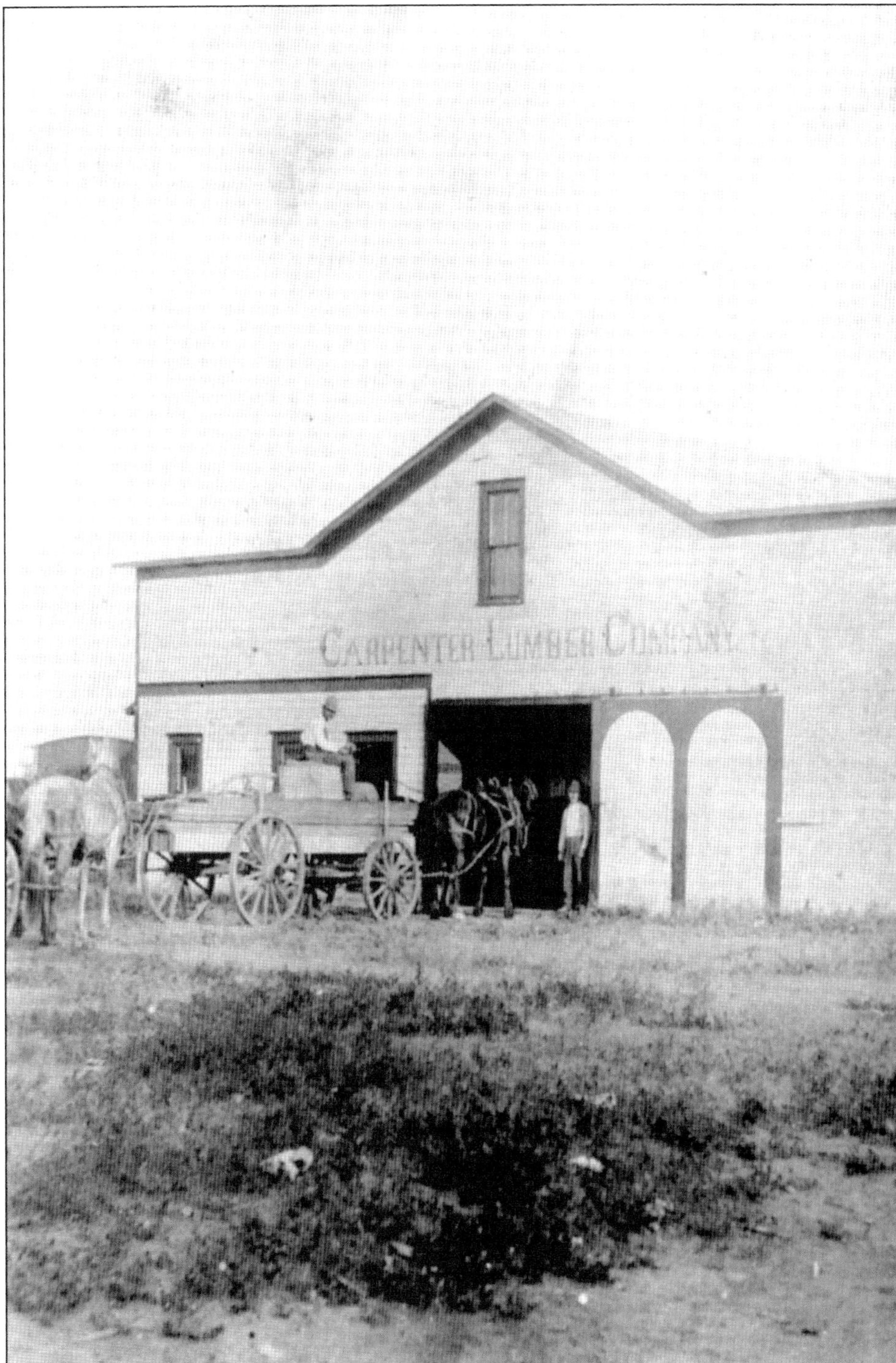

A scene at the lumberyard in Carpenter shows this man with his team of horses and buckboard ready to pick up a load of lumber. This card was made by Owen Publishing Company in Dansville, New York, and has never been used. The lumberyard, not open for many years, was torn down in the late 1990s.

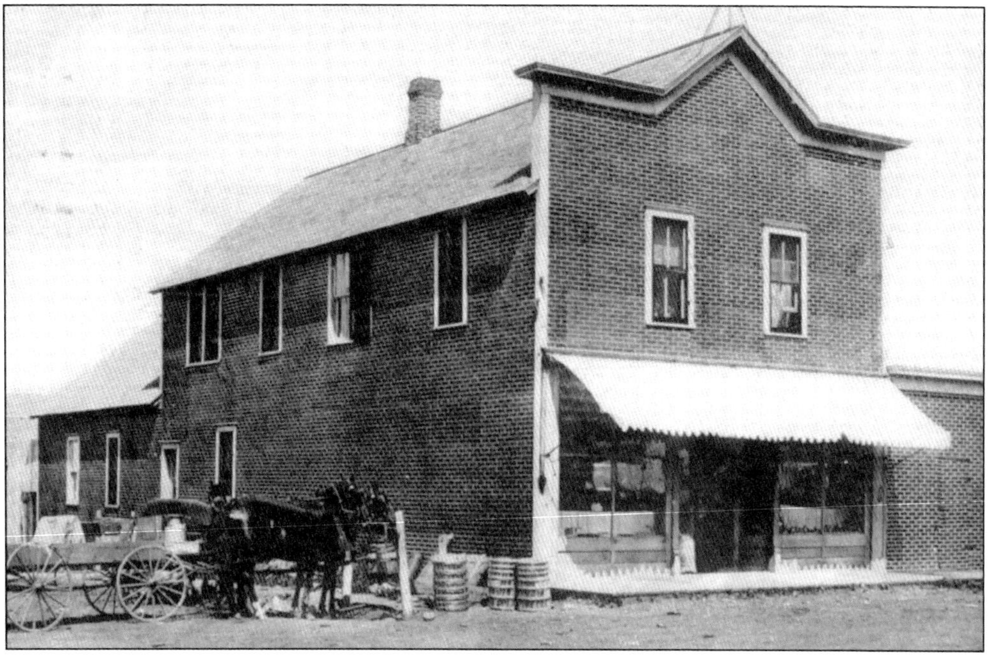

The C. W. Chambers General Merchandise building was packed full of everything in its prime just after the beginning of the 20th century. This printed card was postmarked from Carpenter in 1911 and was sent to Walter Smith at Mitchell, South Dakota.

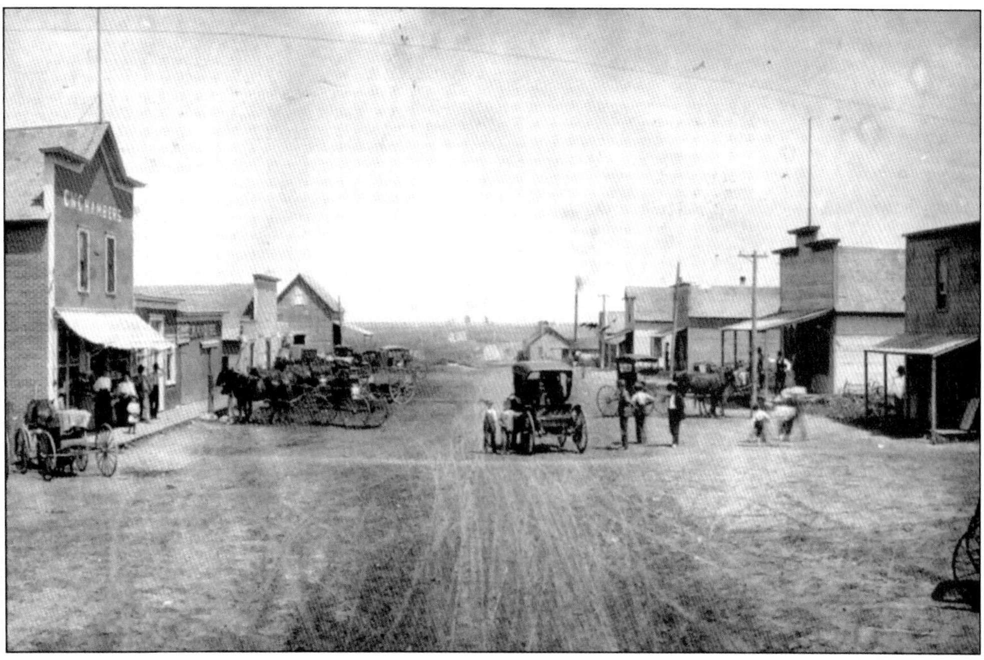

This beautiful street scene of Carpenter with the C. W. Chambers building on the left also shows Dr. Leach with the first car in 1909. Leach had moved to Carpenter in 1907 to take over the practice of Dr. Jones.

Six

Raymond

A prominent settler of the Raymond area homesteaded the land on which Raymond was later located and the town was named for him. J. M. "Jim" Raymond was his name. A former surveyor, he had turned to farming and wanted the railroad to run through his land to shorten the distance that he would have to haul his grain for shipping. When he heard that railroad had planned to build the railway several miles south of where he thought it should be, he somehow obtained access to the surveyor's plans and changed them to run across his land, from Raymond to Clark. This was in 1883. One of the first settlers and first postmasters was Michael Kelly. The first born in the township was Florence Raymond, and the second born was a boy, Jesse Hurlbert.

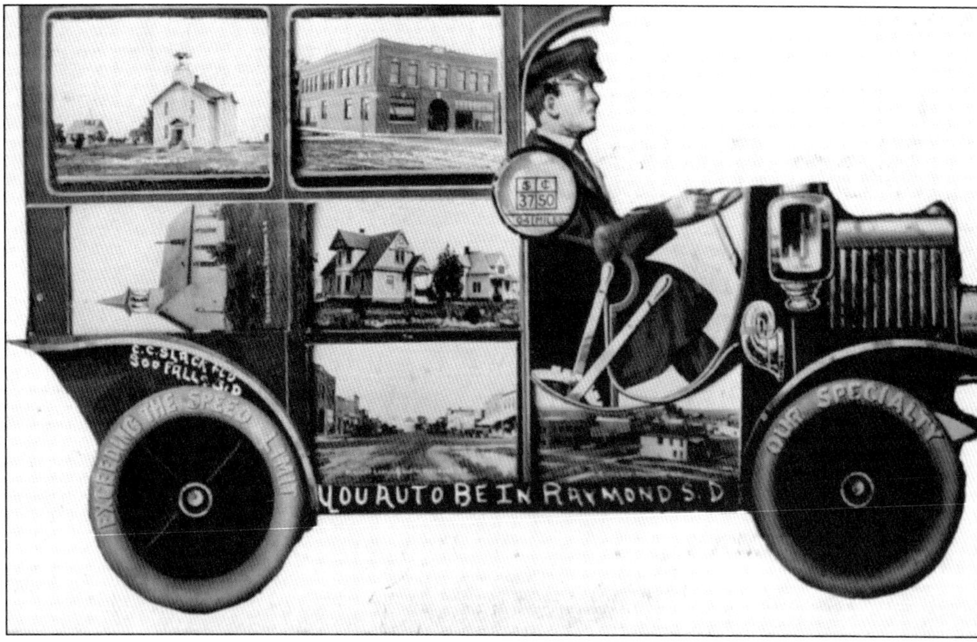

A multi-view card of Raymond, "You auto be in Raymond SD," shows the school, German church, Business Men's Association Building, residence scene, Main Street in a view looking north, and a bird's-eye view. This was an advertising card by J. A. Sussman of Raymond.

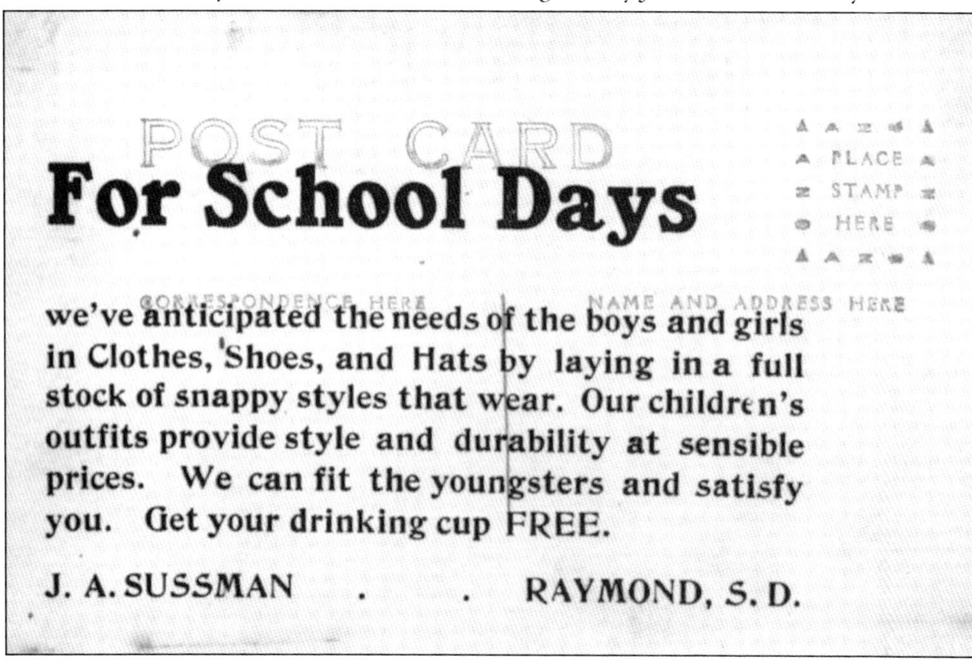

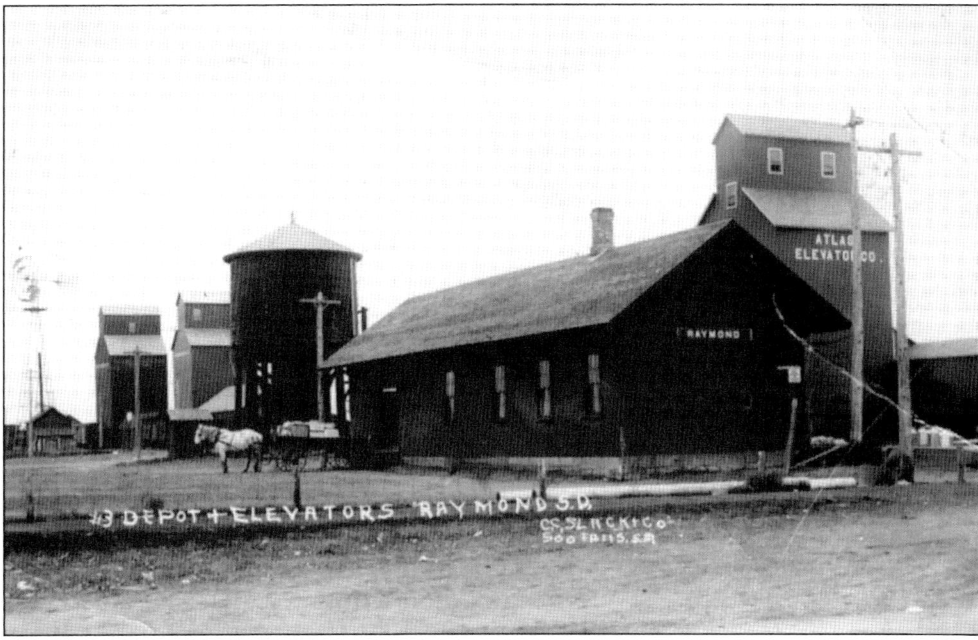

This Slack and Company postcard of Raymond is a fantastic view of the depot, water tower, and Atlas Elevator. Even the horse with the wagon full of goods is great history, as are the cream cans sitting on the loading dock to the back.

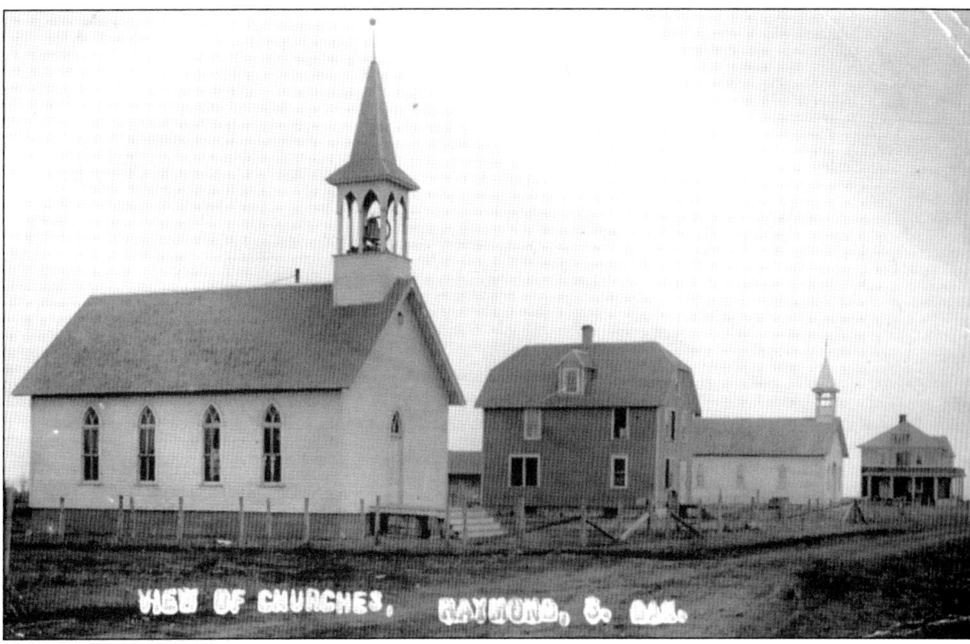

In a view of the churches, the German (Lutheran) church is shown, and the Catholic church sits to the north side. It appears that the house in between is just being built, and the writer of the card refers to this house as "our Preacher's house." This card was sent from Raymond in 1910 to Anka Post in Flanagan, Illinois.

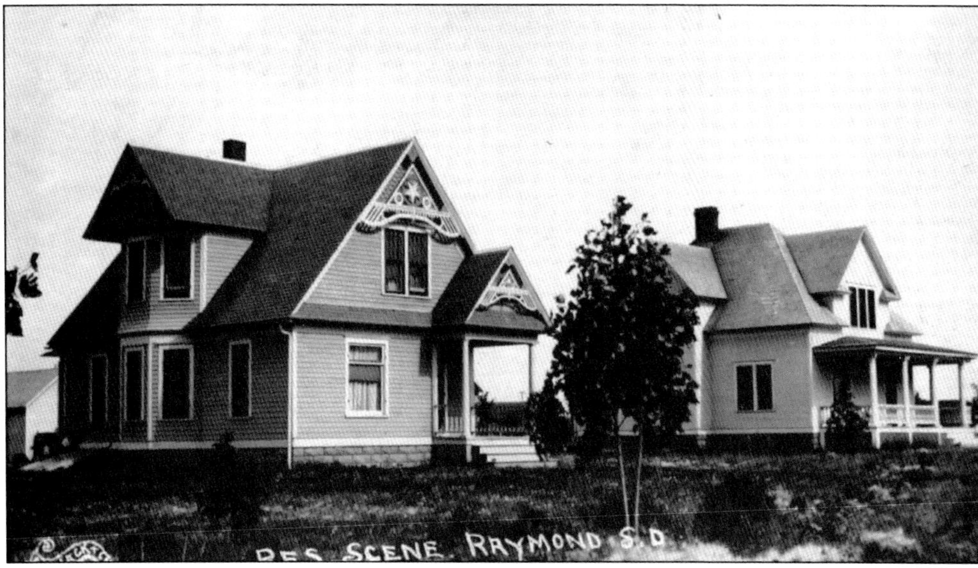

Daisey (Belle) Darling sent this postcard of two beautiful homes showing period architecture to Mrs. Henry Schmidt of Raymond in 1923. The home on the left side was for many years the home of Sophia Riddle, longtime educator in the Raymond area. She died on February 3, 2001, at the age of 94. Not only did her death bring the loss of an educator, but also a South Dakota poet. Riddle had many of her poems published in the *Pasque Petals*, a publication of South Dakota–born poets and their poetry.

MY QUIET TIME

I jump from bed so wide awake
And stealthily slip into my clothes,
Sneak down the stairs to wake no one
This is my quiet time.
I carefully fill the coffee pot,
Glance lovingly around my kitchen,
And set the table for two.
This is my quiet time.

A time to listen to the sounds of spring
Or robins announcing their return;
A time to count my blessings and
Fill my soul with the morning's beauty.
This is my quiet time.
A time to sit, be thankful I'm alive,
A time to plan my day uninterrupted by demands or noise,
A time to gather God into my soul
And rejoice that I can feel so near to Him.
This is my quiet time.
Sophia Riddle, Raymond

This poem by Sophia Riddle was taken from the *Pasque Petals* of May 1978; the official organ of the South Dakota State Poetry Society, a former monthly magazine devoted to South Dakota writers and readers. Riddle had several pieces of her poetry printed in that magazine, which has been out of print for many years.

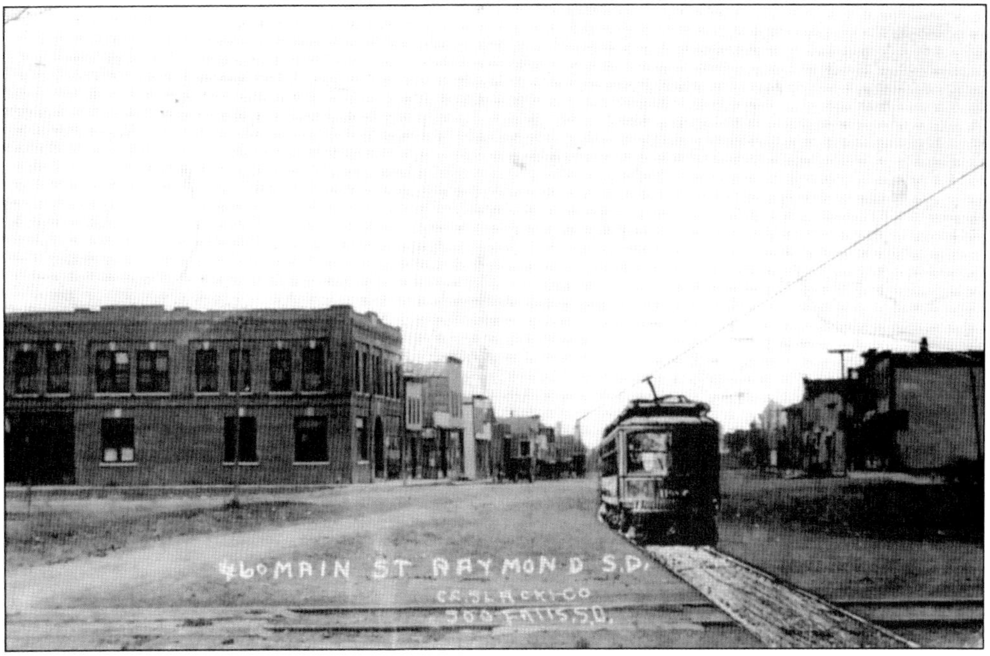

This early Slack and Company card shows the main street of Raymond keeping up with a city. The cable car never ran in Raymond, it is only superimposed on this card sent from Raymond in 1916 from Roland to a Mr. Ruterbaugh in Adair, Iowa.

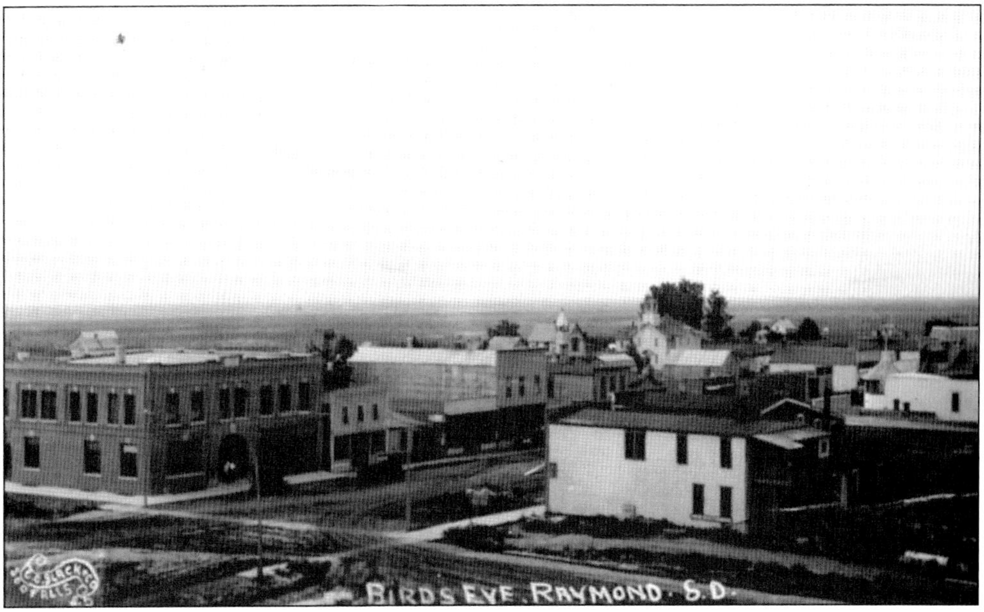

A mix of horses and buggies and automobiles are seen in this bird's-eye view sent from Raymond in 1913. There is a clear view of the old school sitting in front of the big tree.

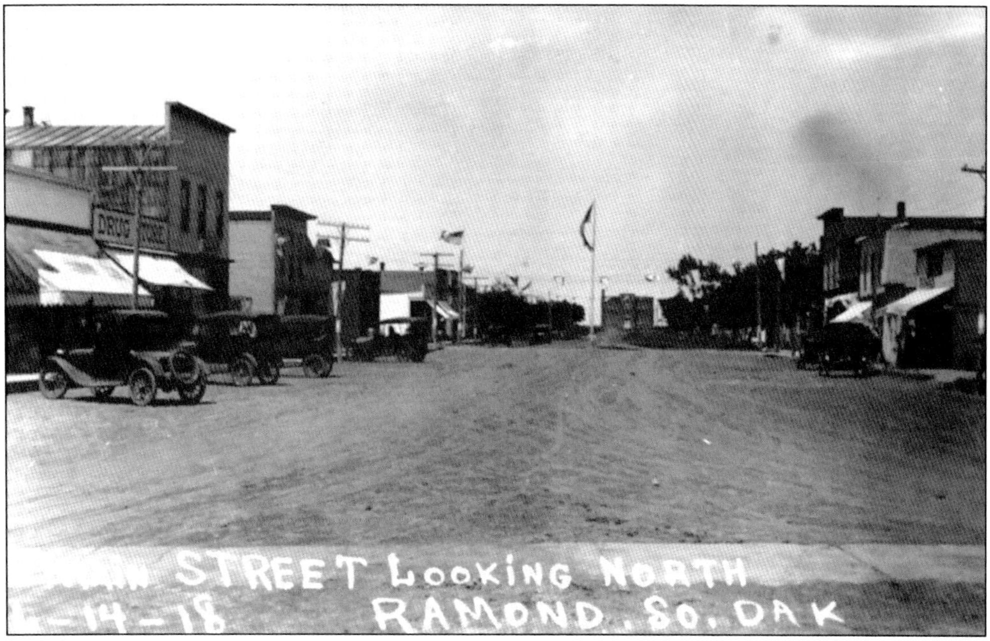

Taken on Flag Day, June 14, 1918, this view is on Main Street looking north. The new school is at the end of the street.

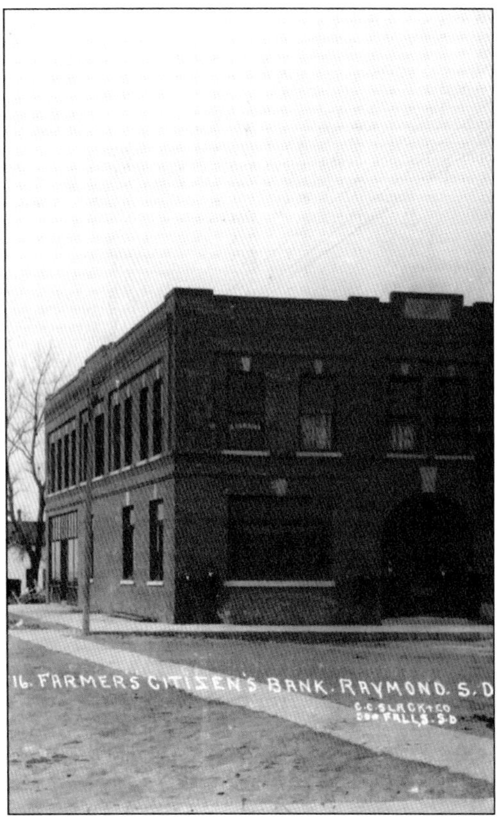

This view of the Farmer's and Citizens Bank Building, around 1911—now the Raymond American Legion Building and Community Center—was sent as a Christmas greeting from the bank in 1912. This card was sent to Henry A. Schmidt at Raymond.

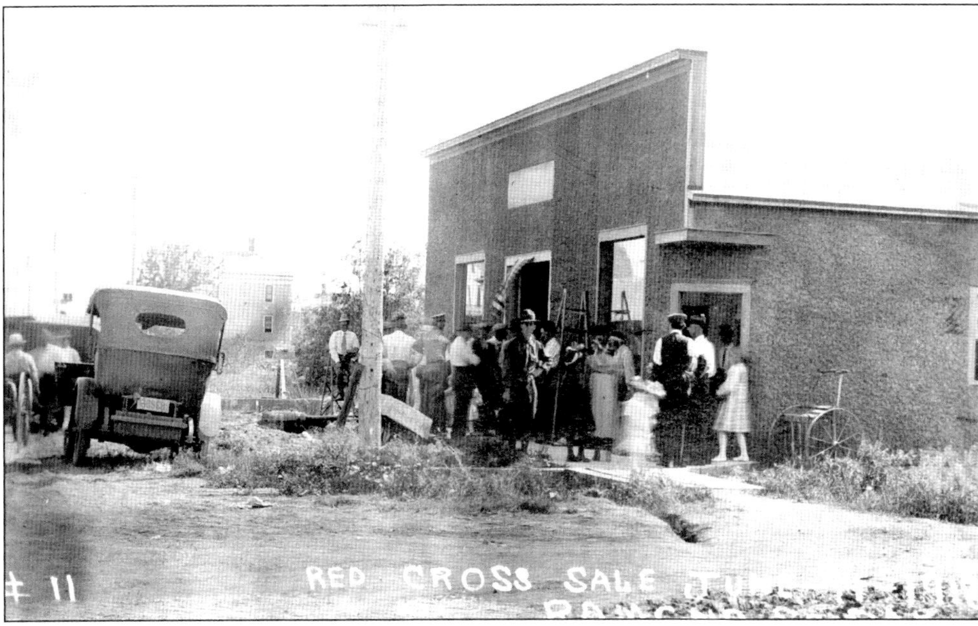

Shown here is the Red Cross sale on Flag Day in 1918 in "Ramond"—notice the spelling!

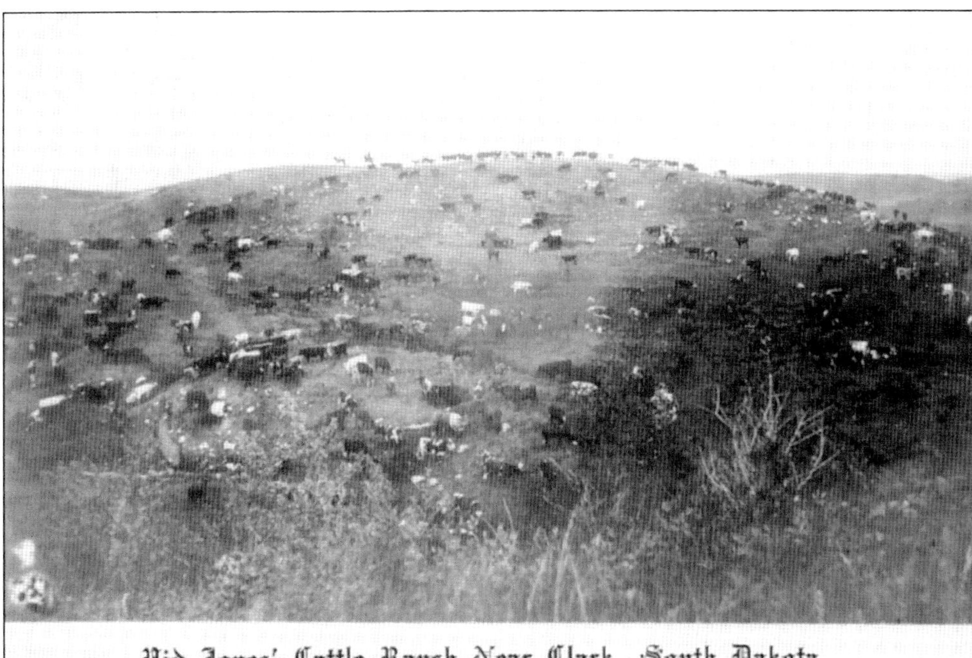

This card, sent in 1908, is of the Vid Jones cattle ranch "Near Clark." Actually, it was near Raymond. C. H. Miller took the photograph.

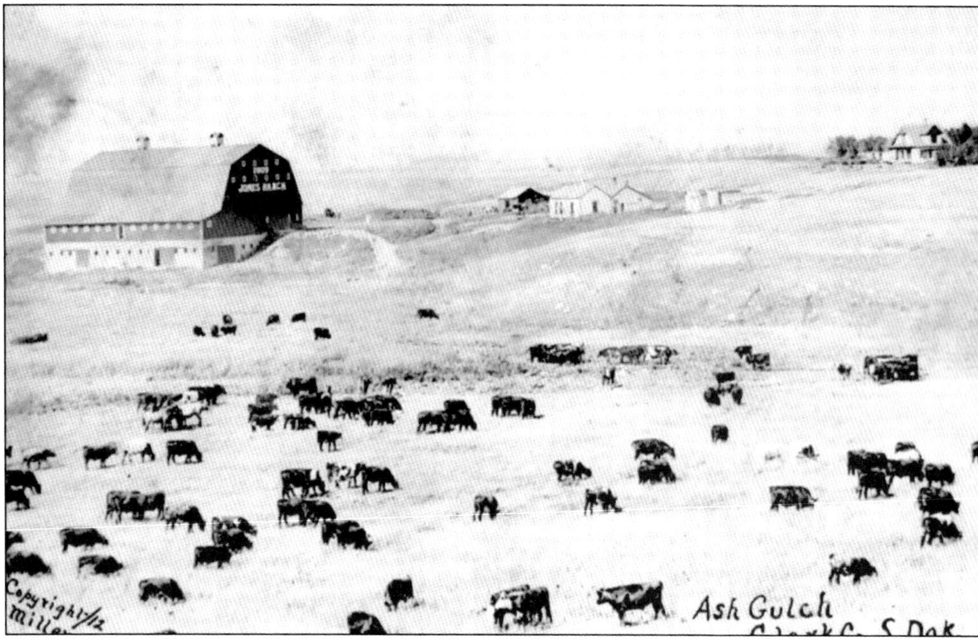

Notice the beauty of Ash Gulch in this C. H. Miller postcard, copyrighted in 1912. The Jones Ranch barn, built in 1909, still stands north of Raymond.

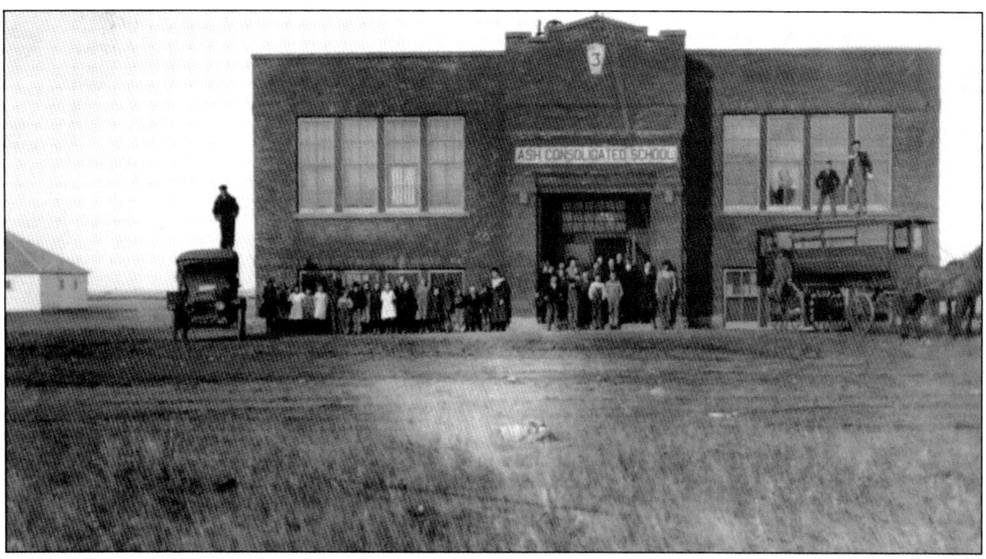

A view of the Ash Consolidated School building located in Ash Township, north of Raymond, is seen here. A milestone was reached for the Ash Township community when it voted to build this school in 1917. Construction started on May 10, 1918, and was completed in time for the opening of school that fall. The last first-grade class started in 1954. See the horse-drawn school bus out in front of the school and the bus garage—stable—located to the left.

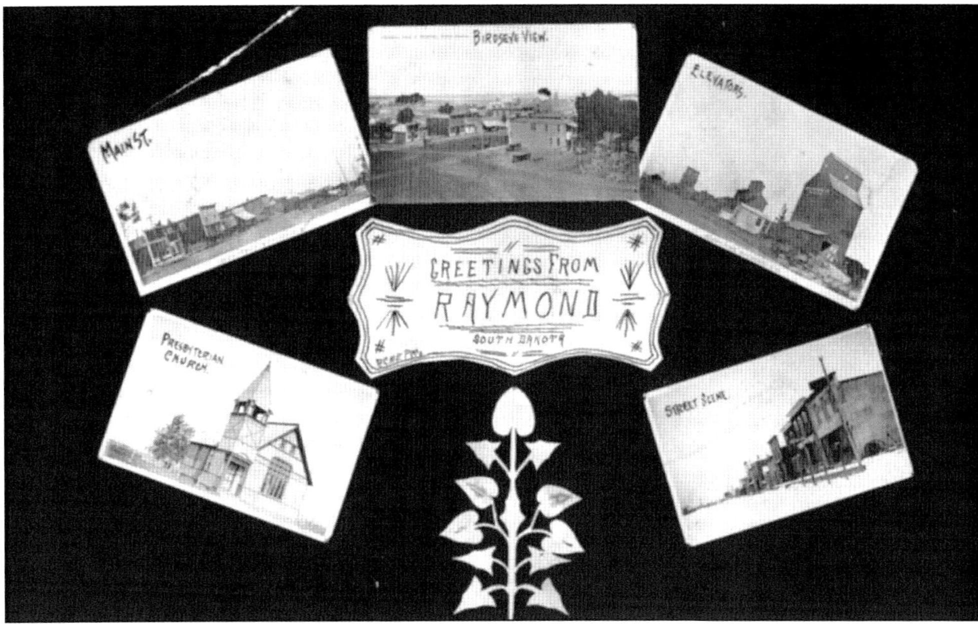

A nice five-scene postcard, written in German, was sent from Raymond in 1910 to John Post in Flanagan, Illinois. This card shows the Presbyterian church, Main Street, a bird's-eye view, elevators of the Eagle Roller Mill Company, a flour-milling business, and a street scene.

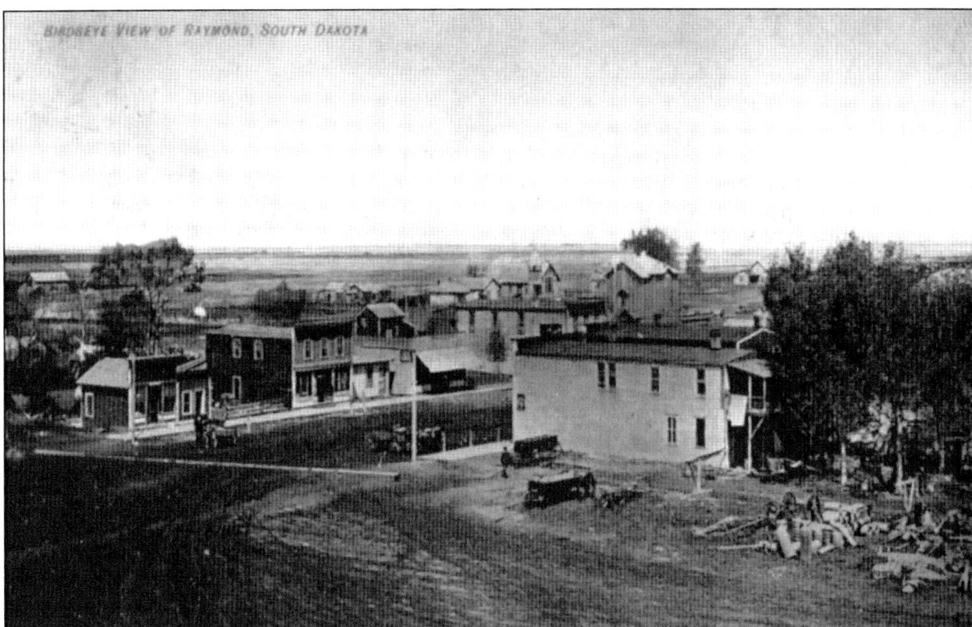

This is a very early hand-tinted bird's-eye view of Raymond, postmarked from Raymond in 1909. The Danforth building has the awning down, and the Nommensen Hardware Building sits with a lot of extra inventory.

DISCOVER THOUSANDS OF LOCAL HISTORY BOOKS FEATURING MILLIONS OF VINTAGE IMAGES

Arcadia Publishing, the leading local history publisher in the United States, is committed to making history accessible and meaningful through publishing books that celebrate and preserve the heritage of America's people and places.

Find more books like this at
www.arcadiapublishing.com

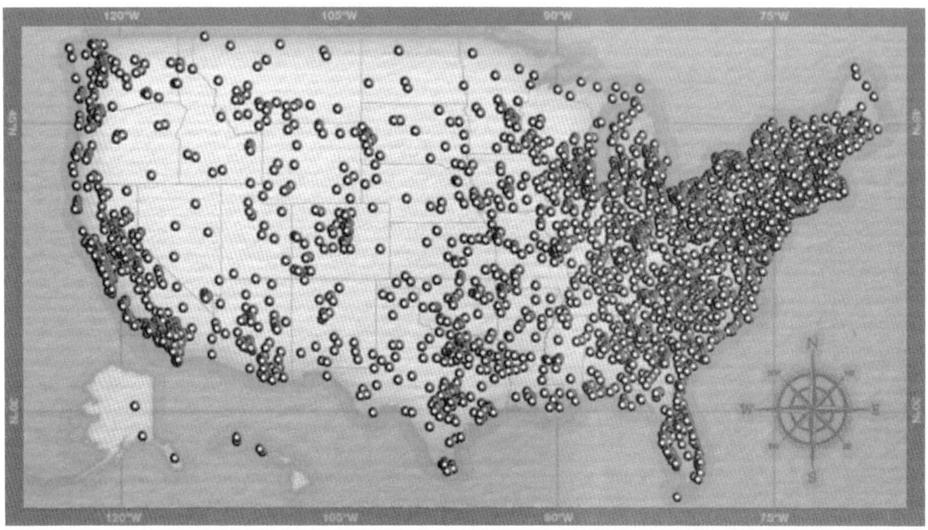

Search for your hometown history, your old stomping grounds, and even your favorite sports team.

Consistent with our mission to preserve history on a local level, this book was printed in South Carolina on American-made paper and manufactured entirely in the United States. Products carrying the accredited Forest Stewardship Council (FSC) label are printed on 100 percent FSC-certified paper.

MADE IN THE USA